Athletic Coaching

COMMUNICATION,
SPORT,
AND
SOCIETY

Lawrence A. Wenner, Andrew C. Billings, and Marie C. Hardin
General Editors

Vol. 3

The Communication, Sport, and Society series is part
of the Peter Lang Media and Communication list.
Every volume is peer reviewed and meets
the highest quality standards for content and production.

PETER LANG
New York • Bern • Berlin
Brussels • Vienna • Oxford • Warsaw

Gregory A. Cranmer

Athletic Coaching

A Communication Perspective

PETER LANG
New York • Bern • Berlin
Brussels • Vienna • Oxford • Warsaw

Library of Congress Cataloging-in-Publication Data

Names: Cranmer, Gregory A., author.
Title: Athletic coaching: a communication perspective / Gregory A. Cranmer.
Description: New York: Peter Lang, 2019.
Series: Communication, sport, and society; v. 3 | 2576-7232
Includes bibliographical references.
Identifiers: LCCN 2019016094 | ISBN 978-1-4331-4766-1 (hardback: alk. paper)
ISBN 978-1-4331-4765-4 (paperback: alk. paper) | ISBN 978-1-4331-4767-8 (ebook pdf)
ISBN 978-1-4331-4768-5 (epub) | ISBN 978-1-4331-4769-2 (mobi)
Subjects: LCSH: Coaching (Athletics) | Communication in sports.
Coach-athlete relationships.
Classification: LCC GV711 .C84 2019 | DDC 796.07/7—dc23
LC record available at https://lccn.loc.gov/2019016094
DOI 10.3726/b15719

Bibliographic information published by **Die Deutsche Nationalbibliothek**.
Die Deutsche Nationalbibliothek lists this publication in the "Deutsche
Nationalbibliografie"; detailed bibliographic data are available
on the Internet at http://dnb.d-nb.de/.

The paper in this book meets the guidelines for permanence and durability
of the Committee on Production Guidelines for Book Longevity
of the Council of Library Resources.

Printed in the United States of America

For Arthur Halbeisen and my two Belles

TABLE OF CONTENTS

Acknowledgements   ix
List of Abbreviations   xi

Chapter 1: A Communicative Approach to Athletic Coaching   1
Chapter 2: Defining Effective Coaching   21
Chapter 3: The Instructional Perspective: Coaches as Instructors   43
Chapter 4: The Organizational Perspective: Coaches as Managers   63
Chapter 5: The Group Perspective: Coaches as Group Members   85
Chapter 6: The Interpersonal Perspective: Coaches as Relational
            Partners   105
Chapter 7: Setting a Scholarly Agenda: Building Toward
            a Holistic Framework   125
Chapter 8: Building Athletic Coaching Theory: Extending
            Confirmation Theory to Athletic Coaching   145

ACKNOWLEDGEMENTS

I owe so much to the scholars who influenced me. Thank you to Dr. Scott A. Myers and the faculty at West Virginia University for encouraging me to follow my passion. Thank you to Jeffrey Kassing and Paul Turman, whose work brought respect to the academic pursuit of coaching within Communication Studies and established the foundation upon which I built my research. It would be impossible to fill your shoes, but following in your footsteps has been quite an enlightening experience. Finally, thank you to Kristine Maul (M.A., Stockton University) for assisting in the copy editing of this monograph.

ABBREVIATIONS

AAU	Amateur Athletic Union
BATs	Behavior Alteration Techniques
CCI	Coach Confirmation Instrument
CCT	Coach Confirmation Theory
IACS	International Association for Communication & Sport
ICA	International Communication Association
IRB	Institutional Review Board
LMX	Leader Member Exchange
MDLM	Multidimensional Leadership Model
NASPE	National Association for Sport and Physical Education
NCA	National Communication Association
PCA	Positive Coaching Alliance
PP	Project Play
SHAPE America	American Alliance for Health, Physical Education, Recreation and Dance

· 1 ·

A COMMUNICATIVE APPROACH TO ATHLETIC COACHING

To me, the coaching profession is one of the most noblest and far-reaching in building [adults]. No [person] is too good to be an athletic coach for youth.—Amos Alonzo Stagg[1]

The role of sport in society has grown throughout the 20th and into the 21st century. Sport is a ubiquitous component of social discourse and shapes how we come to understand our societal structures, as well as our roles and experiences within those structures (Kassing et al., 2004; Pedersen, 2013a; Wenner, 2015). The influence and presence of sport is only possible through a complex web of interactions between interdependent stakeholders (i.e., participants, media, organizations, and fans), known as the community of sport (Billings, Butterworth, & Turman, 2018). Each member of this community has a vital role in the communicative performance of sport. The value of sport as a context of human achievement and development, however, would be significantly lacking if it were not for athletic coaches. Coaches are the conduits of knowledge that allow athletes to refine their abilities, sources of inspiration and support that keep athletes involved in sport, and organizers of sporting activities and team climates. As such, coaches are central figures in sport participation, influencing athletes' physical performances, relationships with teammates, and development (Kassing et al., 2004; Potrac, Denison, & Gilbert, 2013).

Perhaps the importance of their roles is why coaches are viewed as mythical figures, who warrant admiration (Billings et al., 2018). Reverence for coaches permeates popular and sporting culture. We, the public, canonize coaches' motivational speeches (e.g., Knute Rockne's "Win one for the Gipper" halftime speech) through committing them to memory and commemorating them in social artifacts (Maisel, 2003). We revere and recite their teams' accomplishments, like Dan Gable's record at the University of Iowa (i.e., 355-21-5), which included 21 straight Big Ten team titles and 15 NCAA team titles (Turman, 2017). We utilize their coaching philosophies as guides for our non-sporting lives, such as John Wooden's famous Pyramid of Success (Edelhauser, 2007). We position them as social and religious leaders that shape our youth, like University of Colorado's former football coach Bill McCartney and his organization, *Promise Keepers* (Hoffer, 1995). We immortalize them within film, including the likes of high school coaches Ken Carter (i.e., a former basketball coach from Richmond High School, CA and subject of *Coach Carter*) (Gale, Robbins, Tollin, & Carter, 2005) and Gary Gaines (i.e., a former football coach at Permian High School, TX and subject of *Friday Night Lights*) (Grazer & Berg, 2004).

Surprisingly, despite the historical and social significance given to coaches, athletic coaching—whether voluntary, part-time, or full-time—has garnered little consideration within academia until the late 20th century (Gilbert, 2002; Gilbert & Trudel, 2004; Potrac et al., 2013). Since the 1970s, scholars from a group of Western nations (i.e., United Kingdom, United States, Canada, Australia, and New Zealand) have increasingly pursued research on coaching (Duffy et al., 2011; Gilbert, 2002). This body of scholarship, known as coaching science, is comprised of disconnected studies that span multiple fields, including sport management, psychology, and sociology (Gilbert & Trudel, 2004). The limited and fragmented nature of coaching science research is of concern because training programs and innovations in coaching practice are dependent upon the cultivation and synthesis of empirical knowledge. As such, scholars have engaged in efforts to expand upon and unify understandings of coaching (e.g., Jones, 2006; Lyle & Cushion, 2010; Potrac et al., 2013).

Attempts to unify and synthesize coaching science research have excluded the communicative perspective of coaching, which originated within the field of communication studies during the end of the 20th century (Kassing & Infante, 1999; Rocca, Martin, & Toale, 1998), and is now a component of the emerging subfield of sport communication (Wenner, 2015). For instance, the *Routledge Handbook of Sports Coaching* features no communication scholars and only two chapters even tangentially related to communicative behavior (i.e., Becker, 2013; Ronglan & Aggerholm, 2013). Further, the behavioral approaches within coaching science research reference general qualities of communication (e.g., supportive, individualized, fair, appropriate, consistent) rather than specific behaviors or messages (Becker, 2009, 2013). These approaches also rely on understandings of behavior that vary by study in lieu of formalized understandings of human interaction (Becker & Wrisberg, 2008; Potrac, Jones, & Armour, 2002). In contrast, researchers who operate from a communicative perspective identify and empirically examine the effectiveness of specific messages or nonverbal behaviors (e.g., Cranmer, Anzur, & Sollitto, 2017; Cranmer & Brann, 2015; Kassing & Pappas, 2007; Turman, 2003b, 2008; Webster, 2009). The nuance and specificity of communicative scholarship, in conjunction with its emphasis on generalizable results, provides it with a degree of applicability that is missing from other bodies of coaching literature (Duffy et al., 2011; Potrac et al., 2002). In other words, communication research offers prescriptive value because it provides coaches with specifics regarding *what to say* or *what to do* to be more effective. These practical implications are missing from coaching science literature at large.

A formative barrier to the integration and application of coach communication research is that this literature lacks synthesis. The disconnected nature of coach communication research hinders its growth and accessibility for scholars and practitioners. In recent decades, researchers within sport-related fields—including those in coaching science (Gilbert, 2002; Gilbert & Trudel, 2004; Potrac et al., 2013) and sport communication (Abeza, O'Reilly, & Nadeau, 2014; Ishak, 2017; Kassing et al., 2004; Pedersen, 2013b; Wenner, 2015)—have faced similar situations and resolved these problems through reviews of published research. These efforts are imperative as:

> The absence of literature reviews and analyses of published research on coaching seriously limits the ability of (a) researchers to set research agendas and situate their work in the larger content of coaching science, (b) coaches to access and realize the potential of coaching research, and (c) coach educators to integrate the full scope of coaching research into coach education programs. (Gilbert & Trudel, 2004, p. 388)

Analyzing and synthesizing the empirical record on coach communication is a crucial first step toward the continual development and application of academic knowledge.

The purpose of this text, therefore, is threefold: (a) to provide an account and forward an agenda that helps develop scientific exploration of coach communication, (b) form connections between existing coach communication perspectives, and (c) maximize the practical value of communicative research for coaches through promoting applied and generalizable means of inquiry. This purpose benefits many audiences, including emerging coach communication scholars who are developing an initial understanding of this literature, established coach communication scholars who are negotiating the structure and direction of our efforts, interdisciplinary coaching scholars who seek a representation of a communicative perspective of coaching, and coaches who may use this text as a self-reflective tool for pedagogical refinement.

This chapter aims to answer three preliminary questions as a means of providing a foundation upon which the purpose of this text may be accomplished. The first question is *why should anyone, regardless of field of specialization, consider the examination of athletic coaching as a scholarly, worthwhile pursuit?* The second question is *why is a communicative perspective to coaching appropriate and, more importantly, needed?* The third question is *what is the scholarly context in which the communicative perspective of coaching is embedded?*

Need for Coaching Research

The scientific inquiry into coaching is a meaningful pursuit for a multitude of reasons. The foremost of which is that the athlete-coach relationship is a significant context of human interaction. Coaches are entrusted with the social, cognitive, physical, and moral development of their athletes (Super, Verkooijen, & Koelen, 2018). As such, coaches are agents of influence, who inspire interest in participating in sport (Coakley & White, 1992; Fraser-Thomas, Côté, & Deakin, 2008; McPherson, 1981) and impart information that shapes athletes' social schema for years to come (Cranmer & Myers, 2017; Kassing & Pappas, 2007). More specifically, interactions with coaches directly or indirectly account for numerous facets of athletes' emotions, relationships, physical skillsets, psychological processes, and self-perceptions (Vella, Oades, & Crowe, 2011). Coaches' control over sporting environments (e.g., practice schedules and routines) and the dissemination of information may explain their influence. Meân (2013) argued that the manner in which sport is structured and managed by coaches determines the outcomes experienced by athletes. Meân's argument underscores that coach education and training are imperative to organizing sport in a manner that maximizes the potential benefits of athletic participation.

Unfortunately, coaches' reliance on education curriculums, programs, and research are severely lacking in the United States. A survey conducted by the Aspen Institute and featured within the *State of Play 2017* demonstrated that over two-thirds of coaches lack training in a host of crucial areas, including general safety and injury prevention, sport specific skills and tactics, concussion management, motivational techniques, CPR and basic first aid, and physical conditioning (Project Play, 2018). Even coaches who have degrees in physical education are exposed to limited, if any, research on coaching sports teams as part of their formal college education (Gilbert & Trudel, 2004; Jones & Turner, 2006). Thus, it is unsurprising that coaches who have had formal training describe it as insufficient (Irwin, Hanton, & Kerwin, 2004). In the absence of quality education, "… coaches base their coaching on feelings, intuitions, events and previous experience that trigger actions" (Cushion & Lyle, 2010, p. 1). Although these heuristics may serve some coaches well, empirical evidence indicates that education and training coincide with more effective coaching and better sporting experiences for athletes (Agans, Ettekan, & Stack, 2016; Project Play, 2018). As a result, access to qualified and well-trained coaches is included within the *Bill of Rights for Young Athletes* (Denlinger, 1977) and *Secondary School Student-Athletes' Bill of Rights* (National Athletic Trainers Association, 2015).

Scholars and practitioners have engaged in numerous efforts to develop pedagogical resources and knowledge that might assist coaches and further develop the coaching profession in an effort to fulfill these rights (Duffy et al., 2011; Lyle & Cushion, 2010). A number of organizations have taken up the efforts to foster coach education. Globally, these organizations include the *Coaching Association of Canada*, *European Coaching Council*, the United Kingdom's *National Coaching Foundation*, and *UK Sport* (Duffy et al., 2011). Within the United States, three organizations—among others—have made headway in the initiative towards developing the coaching profession. The first is the *Positive Coaching Alliance* (PCA), which is a nonprofit organization that seeks "to transform the youth sports culture into a development zone where all youth and high school athletes have a positive, character-building experience that results in better athletes, better people" (Positive Coaching Alliance, 2018). The PCA teaches prosocial coaching techniques to youth and high school coaches, which it has distributed via more than 20,000 in-person workshops, hundreds of thousands of online training sessions, and partnerships with nearly 4,000 youth sport organizations (Positive Coaching Alliance, 2018). For example, Little League (2018) has partnered with the PCA since 2006 to provide coaches with resources (e.g., demonstration videos and plans for practices) to teach sport and life skills to young players. The total estimated social impact of the PCA exceeds 8.6 million athletes. Encouragingly, PCA training increases coaches' abilities to build relationships with athletes and inspire continued participation, especially when those coaches are paired with the same group of athletes over periods of time (Agans et al., 2016).

The second organization is the Aspen Institute, which is a United States based, international think tank that promotes leadership and the exchange of ideas. One of the many initiatives of the institute is *Project Play* (PP), which "develops, shares and applies knowledge that helps build healthy communities through sports" (Project Play, 2018). Project Play focuses on an eight-pronged solution (i.e., "the play")—one aspect of which is building knowledge about athletic coaching and providing training to coaches—to a troublesome youth sporting culture that has high degrees of professionalism, commodification, and specialization. To date, PP has collaborated with more than 100 sporting organizations (e.g., Nike, ESPN, Major League Baseball, National Basketball Association, National Hockey League, and the United States Olympic Committee) to provide seminars and conferences for sporting stakeholders to implement "the play" into practice (Project Play, 2018). Although PP takes a holistic approach to improving the sporting experiences of young athletes, as part of its 2020 plan, it encourages the cultivation and provision of quality coach training that is based upon scholarship.

The third organization is the *National Association for Sport and Physical Education* (NASPE), which is part of the larger *American Alliance for Health, Physical Education, Recreation and Dance* (i.e., also known as SHAPE America). NASPE is a nonprofit organization that consists of more than 15,000 physical educators, coaches, teachers, athletic directors, and researchers (National Association for Sport and Physical Education, 2018). The commitment of NASPE and SHAPE America to assist in spreading scholarly research on coaching is evident in their publishing of a professional journal—*Strategies: A Journal for Physical and Sport Educators*—that uses empirical research to provide practical advice to coaches, identify best coaching practices, and discuss current issues and trends in sport-related professions. NASPE and SHAPE America further utilized academic research to guide its *Revised National Standards for Sports Coaches* (SHAPE America, 2017), which features 40 standards of effective coaching that are organized into seven core responsibilities (e.g., build positive relationships, strive for continuous improvement, and develop a safe environment). Together, these three organizations demonstrate the existence of an established and well-supported professional network that seeks to implement coaching research. This network offers a promising means for the translation of research into practice, and increases the potential impact of novel insights into coaching.

The value of continuing innovative coaching research is magnified by participation data. As Duffy (2010) noted, coaching is a ubiquitous service with millions of coaches, and even more athletes, engaging in sport around the world. Data specific to the United States indicates more than 21.5 million 6-17 year old children participate in organized sport throughout the country (Kelley & Carchia, 2013), with nearly 8 million of them participating in high school athletics (National Federation of State High School Associations, 2017). The age of the majority of these athletes is noteworthy. Organized sport most readily includes youth and adolescent athletes, who are in important stages of emotional, psychological, social, moral, and physical development (Atkinson, 2009). The *State of Play 2017* revealed that 71.5% of youth 6–12 years old participate in sport (Project Play, 2018). These individuals will come to draw values, assumptions, and patterns of behavior from their interactions with coaches (Cranmer & Myers, 2017; Kassing & Pappas, 2007). The context of sport is further relevant for development because, for many children, sports are one of the first and most common sources of exposure to highly structured, group environments that feature shared tasks (Coakley, 1993; McPherson, 1981). As such, sports become an important context for learning how to manage the social dynamics within collectives that share a purpose. Any context or relationship that influences the experiences of so many individuals during such a crucial period within their lifespan warrants investigation.

It is abundantly clear that there is a great deal of rationale to continue the development of coaching research. Specifically, this scholarship has practical and meaningful value for the development of a sizable population, and organizational structures are in place to aid in the application of its insights. Perhaps this underlying rationale explains why interest in coaching has grown throughout the late 20th century and now constitutes a budding topic of inquiry (Gilbert & Trudel, 2004). However, the research that derived from this early interest is characterized as underdeveloped, simplified, and largely exploratory (Cassidy, Jones, & Potrac, 2009; Cushion & Lyle, 2010). Although these characterizations are not surprising, given the novelty of coaching as an academic pursuit, clarity regarding terminology and the conceptualization of coaching are recognized as essential for overcoming these early shortcomings (Duffy, 2010; Lyle, 2002).

Coaching as Communication

A central limitation of coaching science research is that it relies on inconsistent conceptualizations that overlook the communicative nature of coaching. The foundation of scientific inquiry is rooted in the ability to conceptualize the objects, relationships, and processes investigated by researchers (LeFebvre, 2017). Without consistent and functional definitions of what is being studied across a field of inquiry, building bodies of knowledge with heuristic and practical implications becomes difficult; for it is through shared understanding that connections between specific studies are made and novel insights are discovered and tested. Cushion and Lyle (2010) underscored the importance of this shared understanding by suggesting that "conceptualization creates a mechanism for representing the coaching process, without which there is no adequate basis of understanding, analysis or modelling" (p. 2). Unfortunately, Jones (2006) described the state of coaching science research in the following manner:

> Despite a recent upsurge in scholarly interest, coaching remains an ill-defined and under-theorized field. Indeed, it has been argued that no conceptual framework currently exists which adequately deals with the complex reality within which coaches work and how they can better manage it. (p. 3)

Developing conceptualizations, however, requires rigorous evaluations through which understandings of an object, relationship, or process become clearer and more precise. LeFebvre (2017) noted that as scholarly understanding is refined, "pre-existing conceptualizations affirmed by the field, extensively tested, and adopted across numerous studies have advantages; nevertheless, nuances can occur and often multiple conceptualizations exist in a variety of contexts" (p. 1838). Thus, building quality conceptualizations requires time and empirical investigation, but the incremental nature of this process may result in a plurality of understandings that differ in nuanced ways. Coaching science research has demonstrated these sentiments well, with early research failing to effectively conceptualize coaching—a barrier that has stunted its development (Duffy, 2010; Duffy et al., 2011; Jones, 2006; Lyle, 2002). Yet, with efforts to refine the conceptualization of coaching throughout the past two decades, a variety of definitions have been forwarded, including those that span sociological, pedagogical, instructional, humanistic, and science performance perspectives (Cushion & Lyle, 2010; Lyle, 2002).

Although there are various definitions of coaching within coaching science research, these definitions share three common features that partially address the context and function of coaching. The first feature is that coaching is a *complex process that requires degrees of flexibility, innovation, and improvisation*. For example, scholars have argued that "coaching is in fact largely uncontrollable, incomprehensible and imbued with contradictory values" (Cushion & Lyle, 2010, p. 4) or "… [it] is an inherently non-routine, problematic and complex endeavor …" (Jones, 2006, p. 3). The feature of complexity acknowledges that coaching occurs within a chaotic environment that requires altering techniques and strategies because of athletes' abilities, individual or team score, human error on the part of athletes or officials, injuries, chance, or other game situations. The underlying complexity of coaching brings with it a tension that renders neat and straightforward definitions as overly simplistic and too narrow to encompass the full scope of the realities of coaching. Yet, overly complex definitions are cumbersome and limit the practicality of conducting and applying research.

The second common feature is that coaching *serves a developmental function through which coaches pass expertise to athletes*. For instance, according to the European Coaching Council (2007) coaching centers around "the guided improvement, led by a coach, of sports participants and teams in a single sport and at identifiable stages of the athlete/sportsperson pathway" (p. 5). Jones (2006) summarized the importance of developing athletes in the following manner: "… at the heart of coaching lies the teaching and learning interface, and the myriad ways through which coaches influence athletes to develop and improve" (p. 3). Conceptualizations that emphasize the developmental nature of coaching accentuate the importance of improving the comprehension and performance of athletes, as well as the assessment of such development (Sherman, Crassini, Maschette, & Sands, 1997). Such definitions of coaching also recognize an explicit purpose of coaches, which provides a basis for subsequent and partial assessments of effectiveness (see Chapter 2).

The third feature of the conceptualizations of coaching is that *coaching occurs within the contexts of human relationships*. This feature considers that coaching is a social activity that is shaped by the relational climates in which it occurs (Cushion & Lyle, 2010; Jones, 2006). Potrac et al. (2002) summarized this feature by suggesting "… coaches operate as social beings within a social environment, with the coaching process being inextricably linked to both the constraints and opportunities of human interaction" (p. 184). The relational nature of coaching allows for the recognition of the interplay between coaches' and athletes' cognitions, emotions, and behaviors, which manifest within interaction and influence the subsequent interpretations of interaction (Jowett, 2017; Jowett & Poczwardowski, 2007). This feature is important because the connection between athlete and coach is an important determinant of the success of coaching efforts (Jowett, 2017).

Despite the variation in conceptualizations of coaching, the exchange of messages and the construction of meaning, which are integral to the communicative perspective, are noticeably absent from coaching science research. The absence of these communicative features from conceptualizations of coaching is odd given that coaching science scholars recognize that coaching is rooted within interaction. Yet, these scholars overlook the features and processes that come to define the nature and the subsequent aftermath of interaction. More surprisingly, coach communication researchers have not explicitly provided a definition of coaching within the empirical record. The advancement of a communicative understanding of coaching, however, is beneficial as it provides a unified framework in which interaction, behavior, and speech can become focal points for coaching scholars. These concepts merit further attention, as successful coaching is dependent upon soft skills, especially communication (Turman, 2017).

A communicative conceptualization of coaching, therefore, is of value because it better encompasses interaction and is actionable. With this in mind, coaching might be better understood as *a social process, which is embedded within the larger social and cultural structures of sport, through which meaning is exchanged between coaches and athletes via verbal and nonverbal symbols, as coaches seek to promote athlete or team development and performance, as well as manage the dynamic sporting environments in which that development and performance occurs.* The provision of this conceptualization marks a potential change in direction for coaching researchers by emphasizing that specific verbal and nonverbal messages facilitate athletes' and teams' development and performances, and allow coaches to manage the complexities of the sporting environment. Further, this conceptualization recognizes the larger social and cultural structures in which human interaction occurs and is influenced (Alberts, Nakayama, & Martin, 2012). This conceptualization also offers scholars multiple levels of analysis, including a micro-level that focuses on specific acts and messages within interactions involving coaches and a macro-level that acknowledges cultural structures in which coaching and sport occur. Thus, this understanding of coaching is broad enough to include a host of variables that relate to human development, performance, mutual influence, information processing and sharing, and responses to environmental change. These features are strengths and may advance coaching research and education.

Development of Coach Communication

In order to fully comprehend, appreciate, and apply a body or research, it is necessary to understand the context from which it arises. Within this chapter, the importance and nature of coach communication research is framed within the larger academic body of coaching science. This initial formulation is useful for illustrating the uniqueness of coach communicative research and highlighting intersections upon which future interdisciplinary knowledge may be generated. However, it is imperative to recognize that coach communication scholarship developed in a specific milieu that is distinct from the fields of psychology, management, and sociology. Such a distinction is evident in communication scholars' reliance upon alternative contexts of communication research (e.g., instructional communication) for concepts and frameworks (e.g., Cranmer & Goodboy, 2015; Kassing & Infante, 1999; Rocca et al., 1998; Turman, 2008) rather than integrating those from coaching science literature. As a result of these decisions, coach communication research developed in relative isolation, with a limited amount of noticeable influence from outside fields of inquiry—Turman's (2001, 2003a) earliest works being notable exceptions. The benefit of this isolation is that coach communication literature examines a variety of behaviors (e.g., immediacy and verbal aggression) and messages (e.g., memorable and supportive messages) that are absent from the remainder of coaching science literature. The communicative perspective, therefore, offers unique and valuable insight toward building an understanding of coaching. The detriment of this isolation, however, is that it creates barriers (e.g., detached conceptualizations, variables, theories, and lines of research) that make the integration of said knowledge difficult. These barriers may explain why coaching scholars in sport psychology, sociology, and management rarely cite the scholarship of communication researchers.

Modern coach communication scholars operate within the subfield of sport communication, but largely rely on literature from the discipline of communication studies (Kassing et al., 2004; Wenner, 2015). *Sport communication* considers the "process by which people in sport, in a sport setting, or through a sport endeavor, share symbols as they create meaning through interaction" (Pedersen, Laucella, Miloch, & Fielding, 2007, p. 196). Although the origins of sport communication can be traced back to either Riding's (1934) exploration of slang in sport journalism or Real's (1975) examination of the spectacle of the Super Bowl, it has only consistently emerged within the empirical record during the late 20th and early 21st century (Pedersen, 2013a, 2013b; Wenner, 2015).

A defining element of sport communication is its heterogeneity, as it spans intrapersonal, interpersonal, intercultural, organizational, mediated, and rhetorical modes of communication (Billings et al., 2018). With such diversity of interests, sport communication is quite fractured, and there have been numerous attempts to organize or determine its scholarly location(s), including by topics of inquiry (Abeza et al., 2014; Pedersen, 2013b), communicative processes (Kassing et al., 2004), or dispositions within scholarship (Wenner, 2015). All of these efforts recognize that sport communication is dominated by those interested in media (social and mass) and cultural or rhetorical studies. For instance, the *Routledge Handbook of Sport Communication* focused on mediated content, practices within journalism, and the critical/ rhetorical examination of sporting cultures, but did not include a single chapter on coaching (Pedersen, 2013c). Likewise, Abeza et al.'s (2014) audit of the *International Journal of Sport Communication* found that less than 4% of publications addressed interpersonal or organizational communication with sport—none of those articles considered coaching. The media and cultural-centric nature of sport communication is likely due to the academic infrastructures (e.g., journals, programs, and conferences) that were available before the formal emergence of sport communication as a subfield, including those within journalism, media studies, management, and sociology (Abeza et al., 2014).

The absence of coach communication research from the aforementioned overviews of sport communication should not be interpreted as evidence that coaching research does not belong within sport communication. Instead, this absence is an opportunity to address two realities. First, coach communication research is an integral component of sport communication. The contribution of coaching to sport communication is at the heart of the process of *enactment of sport*, which focuses on the communication that surrounds the performance of sport (Kassing et al., 2004). Coaches are the conduits of information that connect sport organizations and structures to athletes, teach skills and team strategy, manage interactions and disputes between teammates and opposition, set and model appropriate forms of interaction with sources of authority, and influence the life lessons taken from sport. In other words, by examining coaching, scholars learn about the everyday interactions through which sports are taught, structured, maintained, and performed. Without these interactions, the organized and skilled versions of sports featured within sport media and popular culture would not exist. Moreover, coaches exert more influence on athletes' involvement with sport than forms of popular media (Coakley, 1993; Cranmer & Myers, 2017; McPherson, 1981). Simply, the value of coaching research is undeniable for illuminating the foundational interactions upon which larger sporting structures are built.

Second, a budding body of research on coach communication exists, if one knows where to look for it. Historically, coach communication research has been published within the discipline of communication studies, which is concerned with investigating and understanding human interaction and the construction of meaning (Wenner, 2015). Many coach communication manuscripts are published in journals affiliated with the National Communication Association or regional communication associations. For example, coach communication research can be found in journals such as *Communication Research Reports* (Cranmer & Sollitto, 2015; Kassing & Infante, 1999; Rocca et al., 1998; Turman, 2006; Turman & Schrodt, 2004), *Communication Education* (Turman, 2003a, 2007), *Journal of Applied Communication Research* (Turman, 2005), *Communication Studies* (Cranmer & Buckner, 2017), and *Western Journal of Communication* (Cranmer & Goodboy, 2015; Turman, 2008). Early coach communication scholars relied on the conferences of these associations as preliminary outlets for their scholarship, especially within divisions and interest groups that focus on instructional, organizational, group, or interpersonal communication. In return, these divisions and interest groups provided frameworks, theories, variables, and metaphors from which coaching was understood. Naturally, these infrastructures fostered distinct perspectives of coaching (i.e., coaches as instructors, managers, group members, or relational partners) over the past two decades. Each of these perspectives yield unique insight into differing aspects of the roles and obligations of coaches, as well as how sporting contexts create variation in athlete-coach relationship dynamics and the prioritization of effective coaching outcomes. Similar comparative perspectives were utilized by psychologists, who initially viewed coaching through parental or marital frameworks (Jowett, 2008; Jowett & Meek, 2000; Jowett, Paull, & Pensgaard, 2005). Chapters 3, 4, 5, and 6 of this text consider the underlying assumptions, utility, lines of research, and futures of the instructional, organizational, group, and interpersonal perspectives, respectively.

Recent shifts within the field of sport communication, however, have begun to centralize research, including that of coaching, into a more integrated pursuit (e.g., Ishak, 2017; Rodriguez, 2017). This shift may be the consequence of the availability of more unified platforms for scholarship, including Sage's *Communication & Sport* and sport specific divisions/interest groups at the National Communication Association (NCA), International Communication Association (ICA), or the International Association for Communication & Sport (IACS). In other words, today's coach communication researchers are free to entwine research perspectives more readily because singular perspectives no longer define the outlets of their scholarship. This reality is evident in Cranmer and colleagues recent blending of the organizational and interpersonal perspectives (Cranmer, 2016; Cranmer, Arnson, Moore, Scott, & Peed, 2019). Understanding what connects the existing perspectives may demonstrate the intricacies of the interplay and tensions between coaches' roles, as well as reveal potential blind spots that exist on the fringes between perspectives. Chapter 7 and 8 of this text consider these holistic issues by setting scholarly agendas, identifying opportunities to refine future research, and forwarding theoretical frameworks that may assist in the integration of communication research.

Conclusion

Sport is a profound component of our society. One reason for sport's salience is the tremendous rate at which individuals participate in organized sport during important developmental stages of life. These experiences come to socialize participants into sport and society (Coakley, 1993; McPherson, 1981). In order to maximize beneficial experiences and athlete development, sporting environments must function properly and under the supervision of well-trained coaches (Agans et al., 2016; Meân, 2013). Academic research is invaluable in aiding private and governmental organizations in their attempts to provide this education to coaches (National Association for Sport and Physical Education, 2018; Positive Coaching Alliance, 2018; Project Play, 2018). Unfortunately, the utility of current coaching science research is limited (Duffy, 2010)—arguably by its failure to fully recognize the importance of specific behaviors, messages, and the construction of meaning within sport. A communicative perspective of coaching, therefore, is crucial to the effort to assist scholarly and practitioner communities alike.

Note

1. Elite Sport Leadership Central (2019). Impact quotes. *Elitesportleader.com*. Retrieved from http://www.elitesportleader.com/themes/be-committed/quotes/

References

Abeza, G., O'Reilly, N., & Nadeau, J. (2014). Sport communication: A multidimensional assessment of the field's development. *International Journal of Sport Communication, 7,* 289–316.

Agans, J. P., Ettekan, A. V., & Stack, C. (2016, September). *PCA impact comparison study: Report of findings.* Unpublished manuscript, Positive Coaching Alliance. Retrieved from http://positivecoach.org/media/276708/pca_impactcomparisonstudy_final091316.pdf.

Alberts, J. K., Nakayama, T. K., & Martin, J. N. (2012). *Human communication in society* (3rd ed.). Upper Saddle River, NJ: Pearson.

Atkinson, J. L. (2009). Age matters in sport communication. *The Electronic Journal of Communication, 19.* Online Journal. Retrieved from http://www.cios.org/EJCPUBLIC/019/2/019341. html

Becker, A. J. (2009). It's not what they do, it's how they do it: Athlete experiences of great coaching. *International Journal of Sports Science & Coaching, 4,* 93–119.

Becker, A. J. (2013). Quality coaching behaviours. In P. Protrac, W. Gilbert, & J. Denison (Eds.), *The Routledge handbook of sports coaching* (pp. 184–195). New York, NY: Routledge.

Becker, A. J., & Wrisberg, C. A. (2008). Effective coaching in action: Observations of legendary collegiate basketball coach Pat Summitt. *The Sport Psychologist, 22,* 197–211.

Billings, A. C., Butterworth, M. L., & Turman, P. D. (2018). *Communication and sport: Surveying the field* (3rd ed.). Los Angeles, CA: Sage.

Cassidy, T., Jones, R., & Potrac, P. (2009). *Understanding sports coaching: The social, cultural and pedagogical foundations of coaching practice* (2nd ed.). New York, NY: Routledge.

Coakley, J. (1993). Sport and socialization. *Exercise and Sport Sciences Reviews, 21,* 169–200.

Coakley, J., & White, A. (1992). Making decisions: Gender and sport participation among British adolescents. *Sociology of Sport Journal, 9,* 20–35.

Cranmer, G. A. (2016). A continuation of sport teams from an organizational perspective: Predictors of athlete-coach leader-member exchange. *Communication & Sport, 4,* 43–61.

Cranmer, G. A., Anzur, C. K., & Sollitto, M. (2017). Memorable messages of social support that former high school athletes received from their head coaches. *Communication & Sport, 5,* 604–621.

Cranmer, G. A., Arnson, E., Moore, A., Scott, A., & Peed, J. (2018). High school athletes' reports of confirmation as a function of starting status and leader-member exchange. *Communication & Sport*, 7, 510–528. doi:10.1177/2167479518783838

Cranmer, G. A., & Brann, M. (2015). "It makes me feel like I am an important part of this team": An exploratory study of coach confirmation. *International Journal of Sport Communication*, 8, 193–211.

Cranmer, G. A., & Buckner, M. (2017). High school athletes' relationships with head coaches and teammates as predictors of their expressions of upward and lateral dissent. *Communication Studies*, 68, 37–55.

Cranmer, G. A., & Goodboy, A. K. (2015). Power play: Coach power use and athletes' communicative evaluations and responses. *Western Journal of Communication*, 79, 614–633.

Cranmer, G. A., & Myers, S. A. (2017). Exploring Division-I student-athletes' memorable messages from their anticipatory socialization. *Communication Quarterly*, 65, 125–143.

Cranmer, G. A., & Sollitto, M. (2015). Sport support: Received social support as a predictor of athlete satisfaction. *Communication Research Reports*, 32, 253–264.

Cushion, C., & Lyle, J. (2010). Conceptual development in sports coaching. In J. Lyle & C. Cushion (Eds.), *Sports coaching: Professionalisation and practice* (pp. 1–13). Edinburgh: Churchill Livingstone.

Denlinger, K. (1977, November 16). A bill of rights. *The Washington Post*. Retrieved from https://www.washingtonpost.com/archive/sports/1977/11/16/a-bill-of-rights/0f39c954-ff8e-4f9a-8f5f-835906af42dc/?utm_term=.14096611e078

Duffy, P. (2010). Preface. In J. Lyle & C. Cushion (Eds.), *Sports coaching: Professionalization and practice* (pp. vii–x). Edinburgh: Churchill Livingstone.

Duffy, P., Hartley, H., Bales, J., Crespo, M., Dick, F., Vardhan, D., … & Curado, J. (2011). Sport coaching as a "profession": Challenges and future directions. *International Journal of Coaching Science*, 5, 93–123.

Edelhauser, K. (2007, March 27). John Wooden's pyramid still standing. *Entrepreneur*. Retrieved from https://www.entrepreneur.com/article/176282.

European Coaching Council. (2007). Review of the EU 5-level structure for the recognition of coaching qualifications. *European Network of Sports Science, Education and Employment*. Retrieved from https://www.icce.ws/_assets/files/documents/ECC_5_level_review.pdf.

Fraser-Thomas, J., Côté, J., & Deakin, J. (2008). Understanding dropout and prolonged engagement in adolescent competitive sport. *Psychology of Sport and Exercise*, 9, 645–662.

Gale, D., Robbins, B., Tollin, M. (Producers), & Carter, T. (Director). (2005, January 14). *Coach Carter* [Motion picture]. United States: Paramount Pictures.

Gilbert, W. D. (2002, June). *An annotated bibliography and analysis of coaching science: 1970-2001*. Washington, DC: American Alliance for Health, Physical Education, Recreation. Retrieved from www.aahperd.org/rc/programs/upload/grantees_coaching_science.pdf.

Gilbert, W. D., & Trudel, P. (2004) Analysis of coaching science research published from 1970-2001. *Research Quarterly for Exercise and Sport*, 75, 388–399.

Grazer, B. (Producer), & Berg, P. (Director). (2004, October 4). *Friday night lights* [Motion picture]. United States: Universal Pictures.

Hoffer, R. (1995, January 16). Putting his house in order. *Sports Illustrated*. Retrieved from https://www.si.com/vault/1995/01/16/133038/putting-his-house-in-order-bill-mccartney-quit-as-colorados-coach-for-a-greater-quest-healing-his-family.

Irwin, G., Hanton, S., & Kerwin, D. (2004). Reflective practice and the origins of elite coaching knowledge. *Reflective Practice, 5*, 425–442.

Ishak, A. W. (2017). Communication in sports teams: A review. *Communication Research Trends, 36*, 4–38.

Jones, R. L. (2006). *The sports coach as educator: Reconceptualizing sports coaching*. New York, NY: Routledge.

Jones, R. L., & Turner, P. (2006). Teaching coaches to coach holistically: Can problem-base learning (PBL) help? *Physical Education and Sport Pedagogy, 11*, 181–202.

Jowett, S. (2008). Outgrowing the familial coach-athlete relationship. *International Journal of Sport psychology, 39*, 20–40.

Jowett, S. (2017). Coaching effectiveness: The coach–athlete relationship at its heart. *Current Opinion in Psychology, 16*, 154–158.

Jowett, S., & Meek, G. A. (2000). The coach-athlete relationship in married couples: An exploratory content analysis. *The Sport Psychologist, 14*, 157–175.

Jowett, S., Paull, G., & Pensgaard, A. M. (2005). Coach-athlete relationship. In J. Taylor & G. S. Wilson (Eds.), *Applying sport psychology: Four perspectives* (pp. 153–170). Champaign, IL: Human Kinetics.

Jowett, S., & Poczwardowski, A. (2007). Understanding the coach-athlete relationship. In S. Jowett & D. Lavallee (Eds.), *Social psychology in sport* (pp. 3–14). Champaign, IL: Human Kinetics.

Kassing, J. W., Billings, A. C., Brown, R. S., Halone, K. K., Harrison, K., Krizek, B., ... Turman, P. D. (2004). Communication in the community of sport: The process of enacting, (re) producing, consuming, and organizing sport. In P. J. Kalbfleisch (Ed.), *Communication yearbook* (Vol. 28, pp. 373–409). Mahwah, NJ: Erlbaum.

Kassing, J. W., & Infante, D. A. (1999). Aggressive communication in the coach-athlete relationship. *Communication Research Reports, 16*, 110–120.

Kassing, J. W., & Pappas, M. E. (2007). "Champions are built in the off season": An exploration of high school coaches' memorable messages. *Human Communication, 10*, 537–546.

Kelley, B., & Carchia, C. (2013, July 11). Hey, data data—Swing! The hidden demographics of youth sports. *ESPN.com*. Retrieved from http://espn.go.com/espn/story/_/id/9469252/hidden-demographics-youth-sports-espn-magazine

LeFebvre, L. (2017). Variables, conceptualization. In M. Allen (Ed.), *Sage encyclopedia of communication research methods* (pp. 1837–1839). Thousand Oaks, CA: Sage.

Little League. (2018). Partnerships. *LittleLeague.org*. Retrieved from https://www.littleleague.org/partnerships/pca/

Lyle, J. (2002). *Sports coaching concepts: A framework for coaches' behavior*. London: Routledge.

Lyle, J., & Cushion, C. (2010). *Sports coaching: Professionalisation and practice*. Edinburgh: Churchill Livingstone.

Maisel, I. (2003, November 7). The art of locker-room speaking. *ESPN.com*. Retrieved from http://www.espn.com/college-football/columns/story?columnist=maisel_ivan&id=1656370

McPherson, B. D. (1981). Socialization into and through sport involvement. In G. R. F. Lus-chen & G. H. Sage (Eds.), *Handbook of social science of sport* (pp. 246–273). Champaign, IL: Stipes.

Meân, L. J. (2013). The communicative complexity of youth sport: Maintaining benefits, man-aging discourses, and challenging identities. In P. M. Pedersen (Ed.), *Routledge handbook of sport communication* (pp. 338–349). New York, NY: Routledge.

National Association for Sport and Physical Education. (2018). *Play and playground encyclo-pedia*. Retrieved from https://www.pgpedia.com/n/national-association-sport-and-physical-education.

National Athletic Trainers Association. (2015, February 27). Student athletes' bill of rights introduced as a joint resolution in house and senate. *NATA.org*. Retrieved from https://www.nata.org/press-release/022715/student-athletes%E2%80%99-bill-rights-introduced-joint-resolution-house-and-senate

National Federation of State High School Associations. (2017). High school participation increases for 25th consecutive year. *NFHS.org*. Retrieved from http://www.nfhs.org/ParticipationStatistics/PDF/2016-17_Participation_Survey_Results.pdf

Pedersen, P. M. (Ed.). (2013a). Introduction. In *Routledge handbook of sport communication* (pp. 1–6). New York, NY: Routledge.

Pedersen, P. M. (2013b). Reflections on communication and sport: On strategic communica-tion and management. *Communication & Sport, 1*, 55–67.

Pedersen, P. M. (Ed.). (2013c). *Routledge handbook of sport communication*. New York, NY: Rout-ledge.

Pedersen, P., Laucella, P., Miloch, K., & Fielding, L. (2007). The juxtaposition of sport and communication: Defining the field of sport communication. *International Journal of Sport Management and Marketing, 2*, 193–207.

Positive Coaching Alliance. (2018). Mission statement. *PositiveCoach.org*. Retrieved from https://www.positivecoach.org/mission-history/

Potrac, P., Denison, J., & Gilbert, W. (2013). Introduction. In P. Potrac, W. Gilbert, & J. Denison (Eds.), *Routledge handbook of sports coaching* (pp. 1–2). New York, NY: Routledge.

Potrac, P., Jones, R., & Armour, K. (2002). "It's all about getting respect": The coaching behav-iors of an expert English soccer coach. *Sport, Education and Society, 7*, 183–202.

Project Play. (2018). What we do. *AspenProjectPlay.org*. Retrieved from https://www.aspenprojectplay.org/whatwedo/

Real, M. R. (1975). Super Bowl: Mythic spectacle. *Journal of Communication, 25*, 31–43.

Riding, J. W. (1934). Use of slang in newspaper sports writing. *Journalism Quarterly, 11*, 348–360.

Rocca, K. A., Martin, M. M., & Toale, M. C. (1998). Players' perceptions of their coaches' imme-diacy, assertiveness, and responsiveness. *Communication Research Reports, 15*, 445–450.

Rodriguez, D. (2017). *Sport communication: An interpersonal approach*. Dubuque, IA: Kendal Hunt.

Ronglan, L. T., & Aggerholm, K. (2013). Humor and sports coaching: A laughing matter? In P. Protrac, W. Gilbert, & J. Denison (Eds.), *The Routledge handbook of sports coaching* (pp. 222–234). New York, NY: Routledge.

SHAPE America. (2017). National standards for sport coaches by core responsibilities. *Shapeamerica.org*. Retrieved from https://www.shapeamerica.org/uploads/pdfs/2018/standards/National-Standards-for-Sport-Coaches-DRAFT.pdf

Sherman, C., Crassini, B., Maschette, W., & Sands, R. (1997). Instructional sport psychology: A re-conceptualization of sports coaching as sport instruction. *International Journal of Sport Psychology, 28*, 103–125.

Super, S., Verkooijen, K., & Koelen, M. (2018). The role of community sports coaches in creating optimal social conditions for life skill development and transferability—A salutogenic perspective. *Sport, Education and Society, 23*, 173–185.

Turman, P. D. (2001). Situational coaching styles: The impact of success and athlete maturity level on coaches' leadership styles over time. *Small Group Research, 32*, 576–594.

Turman, P. D. (2003a). Athletic coaching from an instructional communication perspective: The influence of coach experience of high school wrestlers' preferences and perceptions of coaching behaviors across a season. *Communication Education, 23*, 73–86.

Turman, P. D. (2003b). Coaches and cohesion: The impact of coaching techniques on team cohesion in the small group sport setting. *Journal of Sport Behavior, 26*, 86–104.

Turman, P. D. (2005). Coaches' use of anticipatory and counterfactual regret messages during competition. *Journal of Applied Communication Research, 33*, 116–138.

Turman, P. D. (2006). Athletes' perception of coach power use and the association between playing status and sport satisfaction. *Communication Research Reports, 23*, 273–282.

Turman, P. D. (2007). The influence of athlete sex, context, and performance on high school basketball coaches' use of regret messages during competition. *Communication Education, 56*, 333–353.

Turman, P. D. (2008). Coaches' immediacy behaviors as predictors of athletes' perceptions of satisfaction and team cohesion. *Western Journal of Communication, 72*, 162–179.

Turman, P. D. (2017). What effects do coaches' communicative messages have on their athletes/teams? In A. K. Goodboy & K. Shultz (Eds.), *Introduction to communication studies: Translating scholarship into meaningful practice* (pp. 121–128). Dubuque, IA: Kendall Hunt.

Turman, P. D., & Schrodt, P. (2004). New avenues for instructional communication research: Relationships among coaches' leadership behaviors and athletes' affective learning. *Communication Research Reports, 21*, 130–143.

Vella, S., Oades, L. G., & Crowe, T. P. (2011). The role of coach in facilitating positive youth development: Moving from theory to practice. *Journal of Applied Sport Psychology, 22*, 33–48.

Webster, C. A. (2009). Expert teachers' instructional communication in golf. *International Journal of Sport Communication, 2*, 205–222.

Wenner, L. A. (2015). Communication and sport, where art thou? Epistemological reflections on the moment and field(s) of play. *Communication & Sport, 3*, 247–260.

· 2 ·

DEFINING EFFECTIVE COACHING

Winning is fun … Sure. But winning is not the point. Wanting to win is the point. Not giving up is the point. Never letting up is the point. Never being satisfied with what you've done is the point.—Pat Summitt[1]

One of the few ideas around which there is consensus among coaching scholars and practitioners is that their efforts should encourage effective coaching (Horn, 2002; Potrac, Denison, & Gilbert, 2013; Rhind & Jowett, 2012; Turman, 2008). This consensus, however, is hollow, as what constitutes effectiveness is not readily agreed upon or clear. What is clear is that coaching effectiveness is a multifaceted and complex concept that varies based on context (Becker, 2009; Nash, Sproule, & Horton, 2011; Vella, Oades, & Crowe, 2011). Yet, formalizing an understanding of coaching effectiveness provides a shared focus and purpose for researchers and allows for better integration of findings across studies (Duffy, 2010). The purpose of this chapter is to forward an understanding of coaching effectiveness that recognizes specific domains of outcomes and the pertinent contextual features that determine how effectiveness is valued and achieved.

Before such a purpose can be fulfilled, it is important to explicate how effectiveness is understood within this chapter. One approach for understanding effective coaching is to determine the telos of a coach. *Telos* is a Greek term that is rooted within Aristotelianism, and refers to the purpose or goal of an object, person, or practice. A telos-centric approach asserts that it is only by asking what is the purpose or goal of a coach that one can understand effective coaching. As aforementioned in Chapter 1, the purpose of coaching is to foster the development and performance of athletes and teams through verbal and nonverbal symbols, as well as manage sporting environments in an effort to facilitate those aims. Outcomes that are shaped by interaction and associated with these goals are, therefore, indicators of effective coaching. A telos approach provides a communicative and athlete-centered view of effective coaching, whereby coaches' behaviors and words are effective (or not) based upon athletes' experiences and performances. This approach offers prescriptive information that can empower coaches and guide their pedagogical, managerial, and interpersonal practices.

The value of a telos-centric approach is further evident in its alignment with the objectives of the non-profit organizations highlighted in Chapter 1. The PCA promotes the use of specific, prosocial coaching behaviors and techniques, which highlights coaches' communication as the central mechanism of their effectiveness (Positive Coaching Alliance, 2018). Project Play advocates that effective coaches inspire particular states within athletes (e.g., increased physical abilities, confidence, and motivation), which positions athletes' experiences as the primary indicators of a coach's effectiveness (Project Play, 2018). NASPE's *Revised National Standards for Sport Coaches* focuses on the fulfillment of coaching responsibilities (e.g., developing a safe sport environment, conducting practices, and preparing for competition) to determine effectiveness (SHAPE America, 2017). Jointly, these organizations forward an understanding whereby coach effectiveness rests within accomplishing assigned roles through strategic communication, which becomes evident in the experiences of athletes. Such an understanding of effectiveness is also consistent with that of coach communication researchers (Kassing et al., 2004; Turman, 2008).

Domains of Effective Coaching

To facilitate the discussion of effective coaching, this chapter utilizes domains of effectiveness. The term domain refers to groups of outcomes that share features or origins. The codification of domains of effectiveness suggests that coaching, regardless of context, shares similar core functions and valued outcomes—an assertion that must be true for a singular definition of the role/profession of a coach to be tenable. This text asserts that these domains are indicators of effectiveness across levels of athletics, and that all coaches, to some degree, must instruct athletes, organize their teams, manage group dynamics, and relate to athletes as people (i.e., the foci of Chapters 3–6). Yet, it is important to recognize how coaches obtain these domains or weight their importance varies by context. For instance, both Little League and Major League Baseball coaches must teach baseball strategies and skills. The success of said coaches could be assessed via the learning indicators of their athletes. Yet, the complexity of their instruction (e.g., language and content) and pedagogical approaches would unarguably differ in accordance with the characteristics of their athletes (e.g., age and cognitive capacity) and purpose of their leagues. As such, the contextual nature of coaching is acknowledged in the second half of this chapter, as well as the introduction of each of the proceeding four chapters.

Still, there is utility in forwarding codified domains of effectiveness, as it provides coaches with benchmarks from which to assess their performance and scholars with a framework from which to build knowledge (Vella et al., 2011). The criteria for inclusion among these domains was threefold: the selected domains of effective coaching (a) address an aspect of human development (i.e., social, cognitive, emotional, moral, or physical) or athletic performance, (b) are attributable to coaching behaviors or messages, and (c) exist within extant coach communication literature. These criteria are consistent with the telos approach and conceptualization of coaching, as well as ensure the identified domains are within coaches' purview. Six domains were identified with these criteria: learning, relationships, psychological orientations, socialization, team environment, and winning.

Learning

Athlete learning is at the heart of development (Kassing et al., 2004). Nelson and Colquhoun (2013) suggested that "athlete learning is arguably one of those few outcomes that all coaching practitioners desire, irrespective of the context in which they work" (p. 284). Learning manifests in affective, cognitive, and behavioral forms (Waldeck, Plax, & Kearney, 2010). *Affective learning* denotes the internalization of positive regard toward subject matter, learning environment, or instructor. Athletes' affective learning manifests within the internalized appreciation for their sport, the sporting skills featured within instruction, or coaches. The appreciation of instruction and coaches is a determinant of continued sport participation (Coakley & White, 1992;

Fraser-Thomas, Côté, & Deakin, 2008) and facilitates additional forms of cognitive and behavioral learning (Waldeck et al., 2010).

Sport participation requires mental acuity to inform and guide physical performance. Rooted within Bloom's (1956) taxonomy of learning, *cognitive learning* refers to obtaining, remembering, managing, and using information communicated by instructional figures. Athletes' cognitive learning encompasses their acquisition, application, and retention of the complex techniques (e.g., patterns of fine motor skills), strategies (e.g., formations), tactics (e.g., styles of play), and systems that govern performance and the interplay between athletes during competition (e.g., rules of their respective sports). Improved performance as the result of instruction requires athletes to understand and integrate information into their existing knowledge of skills and team strategy. Recognizing athletes' comprehension and processing of instruction is an important way to assess the cognitive development of athletes and effectiveness of coaches (Becker, 2009; Côté & Gilbert, 2009; Vella et al., 2011).

Sport also requires physical performance. *Behavioral learning* references learners' physical actions or skills in response to instruction. Athletes' behavioral learning encompasses their efforts to bring coaches' instruction to fruition on the field of play through their physical efforts. Given that physical development of fine motor skills requires time, behavioral learning is a long-term coaching objective (Nash et al., 2011). The ability to receive instruction from a coach and demonstrate a skill or technique partially determines the outcomes of sporting events. Moreover, behavioral learning is at the center of the coaching process, and is a means of assessing effectiveness (Côté & Gilbert, 2009; Vella et al., 2011). Together, the domain of learning forwards that effective coaches inspire appreciation of sport, facilitate the processing of instruction and feedback, and improve the behavioral performances of athletes.

Relationships

Another domain of effective coaching is developing beneficial and functional relationships for athletes (Côté & Gilbert, 2009; Vella et al., 2011). This domain spans athlete-coach and athlete-teammate relationships, as successful coaches facilitate positive interaction between themselves and amongst their teams. These relationships are relevant to effective coaching to the extent that they facilitate the development or performance of athletes. Because coaching is a social activity dependent upon interaction, the quality and closeness of athletes' relationships with coaches and teammates facilitates development and performance (Jowett, 2017). Yet, sport is a particularly challenging context in which to form relationships because competitive environments provide opportunities for disagreement, face threats, and destructive emotions (e.g., jealousy or anger). As such, boundaries and high-degrees of professionalism are effective relational features that enable accountability, trust, and ensure appropriate forms of interaction (Becker, 2009).

Athletes' perceptions of relationships—which manifest in degrees of trust, respect, and affect for others—are a means of assessing relational quality. Team cohesion is one such perception and encompasses athletes' sense of closeness or belonging with teammates along task and social dimensions (Bollen & Hoyle, 1990). Cohesion offers insight into team relationships and the sense of shared responsibilities or objectives—both of which increase performance (Jones & Kijeski, 2009; Widmeyer, Carron, & Brawley, 1993). Likewise, athletes' perceptions of close athlete-coach relationships shape interactions with teammates (Turman, 2008; Westre & Weiss, 1991) and provide psychosocial resources for development (Cranmer & Myers, 2015). These perceptions also influence how athletes respond to coach communication, with instruction and motivation being easier to achieve with closer relational dynamics (Jowett, 2017).

The observable nature of athlete-coach interactions also indicates relational quality. Coaches are most effective when they establish reciprocal communication that features genuine, open-minded, empathetic, and free exchanges with athletes (Cranmer & Myers, 2015; Jowett, 2017). Effective athlete-coach communication includes providing athletes with the social capital and resources to perform, including information, support, feedback, and attention (Cranmer, 2018; Cranmer & Myers, 2015). Quality coaching is not merely a top-down process, as coaches who are open to athletes' viewpoints and disagreements are better positioned to gain insight regarding strategy, inspire investment, and manage team climates (Cranmer & Buckner, 2017; Cranmer, Buckner, Pham, & Jordan, 2018). The relational domain indicates that effective coaches promote development and performance through cultivating relationships and social climates that facilitate open exchanges and a sense of belonging among teams.

Psychological Orientations

An additional domain of effectiveness recognizes psychological orientations toward sport participation. Coaches' encouragement of orientations that allow athletes to perform successfully, manage stress and uncertainty, and continue their participation in sport are indicators of effectiveness (Horn, 2002; Project Play, 2018). Within coach communication research, two psychological orientations have garnered considerable attention. The first psychological orientation is athletes' motivation (Cranmer, Brann, & Weber, 2018; Mazer, Barnes, Grevious, & Boger, 2013; Turman, 2003). *Motivation* reflects an internal process towards the initiation of effort and direction toward a behavior (Weiss & Ferrer-Caja, 2002). For athletes, motivation references their desire to enact sporting behaviors or participate in sport. It is noteworthy that communication scholars recognize motivation as a continuum ranging from amotivated to motivated, as well as either a state or trait disposition (Waldeck et al., 2010). State motivation is the focal point of communication scholars, who seek to understand how specific interactions with coaches motivate athletes (Cranmer, Brann, et al., 2018; Martin, Rocca, Cayanus, & Weber, 2009; Turman, 2003). Coaching science scholars, however, consider the intrinsic or extrinsic sources of athletes' motivation (Vallerand & Fortier, 1998). Regardless of these differences, coaching scholars and practitioners consider motivation a primary determinant of sporting experiences (Hanrahan & Andersen, 2013; Weiss & Ferrer-Caja, 2002) and coaching effectiveness (Project Play, 2018).

The second psychological orientation is satisfaction, which was the first non-performance outcome studied within coaching science literature (Horn, 2002). *Satisfaction* is the evaluative response of comparing expectations or goals with one's experiences. Sporting experiences are deemed satisfying when athletes' expectations and goals (e.g., have fun, be with friends, learn skills, and be physically active) are met by coaches and sporting environments. Satisfaction is a multifaceted construct that may refer to sport outcomes or processes, task or relational dynamics, and individual or team-level experiences (Chelladurai & Riemer, 1998). Coach behavior is predominant in determining athletes' satisfaction with their sporting experiences (Turman, 2006), relationships (Kassing & Infante, 1999), and specific interactions (Cranmer & Goodboy, 2015; Cranmer & Sollitto, 2015). Fostering environments that are satisfying is one means through which coaches can demonstrate effectiveness (Positive Coaching Alliance, 2018; Project Play, 2018).

Countless additional orientations may indicate effective coaching, and one merely needs to consider sport psychology literature to identify them. Coaching science researchers recognize the effectiveness of promoting self-efficacy or reducing anxiety, as these states coincide with confidence, comfort, and self-worth in relation to competition (Côté & Gilbert, 2009; Project Play, 2018). Other scholars advocate for the promotion of resiliency or restraint in the face of adversity (Vella et al., 2011). Recently, communication scholars have considered athletes' *competitiveness*, which is an achievement orientation to compete and defeat others (Cranmer, Gagnon, & Mazer, 2019). Competitiveness is a disposition that improves performance across a variety of task-oriented contexts, as competitive individuals assume personal or professional costs to build feelings of self-worth through achievement (Mowen, 2004). Competitive athletes enjoy the thrill and uncertainty that comes with facing and defeating opposition. Effective coaches inspire athletes to embrace competition by creating challenging environments that focus on improvement (Cranmer et al., 2019). Collectively, the domain of psychological orientations demonstrates that effective coaches encourage mindsets that allow athletes to develop, perform, evaluate, and function within sporting environments.

Socialization

Socialization is the social process that prepares (i.e., socializes) individuals to participate in society or specific subgroups in society (McPherson, 1981). Athletes are socialized into teams and society through interactions with coaches—among other agents of socialization (i.e., parents, siblings, peers, teachers, and media). Socialization research focuses on two distinct processes: socialization into sport and socialization via sport. *Socialization into sport* concerns how athletes become involved in sport and adjust to their sporting roles and teams (Cranmer, 2017, 2018). During this process, coaches create interest in joining teams (McPherson, 1981), inspire continued participation (Coakley & White, 1992), and provide understandings of tasks and roles (Cranmer, 2017, 2018). Although non-communication scholars focus on athletes' participative decisions (Coakley, 1993; McPherson, 1981), for coaches to be effective athletes must become well-adjusted and productive members of their teams. Athletes' adjustment is often impeded by uncertainty, stress, interpersonal demands (e.g., pressure to socially integrate into the group), task demands (e.g., work overload, time pressures), role demands (e.g., role conflict, role ambiguity), and unmet expectations (Anderson, Riddle, & Martin, 1999). Coaches help overcome these challenges by providing information, feedback, and support to athletes, as well as properly structuring their teams. These resources aid athletes' knowledge of team history (e.g., culture, traditions, myths, customs, stories, and rituals), language and terminology (e.g., acronyms, jargon, and slang), politics (e.g., formal and informal power structures), goals and values, tasks and roles, or relational dynamics (Cranmer, 2018). Such knowledge is crucial for athletes' integration into their teams.

The second process of *socialization via sport* considers how athletes are socialized into society. Coaches are responsible for helping athletes become functional members of society (Côté & Gilbert, 2009; Super, Verkooijen, & Koelen, 2018; Vella et al., 2011). Eime, Young, Harvey, Charity, and Payne (2013) conducted a literature review of 30 studies and concluded that participation in sport, especially team sports, increases athletes' social adjustment (e.g., reduced anxiety, depression, and suicidality), social skills (e.g., greater self-control, assertiveness, and conflict resolution), and identities (e.g., greater self-concept). Some data indicates that sport participation is more valuable than other extracurricular activities (e.g., performance and fine art, faith & service, or academic activities)—although a combination of activities is arguably most beneficial (Hansen, Larson, & Dworkin, 2003). Coaches contribute to this process through structuring sporting environments and modeling behavior (Arthur-Banning, Wells, Baker, & Hegreness, 2009; Lockwood & Perlman, 2008; Meân, 2013). Specifically, effective coaches emphasize cultural means of success (e.g., work ethic, delayed gratification, perseverance) and develop athletes' skill sets that extend beyond sport (e.g., time management, goal setting, or communication skills) (Kassing & Pappas, 2007; Lockwood & Perlman, 2008; Super et al., 2018). The domain of socialization reveals that effective coaches are able to assist their athletes in becoming well-adjusted members of social collectives – both within and outside of sport.

Team Environment

An additional domain is the management of the sporting environment, which is the accumulated atmosphere and structure of a team, towards development and performance (Cushion & Lyle, 2010; Vella et al., 2011). Effective environments facilitate successful coping and functioning in game situations (Becker, 2009; Nash et al., 2011) and balance the development of individuals with the needs of teams (Cushion & Lyle, 2010). Environments are especially important for the social wellbeing and health of athletes. Part of promoting healthy team environments is embracing sportsmanship. *Sportsmanship* refers to the valuing of fair play (e.g., not cheating or causing undue harm to opponents) and respect for opponents, coaches, and officials (Kassing & Barber, 2007; Kassing & Infante, 1999). The development of sportsmanship is important because sport occurs via a series of games, and without sportsmanship continued and

welcomed participation in this series is unlikely. Coaches develop sportsmanship through role modeling sportsmanship behaviors for athletes (e.g., demonstrating respect for officials), creating official team policies (e.g., mandatory
post-game handshakes), and developing cultures that respect rules and denote
goodwill during competition (Arthur-Banning et al., 2009; Kassing & Barber,
2007; Kassing & Infante, 1999).

Environments and team climates also relate to athletes' health. Disturb-
ing trends of specialization, professionalization, and commodification are
commonplace and endanger youth and adolescent athletes. Burnout, psychological distress, and overuse injuries are often the result of these destructive
trends (Hyman, 2009). Another distressing trend within contact sports is
the commonality with which concussions are sustained (Cantu & Hyman,
2012). Effective sporting environments prioritize the physical wellbeing of
athletes. For instance, coaches may adopt team policies that limit exposure to
unnecessary injuries (Cranmer & Sanderson, 2018) or create social climates
that emphasize safety (Cranmer & LaBelle, 2018). Environments that reduce
stigma around reporting injuries and frame the prioritization of one's health
as an obligation to their teams are especially effective (Baugh, Kroshus, Daneshvar, & Stern, 2014; Cranmer & LaBelle, 2018; Sanderson, Weathers, Snedaker, & Gramlich, 2017). Such environments are established through open
communication and close athlete-coach relationships (Cranmer & LaBelle,
2018). The domain of team environment demonstrates that effective coaches
promote social structures and cultures that prioritize the wellbeing of all sporting stakeholders, especially athletes.

Winning

Winning is widely recognized within the public realm as the sole indicator
of coaching effectiveness (Becker, 2009; Turman, 2017). Coaching science
scholars implicitly accept that effective coaching is determined by wins, as
numerous studies attempt to reverse engineer effectiveness through the obser-
vation of coaches with established records of winning (Becker, 2009; Jowett
& Cockerill, 2003; Nash et al., 2011; Potrac, Jones, & Armour, 2002). Winning is cautiously included as a domain of effectiveness within this text. This
caution is merited for two reasons. First, the emphasis of winning serves to
the detriment of other indicators of effectiveness (e.g., sportsmanship or life
skills) and contradicts the purpose of many developmental sports leagues
(Turman, 2017). For instance, the prioritization of winning is associated with

ineffective styles of instruction that focus on individual task mastery, which decreases motivation, enjoyment, and skill acquisition among youth participants (Lockwood & Perlman, 2008). The overemphasis on winning also contributes to burnout and disinterest in sport (Coakley & White, 1992). Second, the comparative contributions of coaching and athlete talent to winning are debatable. For instance, one study indicated that Division-I football players' talent (i.e., determined by recruiting websites) accounted for as much as 60–80% of team in-conference winning percentage (Caro, 2012). The importance of athletes' raw abilities might be more relevant within youth and adolescent sports, which feature more variation in physical development and abilities (Atkinson, 2009). Put differently, a novice coach with talented and physically developed athletes will likely defeat an expert coach with lesser athletes. There is a reason for the coaching colloquialism: *It's not about the X's and O's, it's about the Jimmies and Joes.*

Despite these concerns, with all things equal, effective coaches theoretically should win more. It is not the intention of this text to discourage coaches from winning games. Competition is a defining aspect of sport, and serves athlete development by providing opportunities to manage oneself in victory and defeat. However, scholarly discourse around winning must be reshaped. Winning is but one of many means to assess coaches' effectiveness. More importantly, coaching is indirect in its influence on winning. In other words, coaches assist athletes via their instruction but do not have direct control over the outcomes of games. Instead, sporting outcomes are influenced by a host of variables, including athletes' abilities, opponents' abilities, referees' decisions, and chance. With this in mind, context should determine the emphasis on winning, with careful consideration toward its importance.

Contextual Nature of Coach Effectiveness

A "one-size fits all" approach to coaching effectiveness is misguided and overlooks the contextual elements and dynamism that define coaching (Duffy et al., 2011; Trudel & Gilbert, 2006). It is unarguable that most coaches consider their efforts successful if their athletes learn sporting skills and strategies, form quality relationships with coaches and teammates, develop mindsets that aid their performance, integrate into their roles and society, play in safe environments, and win games. As such, the domains of effectiveness are a reasonable starting point for evaluating coaches. However, how these domains are achieved and the manner in which they are emphasized should not be uniform across all sporting environments (European Coaching Council, 2007). Scholars and practitioners need to consider athlete and coach characteristics, as well as the nature of particular sports or leagues when contemplating effectiveness (Becker, 2009; Horn, 2002; Nash et al., 2011).

Athletes' Characteristics

Athletes' characteristics and dispositions influence their expectations, evaluations, and responses to coaching (Horn, 2002). Coaches must consider these features when determining how to achieve effectiveness. Indeed, all communication is receiver oriented, as meaning is established within the minds of others. Coaching scholars recognize the communicative and psychological characteristics of athletes as important features within athlete-coach interaction. For instance, athletes with low self-esteem respond most favorably to coaches' reinforcement and encouragement but most negatively to an absence of support (Smith & Smoll, 1990). Other considerations might include the demographic profiles of athletes, including their sex. To date, practitioners and communication scholars have largely de-emphasized the importance of such demographics within coaching. Yet, a limited number of studies have demonstrated that aggressive interactions are more normative among male athletes (Martin et al., 2009; Turman, 2003). This limited data indicates athletes' interactions with coaches, self-expressions, and some team norms may vary by sex. Coaches should keep the potential influence of such orientations and features in mind when selecting coaching behaviors and techniques, and should strive to meet expectations and societal norms when appropriate.

Other important characteristics include athletes' physical and cognitive development (Lockwood & Perlman, 2008). A life-span approach to coaching requires the recognition of the different motivations, needs, and abilities of groups of athletes ranging from youths to adults. Coaches must understand that youth athletes are differentiated from adults, and are still developing physically (e.g., in size, strength, speed, and coordination) and mentally (e.g., cognitive ability) (Atkinson, 2009). For instance, children's motivations for participating in sport (i.e., to have fun, be with friends, learn, and exercise) are less outcome driven than adult athletes (Coakley, 2007). Therefore, coaching behaviors that are focused on the performance process (i.e., basic skill development and enjoying participation) are most appropriate for young athletes, with the increased emphasis on performance outcomes (e.g., scoring) becoming more suitable as athletes age (Chaumenton & Duda, 1988). These developmental realities reveal that complex instruction and strategy, as well as the emphasis on competition and winning, should be avoided until athletes mature and develop. Unfortunately, youth sport (i.e., that for children aged 6–14 years old) often occurs in social climates that include public reprimands and emphasize winning as a means of validation for parents and coaches (Meân & Kassing, 2007).

Coaches must also consider athletes' physical abilities when coaching. Effective coaching rests within identifying and maximizing the strengths of athletes (Vella et al., 2011). Coaches are often favorable toward and invest more resources in athletes with greater abilities. For instance, starting athletes form closer relationships with coaches (Case, 1998; Cranmer, 2016), have greater voice in the functioning of their teams (Cranmer & Buckner, 2017; Kassing & Anderson, 2014), and receive more useful feedback and instruction (Cranmer, Arnson, Moore, Scott, & Peed, 2019; Cranmer & Goodboy, 2015; Turman, 2006). These patterns inhibit the skill development of less talented athletes by diverting and pooling resources among starters (Cranmer, Arnson, et al., 2019), and ultimately may lead to disinterest or exit from sport (Coakley & White, 1992; Lockwood & Perlman, 2008). Effective coaches must balance efforts to coach athletes according to their abilities, without letting such efforts detract from the sporting environments that they create. An athlete-centric approach is a valuable mindset for ensuring that coaches maximize their effectiveness through individualizing athletes' sporting experiences.

Coach Characteristics

Coaching requires self-awareness of one's own personality and skillsets, as these characteristics guide the ability to instruct, manage, and relate to athletes (Nash et al., 2011). Self-awareness and reflection are crucial mechanisms through which coaches identify modes of interaction that work for them (Cassidy, Jones, & Potrac, 2009; Gilbert & Trudel, 2004). One such characteristic that coaches must reflect upon is their sporting knowledge (Becker, 2009; European Coaching Council, 2007). Côté, Young, North, and Duffy (2007) argued that effective coaching consists of "… the competences that coaches require when interacting with athletes …" (p. 4). These competences include coaches' *professional* (i.e., related to sporting skills and pedagogical strategies), *interpersonal* (i.e., how to form and maintain relationships), and *intrapersonal* knowledge (i.e., that which comes from self-reflection and considering one's schemas) (Gilbert & Côté, 2013). These forms of knowledge are cultivated from formal (e.g., university education, certificate programs), non-formal (e.g., conferences, workshops, colloquiums), and informal sources (e.g., mentoring, coaching experience, athletic career) (Nelson, Cushion, & Potrac, 2006). Knowledge is undeniably important for coaches to possess, as effective coaching would be impossible without it. Yet, knowledge itself does not constitute coaching effectiveness, but rather is a prerequisite for effectiveness. Put differently, *how coaches use their knowledge* determines their effectiveness. Coaches should strive to cultivate their sporting knowledge and focus on outcomes for which they are best suited to address.

The role of coaches within a team might also influence what outcomes of effectiveness they prioritize (European Coaching Council, 2007). Coaching staffs, especially for large team sports, usually include multiple individuals. Coaches are assigned titles (e.g., head coach, head assistant coach, or coordinator) and specific roles that correspond with a position (e.g., pitching coach in baseball), group of positions (e.g., offensive coordinator in football), or skillset (e.g., distance running in track and field). On large teams, head coaches act as managers who select assistant coaches, to whom they delegate responsibilities and the majority of interactions with athletes (Cranmer, 2018). Within such a structure, assistant coaches are responsible for much of the technical and instructional feedback and are the primary contact points for most athletes. An assistant coach's role, therefore, may be to emphasize athletes' learning, psychological states, and relationships. In contrast, head coaches within these systems are more responsible for macro elements of team functioning (e.g., goals, schedules, and routines). Head coaches, thus, should be more concerned with collective outcomes like socializing athletes into teams, creating healthy sporting environments, and winning.

Finally, effective coaching may be individualized to the vision and mission of specific coaches, based upon the importance they assign particular domains (Becker, 2009; Nash et al., 2011). A common guiding document utilized among sport practitioners is a coaching philosophy, which formalizes their views of the role of coaches and the nature of athlete-coach relationships within sport (Jenkins, 2010). The intention behind these documents is to guide coaching practices and serve as a template from which coaches can evaluate their efforts (Cassidy et al., 2009). Philosophies, therefore, influence how coaches come to individualize their understandings of effectiveness. For instance, if a coach emphasizes the development of athletes as citizens within their philosophy, outcomes associated with socialization via sport should be focal points in determining their effectiveness. Coaches who prioritize creating welcoming and safe environments may consider athletes' relationships with coaches and teammates, team cultures, or athletes' wellbeing. In this regard, there should be leeway (within reason) to evaluate coaches (at least partially) based upon their own aims. Self-awareness is key for increasing coaching effectiveness, as aligning coaching efforts with one's abilities, positions, and aims facilitates authentic athlete-coach interactions.

Nature of Sport

The emphasis on particular outcomes of effective coaching and appropriate coaching techniques are partially determined by sporting environments, including the type of sport, team size, or sport and league cultures (Horn, 2002; Smoll & Smith, 1989). For example, competition varies across participation-oriented and performance-oriented sports leagues (Duffy et al., 2011). Participation-oriented leagues (e.g., developmental or recreation leagues) emphasize development and are designed for beginners or those who play for enjoyment (Trudel & Gilbert, 2006). Performance-oriented sports leagues (e.g., Amateur Athletic Union or professional sports leagues) stress the outcomes of games, are for full-time or highly devoted athletes, and require greater investment of resources (e.g., finances, time, or emotion) (Trudel & Gilbert, 2006). The type of sports league an athlete participates in should be considered in evaluations of coaching. Positive relationships, athletes' psychological states, and healthy environments should be stressed in all participation-oriented sports leagues. It is also logical to prioritize the teaching of basic skills and strategies within developmental leagues consisting of beginners. Within performance-oriented sports leagues, winning becomes more important with the increase of resource investments (Horn, 2002); this is not to say that other outcomes of effective coaching become irrelevant.

Other contextual factors, like the interdependence within the structure of sports, are important to consider (Evans, Eys, & Bruner, 2012). Sports vary in interdependence, which is evident in a continuum of individual to interdependent sports. *Individual sports* are those in which individuals compete by themselves without dependence upon teammates. The comparison between individual performances entirely determines outcomes (i.e., there are no teams). *Independent sports* are defined by the summation of individual efforts into a team score that is compared to the score of other teams to determine a collective outcome. *Interdependent sports* (e.g., football, baseball, basketball, and hockey) require interdependence between athletes as their simultaneous and collaborative efforts determine team outcomes. As interdependence between athletes increases, quality communication and relationships are required for teams to be successful (Turman, 2003, 2008). Thus, as interdependence increases across sports, relationships between athletes and socialization into teams are of greater value. It should be noted that there are no true individual sports within American educational systems (i.e., middle school, high school, and college), as sports that could be organized as such (e.g., track, cross country, swimming, and wrestling) are organized as team sports. These educational systems serve as the context for most athletic participation among adolescents and for the majority of communication scholars' research on coaching. Therefore, much of the research highlighted within this text focuses on team sports.

The timing within a sporting cycle also shapes the effectiveness of coaches. Periods within sporting seasons serve distinct functions. Coaches may alter their focus and efforts to suit the purpose of these periods (Lockwood & Perlman, 2008; Turman, 2001, 2003). For example, strength and conditioning sessions are for developing the physical abilities of athletes, practices are formalized periods to work on skill development and the execution of strategy, film sessions are opportunities to refine cognitive understanding of the performance of oneself and opponents, games are periods to implement skills and strategies against live competition, and post-season games are hyper-competitive games. The importance of outcomes of effective coaching may coincide with these periods differently. For instance, athlete learning is germane to film sessions and practices, winning is of consequence during games and more so during post-season games, and athletes' relationships may be solidified early within a season as teams form. Effective coaches maximize the potential and purpose of each of these circumstances to improve athlete development and performance. Effective coaches come to be aware of their settings and sporting contexts and adjust accordingly.

Conclusion

Coaching effectiveness is at the heart of the communicative perspective of coaching. Using a telos-centric approach to coaching, this chapter is a foundation from which scholars may enhance the experiences of athletes. The telos of coaches indicates that effective coaches use their communication to aid in athletes' development and performances, including through managing the sporting environment. Effectiveness, therefore, spans a multitude of domains, including those associated with athletes' experiences (i.e., learning, relationships, psychological states, and socialization), the sporting environment (i.e., team climates), and outcomes of games. The importance of these domains and the means through which they can be achieved are highly contextualized by the characteristics of athletes, coaches, and sports. With this in mind, coaches must consider the context in which they coach as a guide for prioritizing and fostering domains of effectiveness. Such complexity is evident in the utility of multiple perspectives of coaching (i.e., instructional, organizational, group, and interpersonal), which are reviewed in Chapters 3 through 6.

Note

1. Brainy Quote. (2019). Pat Summitt quotes. *BrainyQuote.com*. Retrieved from https://www.brainyquote.com/quotes/pat_summitt_777388

References

Anderson, C. M., Riddle, B. L., & Martin, M. M. (1999). Socialization processes in groups. In L. R. Frey, D. S. Gouran, & M. S. Poole (Eds.), *The handbook of group communication theory and research* (pp. 139–163). Thousand Oaks, CA: Sage.

Arthur-Banning, S., Wells, M., Baker, B., & Hegreness, R. (2009). Parents behaving badly? The relationship between the sportsmanship behaviors of adults and athletes in youth basketball games. *Journal of Sport Behavior, 32*, 3–18.

Atkinson, J. L. (2009). Age matters in sport communication. *The Electronic Journal of Communication, 19*. Online Journal. Online Journal. Retrieved from http://www.cios.org/EJC PUBLIC/019/2/019341.html

Baugh, C. M., Kroshus, E., Daneshvar, D. H., & Stern, R. A. (2014). Perceived coach support and concussion symptom-reporting: Difference between freshmen and non-freshmen college football players. *Journal of Law, Medicine, and Ethics, 42*, 314–322.

Becker, A. J. (2009). It's not what they do, it's how they do it: Athlete experiences of great coaching. *International Journal of Sports Science & Coaching, 4*, 93–119.

Bloom, B. S. (1956). *Taxonomy of educational objective: Handbook I: Cognitive domain*. New York, NY: McKay.

Bollen, K. A., & Hoyle, R. H. (1990). Perceived cohesion: A conceptual and empirical examination. *Social Forces, 69*, 479–504.

Cantu, R. C., & Hyman, M. (2012). *Concussions and our kids: America's leading expert on how to protect young athletes and keep sports safe*. New York, NY: Mariner.

Caro, C. A. (2012). College football success: The relationship between recruiting and winning. *International Journal of Sports Science & Coaching, 7*, 139–152.

Case, R. (1998). Leader member exchange theory and sport: Possible application. *Journal of Sport Behavior, 21*, 387–395.

Cassidy, T., Jones, R., & Potrac, P. (2009). *Understanding sports coaching: The social, cultural and pedagogical foundations of coaching practice* (2nd ed.). New York, NY: Routledge.

Chaumenton, N., & Duda, J. (1988). Is it how you play the game or whether you win or lose? The effect of competitive level and situation on coaching behaviors. *Journal of Sport Behavior, 11*, 157–174.

Chelladurai, P., & Riemer, H. A. (1998). Measurement of leadership in sport. In J. L. Duda (Ed.), *Advances in sport and exercise psychology measurement* (pp. 227–253). Morgantown, WV: Fitness Information Technology.

Coakley, J. (1993). Sport and socialization. *Exercise and Sport Sciences Reviews, 21*, 169–200.

Coakley, J. (2007). *Sport and society: Issues and controversies* (9th ed.). New York, NY: McGraw Hill.

Coakley, J., & White, A. (1992). Making decisions: Gender and sport participation among British adolescents. *Sociology of Sport Journal, 9*, 20–35.

Côté, J., & Gilbert, W. (2009). An integrative definition of coaching effectiveness and expertise. *International Journal of Sports Science & Coaching, 4*, 307–323.

Côté, J., Young, B., North, J., & Duffy, P. (2007). Towards a definition of excellence in sport coaching. *International Journal of Coaching Science, 1*, 3–16.

Cranmer, G. A. (2016). A continuation of sport teams from an organizational perspective: Predictors of athlete-coach leader-member exchange. *Communication & Sport, 4*, 43–61.

Cranmer, G. A. (2017). A communicative approach to sport socialization: The functions of memorable messages during Division-I student-athletes' socialization. *International Journal of Sport Communication, 10*, 233–257.

Cranmer, G. A. (2018). An application of socialization resources theory: Collegiate student-athletes' team socialization as a function of their social exchanges with coaches and teammates. *Communication & Sport, 6*, 349–367.

Cranmer, G. A., Arnson, E., Moore, A., Scott, A., & Peed, J. (2019). High school athletes' reports of confirmation as a function of starting status and leader-member exchange. *Communication & Sport, 7*, 510–528. doi:10.1177/2167479518783838

Cranmer, G. A., Brann, M., & Weber, K. D. (2018). "Challenge me!": Using confirmation theory to understand coach confirmation as an effective coaching behavior. *Communication & Sport, 6*, 239–259.

Cranmer, G. A., & Buckner, M. (2017). High school athletes' relationships with head coaches and teammates as predictors of their expressions of upward and lateral dissent. *Communication Studies, 68*, 37–55.

Cranmer, G. A., Buckner, M. M., Pham, N., & Jordan, B. (2018). "I disagree": An exploration of triggering events, messages, and success of athletes' dissent. *Communication & Sport, 6*, 523–546.

Cranmer, G. A., Gagnon, R. J., & Mazer, J. P. (2019). A continued application of confirmation theory: Division-I student-athletes' responses to coach confirmation. *Communication*

& Sport. Advanced online publication. Retrieved from https://journals.sagepub.com/doi/pdf/10.1177/2167479518824868

Cranmer, G. A., & Goodboy, A. K. (2015). Power play: Coach power use and athletes' communicative evaluations and responses. *Western Journal of Communication, 79*, 614–633.

Cranmer, G. A., & LaBelle, S. (2018). An application of the disclosure decision-making model to understand high school football players' disclosures of concussion symptoms. *International Journal of Sport Communication, 11*, 241–260.

Cranmer, G. A., & Myers, S. A. (2015). Sports teams as organizations: A leader-member exchange perspective of player communication with coaches and teammates. *Communication & Sport, 3*, 100–118.

Cranmer, G. A., & Sanderson, J. (2018). "Rough week for testosterone": Public commentary around the Ivy League's decision to restrict tackle football in practice. *Western Journal of Communication, 82*, 631–647.

Cranmer, G. A., & Sollitto, M. (2015). Sport support: Received social support as a predictor of athlete satisfaction. *Communication Research Reports, 32*, 253–264.

Cushion, C., & Lyle, J. (2010). Conceptual development in sports coaching. In J. Lyle & C. Cushion (Eds.), *Sports coaching: Professionalization and practice* (pp. 1–13). Edinburgh: Churchill Livingstone.

Duffy, P. (2010). Preface. In J. Lyle & C. Cushion (Eds.), *Sports coaching: Professionalization and practice* (pp. vii–x). Edinburgh: Churchill Livingstone.

Duffy, P., Hartley, H., Bales, J., Crespo, M., Dick, F., Vardhan, D., … & Curado, J. (2011). Sport coaching as a "profession": Challenges and future directions. *International Journal of Coaching Science, 5*, 93–123.

Eime, R. M., Young, J. A., Harvey, J. T., Charity, M. J., & Payne, W. R. (2013). A systematic review of psychological and social benefits of participation in sport for children and adolescents: Informing development of a conceptual model of health through sport. *International Journal of Behavioral Nutrition and Physical Activity, 10*, 98–135.

European Coaching Council (2007, September). Review of the EU 5-level structure for the recognition of coaching qualifications. *European Network of Sports Science, Education and Employment*. Retrieved from https://www.icce.ws/_assets/files/documents/ECC_5_level_review.pdf

Evans, M. B., Eys, M. A., & Bruner, M. W. (2012). Seeing the "we" in "me" sports: The need to consider individual sport team environments. *Canadian Psychology, 53*, 301–308.

Fraser-Thomas, J., Côté, J., & Deakin, J. (2008). Understanding dropout and prolonged engagement in adolescent competitive sport. *Psychology of Sport and Exercise, 9*, 645–662.

Gilbert, W. D., & Côté, J. (2013). Defining coaching effectiveness: A focus on coaches' knowledge. In P. Protrac, W. Gilbert, & J. Denison (Eds.), *The Routledge handbook of sports coaching* (pp. 147–159). New York, NY: Routledge.

Gilbert, W. D., & Trudel, P. (2004) Analysis of coaching science research published from 1970-2001. *Research Quarterly for Exercise and Sport, 75*, 388–399.

Hanrahan, S. J., & Andersen, M. B. (2013). *Routledge handbook of applied sport psychology: A comprehensive guide for students and practitioners*. New York, NY: Routledge.

Hansen, D. M., Larson, R. W., & Dworkin, J. B. (2003). What adolescents learn in organized youth activities: A survey of self-reported developmental experiences. *Journal of Adolescence, 13*, 25–55.

Horn, T. S. (2002). Coaching effectiveness in the sport domain. In T. S. Horn (Ed.), *Advances in sport psychology* (2nd ed., pp. 309–354). Champaign, IL: Human Kinetics.

Hyman, M. (2009). *Until it hurts: America's obsession with youth sports and how it harms our kids.* Boston, MA: Beacon Press.

Jenkins, S. (2010). Coaching philosophy. In J. Lyle & C. Cushion (Eds.), *Sports coaching: Professionalization and practice* (pp. 233–242). Edinburgh: Churchill Livingstone.

Jones, A., & Kijeski, T. (2009, November). *The relationship of team cohesion on performance among college athletic teams competing in coactive team sports.* Paper presented at the meeting of the National Communication Association, Chicago, IL.

Jowett, S. (2017). Coaching effectiveness: The coach–athlete relationship at its heart. *Current Opinion in Psychology, 16*, 154–158.

Jowett, S., & Cockerill, I. M. (2003). Olympic medalists' perspective of the athlete-coach relationship. *Psychology of Sport and Exercise, 4*, 313–331.

Kassing, J. W., & Anderson, R. L. (2014). Contradicting coach or grumbling to teammates: Exploring dissent expression in the coach–athlete relationship. *Communication & Sport, 2*, 172–185.

Kassing, J. W., & Barber, A. M. (2007). "Being a good sport": An investigation of sportsmanship messages provided by youth soccer parents, officials, and coaches. *Human Communication, 10*, 61–68.

Kassing, J. W., Billings, A. C., Brown, R. S., Halone, K. K., Harrison, K., Krizek, B., … Turman, P. D. (2004). Communication in the community of sport: The process of enacting, (re)producing, consuming, and organizing sport. In P. J. Kalbfleisch (Ed.), *Communication yearbook* (Vol. 28, pp. 373–409). Mahwah, NJ: Erlbaum.

Kassing, J. W., & Infante, D. A. (1999). Aggressive communication in the coach-athlete relationship. *Communication Research Reports, 16*, 110–120.

Kassing, J. W., & Pappas, M. E. (2007). "Champions are built in the off season": An exploration of high school coaches' memorable messages. *Human Communication, 10*, 537–546.

Lockwood, P., & Perlman, D. (2008). Enhancing the youth sport experience: A re-examination of methods, coaching style, and motivational climate. *The Journal of Youth Sports, 4*, 30–34.

Martin, M. M., Rocca, K. A., Cayanus, J. L., & Weber, K. (2009). Relationship between coaches' use of behavior alteration techniques and verbal aggression on athletes' motivation and affect. *Journal of Sport Behavior, 32*, 227–241.

Mazer, J. P., Barnes, K., Grevious, A., & Boger, C. (2013). Coach verbal aggression: A case study examining effects on athlete motivation and perceptions of coach credibility. *International Journal of Sport Communication, 6*, 203–213.

McPherson, B. D. (1981). Socialization into and through sport involvement. In G. R. F. Luschen & G. H. Sage (Eds.), *Handbook of social science of sport* (pp. 246–273). Champaign, IL: Stipes.

Meân, L. J. (2013). The communicative complexity of youth sport: Maintaining benefits, managing discourses, and challenging identities. In P. M. Pedersen (Ed.), *Routledge handbook of sport communication* (pp. 338–349). New York, NY: Routledge.

Meân, L. J., & Kassing, J. W. (2007). Identities at you sporting events: A critical discourse analysis. *International Journal of Sport Communication, 1,* 42–66.

Mowen, J. C. (2004). Exploring the trait of competitiveness and its consumer behavior consequences. *Journal of Consumer Psychology, 14,* 52–63.

Nash, C., Sproule, J., & Horton, P. (2011). Excellence in coaching. *Research Quarterly for Exercise and Sport, 82,* 229–238.

Nelson, L., & Colquhoun, D. (2013). Athlete (non)learning: Is it time for an interdisciplinary understanding? In P. Potrac, W. Gilbert, & J. Denison (Eds.), *Routledge handbook of sports coaching* (pp. 284–295). London: Routledge.

Nelson, L. J., Cushion, C. J., & Potrac, P. (2006). Formal, nonformal and informal coach learning: A holistic conceptualisation. *International Journal of Sports Science & Coaching, 1,* 247–259.

Positive Coaching Alliance. (2018). Mission statement. *PositiveCoach.org.* Retrieved from https://www.positivecoach.org/mission-history/

Potrac, P., Denison, J., & Gilbert, W. (2013). Introduction. In P. Potrac, W. Gilbert, & J. Denison (Eds.), *Routledge handbook of sports coaching* (pp. 1–2). New York, NY: Routledge.

Potrac, P., Jones, R., & Armour, K. (2002). "It's all about getting respect": The coaching behaviors of an expert English soccer coach. *Sport, Education and Society, 7,* 183–202.

Project Play. (2018). What we do. *AspenProjectPlay.org.* Retrieved from https://www.aspenprojectplay.org/whatwedo/

Rhind, D. J. A., & Jowett, S. (2012). Working with coach-athlete relationships: Their quality and maintenance. In S. Hanton & S. D. Mellalieu (Eds.), *Professional practice in sport psychology: A review* (pp. 219–248). New York, NY: Routledge.

Sanderson, J., Weathers, M., Snedaker, K., & Gramlich, K. (2017). "I was able to still do my job on the field and keep playing": An investigation of female and male athletes' experiences with (not) reporting concussions. *Communication & Sport, 5,* 267–287.

SHAPE America. (2017). National standards for sport coaches by core responsibilities. *Shapeamerica.org.* Retrieved from https://www.shapeamerica.org/uploads/pdfs/2018/standards/National-Standards-for-Sport-Coaches-DRAFT.pdf

Smith, R. E., & Smoll, F. L. (1990). Self-esteem and children's reactions to youth sport coaching behaviors: A field study of self-enhancement processes. *Developmental Psychology, 26,* 987–993.

Smoll, F. L., & Smith, R. E. (1989). Leadership behaviors in sport: A theoretical model and research paradigm. *Journal of Applied Social Psychology, 19,* 1522–1551.

Super, S., Verkooijen, K., & Koelen, M. (2018). The role of community sports coaches in creating optimal social conditions for life skill development and transferability—A salutogenic perspective. *Sport, Education and Society, 23,* 173–185.

Trudel, P., & Gilbert, W. (2006). Coaching and coach education. In D. Kirk, M. O'Sullivan, & D. McDonald (Eds.), *Handbook of physical education* (pp. 516–539). London: Sage.

Turman, P. D. (2001). Situational coaching styles: The impact of success and athlete maturity level on coaches' leadership styles over time. *Small Group Research, 32*, 576–594.

Turman, P. D. (2003). Coaches and cohesion: The impact of coaching techniques on team cohesion in the small group sport setting. *Journal of Sport Behavior, 26*, 86–104.

Turman, P. D. (2006). Athletes' perception of coach power use and the association between playing status and sport satisfaction. *Communication Research Reports, 23*, 273–282.

Turman, P. D. (2008). Coaches' immediacy behaviors as predictors of athletes' perceptions of satisfaction and team cohesion. *Western Journal of Communication, 72*, 162–179.

Turman, P. D. (2017). What effects do coaches' communicative messages have on their athletes/teams? In A. K. Goodboy & K. Shultz (Eds.), *Introduction to communication studies: Translating scholarship into meaningful practice* (pp. 121–128). Dubuque, IA: Kendall Hunt.

Vallerand, R. J., & Fortier, M. S. (1998). Measures of intrinsic and extrinsic motivation in sport and physical activity: A review and critique. In J. L. Duda (Ed.), *Advances in sport and exercise psychology measurement* (pp. 81–104). Morgantown, WV: Fitness Information Technology.

Vella, S., Oades, L. G., & Crowe, T. P. (2011). The role of coach in facilitating positive youth development: Moving from theory to practice. *Journal of Applied Sport Psychology, 23*, 33–48.

Waldeck, J. H., Plax, T. G., & Kearney, P. (2010). Philosophical and methodological foundations of instructional communication. In D. L. Fassett & J. T. Warren (Eds.), *The Sage handbook of communication and instruction* (pp. 161–179). Thousand Oaks, CA: Sage.

Weiss, M. R., & Ferrer-Caja, E. (2002). Motivational orientations and sport behaviour. In T. S. Horn (Ed.), *Advances in sport psychology* (2nd ed., pp. 101–114). Champaign, IL: Human Kinetics.

Westre, K. R., & Weiss, M. R. (1991). The relationship between perceived coaching behaviors and group cohesion in high school football teams. *The Sport Psychologist, 5*, 41–54.

Widmeyer, W. N., Carron, A. V., & Brawley, L. R. (1993). Group cohesion in sport and exercise. In R. N. Singer, M. Morphey, & L. K. Tennant (Eds.), *Handbook of research on sport psychology* (pp. 672–692). New York, NY: Macmillan.

· 3 ·

THE INSTRUCTIONAL PERSPECTIVE:
COACHES AS INSTRUCTORS

*In the end, it's about the teaching, and what I always loved about coaching was the practices.
Not the games, not the tournaments, not the alumni stuff. But teaching the players during
practice was what coaching was all about to me.*—John Wooden[1]

The term *coach* was a colloquialism for academic tutors during the 19th century in England, and was transferred to the context of athletics because of its instructional nature (Day, 2013). The similarity between instructional settings and sport is not lost on modern scholars either, who argue that sport is an informal educational context in which information is exchanged and learning occurs (Cassidy, 2010; Jones, 2006; Turman, 2008). As a learning context, sport influences the cognitive, physical, and social development of participants (Heath & McLaughlin, 1994; Jones, 2006). Coaches have a central role in athletes' learning and development, as the manner in which they structure sporting activities and interact with athletes determine learning outcomes (Camiré, Forneris, Trudel, & Bernard, 2011).

The instructional perspective frames coaches as instructors, who gather information and insight regarding sport and share it with athletes through verbal and nonverbal communication (Kassing et al., 2004). Athletes are framed as learners, who receive and process coaches' verbal and nonverbal communication in an attempt to understand instruction and bring it to fruition via their physical performance. The purpose of the instructional perspective, therefore, is to understand how coaches can communicate effectively and develop athlete knowledge and performance (Kassing et al., 2004). As such, the effectiveness of coaches is understood via behaviors that cultivate the affective, cognitive, and behavioral learning of athletes (Rocca, Martin, & Toale, 1998), as well as athletes' motivation and evaluations of coaches (Martin, Rocca, Cayanus, & Weber, 2009; Mazer, Barnes, Grevious, & Boger, 2013). The scholarly focus on effective behaviors, which defines the instructional perspective, is rooted in the assumptions that instructional behaviors can validly and reliably be identified, the use of particular behaviors determines instructional effectiveness, and behaviors can be modified to promote greater degrees of learning (Nussbaum, 1992).

Although most coaching scholars recognize the instructional perspective, they seldom reference the parameters in which it is most useful. Admittedly, most, if not all, levels of athletics include some degree of instruction and learning—underscoring Kassing et al.'s (2004) assertion that the instructional perspective "has limitless potential" for explaining the coaching process (p. 383). However, the instructional perspective provides the most unique insight when applied to athletes participating in developmental sporting leagues (e.g., youth, middle school, freshmen, or junior varsity sports leagues), experiencing novel situations (e.g., learning a new playbook or changing positions), or during periods devoted to the improvement of performance (e.g., practices and off-season workouts). These contexts place a premium on the effective communication of specific skills or strategies, feedback on previous performances, and the acquisition of new knowledge and abilities. With this in mind, the instructional perspective is quite apt and offers insight other perspectives simply cannot provide to coaches within these contexts.

While instructional frameworks and concerns apply well to sport (Jones, 2006), coaching is a unique process that differs in several important ways from instruction within traditional classrooms (Cranmer & Goodboy, 2015; Turman, 2008). Notably, sport features a comparative and collective goal of winning. Winning serves as an objective standard—either a team wins a game or it does not based on a number of points, runs, etc.—upon which teams and coaches are evaluated. Further, winning is determined through direct competition with other athletes and is a zero-sum situation in which for one team to win, another (or multiple teams) must lose. The salience of winning within sport and society is evident as outcomes are featured within local newspapers and on social media. These team outcomes often determine the continued tenure of coaches, especially those who coach professional, collegiate, elite club (e.g., Amateur Athletic Union; AAU), and middle and high school athletics. Even within youth sports, which are meant to be less competitive, winning is becoming increasingly important with the specialization and professionalization of young athletes (Meân, 2013). In comparison, grades, which are the central outcome within classrooms, include varying degrees of subjectivity and are rooted in the expertise of the instructor. Moreover, rarely, if ever, are entire classrooms graded together for their collective performances nor through direct competition with other classes in a manner that requires one class to fail for others to succeed. The salience of grades is also reduced in that student performances are not as publicized and instructors' tenure is less dependent on such performances.

Sports teams also feature greater degrees of interdependence between athletes to accomplish their collective goals (Turman, 2003a, 2008). Interdependence varies as a function of the type of sport in question (Evans, Eys, & Bruner, 2012), with team sports requiring the most interdependence between athletes. Yet, even individual sports are commonly structured within team environments, whereby individual performances are influenced by the efforts of teammates indirectly—especially during practice and training. Within traditional classrooms, interdependence between students is only a prominent feature of the learning environment during group work or assignments. As such, interdependence is not a necessary feature of classrooms. This argument is evident in that many students view interdependence as an unnecessary burden that detracts from learning experiences (Goodboy, 2011).

Further, sports teams differentiate members based on their abilities and roles within a team. This is most evident in the labels of *starter* and *reserve*, which indicates comparative ability, or captain status (Case, 1998; Cranmer & Goodboy, 2015). Such labels often determine athletes' abilities to participate in their sports. For interdependent sports, playing time is restricted by the number of participants, length of games, and availability of substitutions. For example, a high school soccer team may only field 11 players, games are restricted to two 40-minute halves, and substitutions may be limited. In contrast, independent sports are restricted by the number of participants and substitutions are not possible mid-contest. For example, a high school cross country team is limited to seven runners during competition. Within both team structures, those designated as starters have greater opportunities to participate. For reserve athletes, playing time is more common when the outcome of a game is already decided or when starters are unable to participate (e.g., tired or injured). These labels are important sources of athletes' identities, roles, and learning opportunities. In comparison, students are not publicly labeled based on their comparative abilities within a traditional classroom environment, and labels that might emerge among students are informal and socially constructed. Likewise, students are not restricted from partaking in assignments because others may be smarter or more talented. In fact, all students are asked to engage in course materials and assignments.

Together, these arguments reveal that sport is a unique learning environment whereby coaches are incentivized to focus on the outcome of winning as the goal of their instruction, as opposed to task mastery. The emphasis on winning guides the strategic investment of instructional resources and efforts (e.g., attention, feedback, and opportunities to demonstrate skills) towards athletes who contribute to team performance (Cranmer & Goodboy, 2015). This unequal distribution creates more enriching learning environments for starters than reserves (Case, 1998; Turman, 2003a). Such environments hinder approaching athlete learning as a process that requires patience, opportunities for refinement of skills, and acceptance of occasional failure—features consistent with traditional approaches to learning (Cassidy, 2010). These unique instructional features should be, but are not always, considered during the evaluation of athlete learning.

Instructional Perspective

Sport communication scholars have incorporated instructional frameworks within their research for some time. Many of the first scholars to examine athlete-coach interaction operated from the instructional perspective and rooted their efforts in the calls to extend instructional research outside of the classroom (Sprague, 2002; Staton, 1989; Witt, 2012). The influence of this perspective is apparent in a sizeable portion of coaching literature (e.g., Cranmer & Goodboy, 2015; Martin et al., 2009; Mazer et al., 2013; Webster, 2009), especially the seminal scholarship of Paul Turman (Turman, 2003a, 2006, 2008; Turman & Schrodt, 2004). Scholars who operate from the instructional perspective address calls to link athlete-coach interaction or coaching behaviors with athletes' learning outcomes (Nelson & Colquhoun, 2013). Four behaviors are repeatedly identified as determinants of athletes' learning: (a) power use, (b) immediacy, (c) clarity and relevance, and (d) verbal aggression.

Coach Power

Effective instruction depends on efforts to influence learners to obtain and utilize information. *Power* refers to "an individual's capacity to influence another person to do something he/she would not have done had he/she not been influenced" (Richmond & McCroskey, 1984, p. 125). It is through communication that influence is granted and accomplished (McCroskey & Richmond, 1983). All social relationships include elements of influence (Waldeck, Kearney, & Plax, 2001), but power is especially relevant within sport, as "coaching is an activity primarily based on social interaction and power" (Jones, 2006, p. 3). During these interactions, coaches use their influence to develop athletes' knowledge and skillsets (Cranmer & Goodboy, 2015; Turman, 2006). Coaches' power use manifests in their power bases and use of behavioral alteration techniques.

Coaches' influence over athletes derives from five bases of power (French & Raven, 1959). One such base is *expert power*, which refers to athletes being pliable out of respect for coaches' expertise or competence. Expert power is evident in assumptions of coaches' knowledge of strategies, styles of play, specific techniques, or training methods. Another base is *referent power*, which reflects athletes' compliance stemming from desires to satisfy and identify with their coaches. Referent power is observable within the interpersonal connections and admiration for coaches as role models. A third base is *reward power*, which encompasses influence that derives from athletes' perceptions that coaches are able to provide them with psychological, social, or tangible benefits. Reward power manifests within athletes' beliefs that coaches may praise or recognize them, give them additional resources (e.g., playing time), or take away punishments or burdensome tasks (e.g., conditioning exercises), if they behave as desired. An additional base is *legitimate power*, which denotes influence from athletes' regard for the formal authority that innately comes with the position of coach. In other words, this type of influence is rooted in athletes' respect for coaching as an occupation. The final power base is *coercive power*, which functions via athletes' perceptions that coaches are able to provide them with psychological, social, or tangible punishments. Coercive power is associated with athletes' beliefs that coaches may embarrass or scold them, assign punitive tasks (e.g., make them run laps), or take away their playing time, if they fail to perform as desired. Although each power base is distinct, these bases are often organized into prosocial (i.e., reward, referent, and expert power) and antisocial forms of power (i.e., legitimate and coercive power), and may be utilized by coaches independently or conjointly.

Coach power also manifests via the specific behavior alteration techniques (BATs) that coaches utilize to gain compliance or influence athletes. Whereas power bases center around athletes' perceptions, BATs are the behavioral techniques that coaches use to enact power with the goal to "motivate, encourage, or foster alternative, on-task behaviors essential for learning" (Kearney & Plax, 1997, p. 96). Coaches rely on 22 BATs—identified within traditional instructional contexts (Kearney, Plax, Richmond, & McCroskey, 1984)—to influence athletes (Martin et al., 2009). Similar to power bases, BATs are organized into prosocial and antisocial categories. For example, prosocial BATs include coaches' attempts to build athletes' *self-esteem* through suggesting that athletes will feel good about themselves or are especially suited to perform a suggested task, or they may emphasize the *immediate rewards* that might be experienced (e.g., enjoyment) by performing a requested behavior. In contrast, antisocial BATs include coaches' inducement of *guilt* in athletes by emphasizing that failure to perform a suggested task will hurt or disappoint others, or threats of *punishment* for failure to perform a requested behavior.

Coaching research indicates that the exertion of influence contributes to athletes' learning best when it relies upon prosocial forms of power. For example, the use of prosocial power facilitates productive instructional environments through increasing the perceived utility and the retention of corrective feedback from coaches, fostering open dialogue between athletes and coaches (Cranmer & Goodboy, 2015), and motivating athletes to play their sports (Martin et al., 2009). In particular, the cultivation of expert and reward power foster greater affective evaluations, as evidence by high school football and basketball players' satisfaction with their sporting experiences (Turman, 2006) and Division-I student-athletes' communication satisfaction with coaches (Cranmer & Goodboy, 2015). Similarly, prosocial BATs foster greater degrees of affective learning for coaches among former high school athletes (Martin et al., 2009). The empirical record forwards a convincing argument that coaches should demonstrate knowledge, create rewarding environments, and relate to athletes to exert influence on team cultures and athletes. These forms of influence create desires to learn and the appreciation of coaches and learning environments.

Data regarding the effects of antisocial power on athlete learning are more complex. Multiple studies have examined high school and collegiate athlete populations and have failed to find significant relationships between legitimate or coercive power and athletes' affective evaluations of coaches and sporting experiences (Cranmer & Goodboy, 2015; Turman, 2006). Although definitive statements about insignificant relationships should generally be avoided, the consistency between studies suggests antisocial power use is an accepted part of the athlete-coach relationship. This assertion appears to be especially true within male athlete-coach dyads, which feature greater degrees of antisocial power use (Martin et al., 2009). Put differently, athletes expect coaches to rely on their formal position and use punishments to influence them. These expectations provide leeway for coaches to use antisocial means of influence and compliance gaining without detrimental responses. The acceptance of antisocial power contrasts findings from traditional instructional settings (e.g., Richmond, 1990; Richmond & McCroskey, 1984). However, this is not to say that coaches' use of antisocial power has no consequences for coaches. Coercive power, in particular, detracts from athlete-coach mutual understanding and makes athletes more sensitive to and less able to retain corrective feedback (Cranmer & Goodboy, 2015). Antisocial power use, thus, may indirectly impede learning via straining lines of communication between athletes and coaches, and rendering instruction as more difficult to deliver. Collectively, power research indicates that while athletes tolerate some degrees of punishment and formal authority as means of influence, learning environments and evaluations of coaches are best fostered through the demonstration of expertise, cultivation of rewarding environments, and maintenance of relationships.

Immediacy

Immediacy is a set of instructional behaviors that reduce the physical or psychological distance between communicators (Mehrabian, 1969). Within learning environments, immediacy captures learners' attention, promotes engaging climates, and develops interpersonal connections with learners—leading to a host of learning indicators (Witt, Schrodt, & Turman, 2010). Immediacy occurs via nonverbal and verbal behaviors. *Nonverbal immediacy* consists of behaviors that close the distance between coaches and athletes, such as making eye contact, smiling, nodding, leaning forward, using gestures, and touching others in an appropriate manner (Andersen, 1979). Common displays of such behaviors within sports are high fives, pats on the back, and the use of eye contact during periods of strategizing or instruction. *Verbal immediacy* refers to the things coaches say to indicate an openness toward communication with athletes (Gorham, 1988). Verbal immediacy is established through the use of verbal cues such as using humor, inclusive language (e.g., we), self-disclosures, and the use of athletes' names. These verbal efforts foster closeness, demonstrate willingness to relate to athletes, and confirm that they are worth more than their physical performances.

The use of immediacy cultivates engaging learning environments through gaining athletes' attention and inspiring interest in instruction. A study examining high school football and basketball players from the Midwest concluded that coaches' use of verbal immediacy increased satisfaction with sporting experiences, social and task attraction to teammates, and social integration into teams (Turman, 2008). Turman theorized that the less structured nature and time commitments of athletics provide coaches with opportunities for extra-sport communication and self-disclosure, which underscore the importance of verbal immediacy within coaching. Verbal immediacy in turn fosters open and comfortable environments, which promote connection with teammates and learning. Interestingly, nonverbal immediacy explained only a limited portion of athletes' perceptions of cohesion with teammates, despite an incredibly well documented record of benefits in the classroom (Witt et al., 2010). Perhaps, given the voluntary nature of sport, most athletes are already engaged and self-motivated—rendering the benefits of nonverbal immediacy less noticeable. Further, the physical and proximal nature of sport may make some aspects of nonverbal immediacy (i.e., closing physical space) inconspicuous.

The utility of nonverbal immediacy, however, is more pronounced within observational studies of elite coaches, including expert Ladies Professional Golf Association instructors (Webster, 2009) and former University of Tennessee's women's basketball coach, Pat Summitt (Becker & Wrisberg, 2008). These studies have indicated that excellent coaches use appropriate touching and proximity to assist in the positioning of athletes and demonstration of techniques. Given the physical nature of sport, appropriate types and degrees of physical interaction are normal and can be quite useful during efforts to teach fine motor skills. Coaches also established nonverbal immediacy through maintaining positive body language (e.g., avoiding crossed arms, keeping their heads up, or nodding in reinforcement), which communicates openness and support for athletes' performances. Together, immediacy research reveals that coaches are able to use communication to reduce the physical and psychological distance between themselves and their athletes as a means to create stimulating learning environments and engage athletes.

Clarity and Relevance

The ability to competently communicate information to learners is at the heart of instruction in any context. It is nearly impossible for learners to synthesize, evaluate, and apply information if they do not understand or appreciate the point of doing so. The effectiveness of instruction, including coaching, is largely encompassed within two rhetorical behaviors: clarity and relevance. *Clarity* refers to behaviors that facilitate the presentation of information in a manner that is understood by learners (Simonds, 1997), and is considered the "… single most influential aspect in feelings of motivation and confidence" for athletes (Buning & Thompson, 2015, p. 357). These behaviors span using organizational cues that denote important information, the structure of coaching, repetition of points, and questioning learners' understandings (Titsworth & Mazer, 2010). Such behaviors are central in determining a variety of learning and motivational indicators. Emphasizing coach clarity recognizes that athletes must successfully process coaches' instructions to bring them to fruition on the field of play. Yet, sporting environments are hectic and athletes are consistently seeking feedback and interpreting coaching behaviors—even those intended to be innocuous. "One of the greatest challenges for coaches, then, is to behave in ways such that the intent behind their words and expressions is clearly communicated and accurately interpreted by most (if not all) of their athletes" (Becker, 2013, p. 190).

Coaching researchers forward various strategies to clarify instruction, including simplifying one's use of jargon or consistently referring to specific techniques and strategies in the same manner (Becker, 2013). The simplification of terminology and schemes is especially important when coaching youth athletes, as it is imperative the language and complexity of strategies are congruent with athletes' cognitive abilities. Overly complex methods of instruction ensure a lack of understanding. Other means of improving clarity require augmenting instruction with rhetorical tools such as examples or analogies that help athletes understand and implement knowledge (Becker, 2009) or questioning that checks understanding (Cassidy, 2010). Another clarity technique that is especially germane to sport is physical demonstrations of techniques (Becker, 2009). Given that sport requires behavioral learning, the visual manifestations of desired actions are an effective means to clarify expectations. Becker and Wrisberg (2008) highlighted the prevalence and effectiveness of such displays within Pat Summitt's coaching, especially her use of illustrations of correct performance in contrast to athletes' flawed performances.

Other important aspects of clarity refer to clearly communicating expectations and preferences for athlete behavior and performance. Through interviews with collegiate softball players, Buning and Thompson (2015) reasoned that coaches must codify and share their standards and expectations—potentially through player contracts, performance evaluation meetings, or coaching philosophies. Although often viewed as reflective documents that aid in coach development, coaching philosophies clarify how learning environments are to function when shared with athletes. Philosophies outline coaches' beliefs and values, as well as established expectations for athlete-coach interactions, the goals of coaches, and provide metrics by which athletes are assessed (Jenkins, 2010). In *Coaching Wrestling Successfully*, Dan Gable (1999)—arguably one of the most successful college coaches in any sport—framed the creation of a coaching philosophy as the foundational first step for all coaches. He argued that sharing these documents with athletes establishes standards for team processes and coach expectations; reduces athlete uncertainty, stress, and complaints; prioritizes aspects of athletes' lives (e.g., family, faith, school, and wrestling); and serves as a reference point from which future instruction is made relevant.

Relevance behaviors denote to a receiver that information is of consequence through linking instructional content with a learner's goals and interests (Frymier & Shulman, 1995). Whereas clarity focuses on athletes' comprehension of coaches' instructions, relevance behaviors inspire attention and personal investment. Becker (2009) argued that the ability to gain the attention of athletes and impart how instruction may benefit them distinguishes elite coaches from their peers. Coaches may increase the perceived relevancy of their instruction via numerous tactics. The use of vocalics is one strategy that elite coaches utilize to underscore the perceived importance of their instruction (Becker, 2009). One may raise their voice or use pausing for dramatic effect to underscore the value of instruction. Through observations of elite golf coaches, Webster (2009) identified three additional strategies that also help increase relevancy. The first strategy is to connect instruction to athletes' previous experiences. Athletes deem feedback as more relevant when it references specific situations or mistakes from past performances. A second strategy is to state how the content of instruction assists athletes in obtaining future goals. This type of instruction may especially be relevant to athletes within independent sports (e.g., swimming or track), which provide more benchmarks of individual accomplishment (e.g., race times) and often feature objective standards one must meet to qualify for future competitive opportunities (e.g., national meets). The third relevancy technique is to connect instruction to future experiences. If instruction is useful for upcoming performances, athletes regard it as of more consequence. An example of this strategy may be linking a technique or strategy during practices or film sessions as a counter to the tendencies of an upcoming opponent.

Although clarity and relevance are seldom the focus of coaching studies, the importance of these behaviors for learning cannot be understated. These behaviors are essential to effective coaching and prerequisites for learning, which may explain why the majority of empirical evidence regarding clarity and relevance has been collected in broad examinations of elite coaches (e.g., elite golf instructors [Webster, 2009], Pat Summitt [Becker & Wrisberg, 2008], and a variety of professional, college, and Olympic coaches [Becker, 2009]). This research highlights that coaches, if they are going to be effective, must be receiver-oriented in their instruction. Simply, coaches are more effective when their communication is accessible and relatable, which can be assured through an athlete-centric viewpoint when explaining sporting skills and strategy.

Verbal Aggression

While the majority of instructional research seeks to identify the beneficial behaviors that coaches enact, there is also value in identifying behaviors that are ineffective or inhibit learning (Nelson & Colquhoun, 2013). One such behavior considered by coaching scholars is verbal aggression. *Verbal aggression* is a destructive communication behavior that centers on the use of symbolic force (i.e., words) to attack another's self-concept (Infante & Wigley, 1986). These attacks can range from insulting a person's appearance, intelligence, and character to threats, teasing, and profanity (Infante, 1987). Being the target of such aggression leads to emotional distress, embarrassment, a damaged self-concept, feelings of inadequacy, and depression (Avtgis & Rancer, 2010; Infante, 1987) — all of which contribute toward hostile learning environments. As such, verbal aggression is detrimental to the formation of instructional relationships and constitutes psychological abuse, if used consistently (Infante & Rancer, 1996). Yet, verbal aggression is widely considered an effective coaching behavior, which is evident in the romanticized views of aggressive coaches (e.g., Bobby Knight) and acceptable norms within sporting culture (Kassing & Sanderson, 2010).

The appropriateness and effectiveness of verbal aggression came to the forefront of public discourse in 2013, when a viral video of Rutgers University men's basketball coach, Mike Rice made national news. Rice was recorded berating and abusing his players during team practices, including calling his players derogatory terms for homosexuals, slang for female genitalia, and a variety of other creative combinations of personal insults and profanity (e.g., sissies, fairies, soft-ass bitches, or idiots). Gilvydas Biruta reflected on his interactions with Rice in the following manner: "If you're going to criticize me as a basketball player, I'm OK with that. But he would criticize me as a person." Biruta decided to transfer from Rutgers because Rice created a hostile learning environment and left him depressed, unmotivated, and unsure of himself (Van Natta, 2013). Rutgers University eventually fired Rice and the affair is credited with raising national awareness toward issues of athlete abuse (i.e., a trend known as the Rice Effect). Since, a series of high profile firings have occurred for maltreatment and the verbal abuse of student-athletes, including Utah University's swimming coach, Greg Winslow; Rutgers University's swimming coach, Petra Martin; and Maryland University's strength and conditioning coach, Rick Court. Still, the prioritization of winning appears to provide aggressive but successful coaches continued opportunities to interact with developing athletes.

Empirical research validates concern about coaches' use of verbal aggression detracting from athlete learning (Kassing & Infante, 1999; Martin et al., 2009; Mazer et al., 2013); So much so, that preserving athletes' psychological concept is noted as an essential coaching behavior (Becker, 2013). For instance, high school coaches' use of verbal aggression decreases athletes' affective learning (Martin et al., 2009), relational satisfaction (Kassing & Infante, 1999), and perceptions of coaches' credibility (i.e., competence, caring, and character) (Kassing & Infante, 1999). These findings were replicated with Division-I student-athletes, who also perceive verbally aggressive coaches as less credible (Mazer et al., 2013). Additionally, verbal aggression reduces athletes' interest in participating in sports (Martin et al., 2009; Mazer et al., 2013). These empirical findings assert that demeaning athletes as an instructional technique alienates them from sporting content and their coaches. Such a communicative approach obstructs the teaching of sporting technique and strategy by promoting disinterest in sport and aversion to coaches.

Although quantitative research is clear that coaches should avoid using verbal aggression, qualitative investigation—as it often does—provides a nuanced understanding of the limited functionality of this behavior. This recognition does not mean that verbal aggression is a constructive behavior that is desirable in a coach. Such a statement would be disingenuous to the majority of evidence and the spirit of the qualitative research on aggression within coaching. In qualitative studies, athletes overwhelmingly considered verbally aggressive coaching as undesirable in examinations of coaches' responses to losing or training mistakes (Sagar & Jowett, 2012) and roles within the formation of team cohesion (Turman, 2003b). Yet, within these studies, a minority of athletes appreciated verbal aggression, especially if they believed it was deserved (Sagar & Jowett, 2012) or coincided with a preferred style of communication (Cranmer & Brann, 2015). Further, coaches' use of teasing and taunting sometimes serves as a mechanism of team bonding when in jest (Turman, 2003b). For instance, Cranmer and Spinda (2017) highlighted an incident during a film session in which a football player was compared to a turtle to mock his lack of explosive plays on the season. The teasing was in jest as the athlete was one of the fastest players on the team and had a history of making big plays, but served as a jovial moment shared between teammates, as well as a respite from intense game preparation. The limited effectiveness of aggression may be specific to certain team cultures and climates, as both Cranmer and Spinda (2017) and Turman (2003b) considered collegiate football teams. Aggression is normative within such hegemonic masculine cultures and is common within male athlete-coach dyads (Martin et al., 2009). Still, a strong relational foundation and the mitigation of face threats are prerequisites in these very narrow circumstances in which verbal aggression is beneficial. These exceptions speak to the complexity of antisocial communication within the athlete-coach relationship, and underscore the need for continued investigations into the role of gender within athlete-coach interaction.

Collectively, verbal aggression research indicates that coaches should avoid the excessive use of yelling, curse words, or personal attacks when addressing athletes, as these behaviors create hostile learning environments and have the potential to damage athletes' self-concepts. With the established consequences of verbal aggression (e.g., depression, anxiety, and loss of confidence), this behavior is in direct contrast with the spirit of human development and prosocial coaching movements. Despite rare and limited functionality, coaches may consider relying on prosocial behaviors that offer similar benefits but without the potential detriments to team climate and athlete-coach relationships.

The Future of the Instructional Perspective

Despite being the most established perspective of athlete-coach communication, the instructional perspective is still underexplored. The continued development of this perspective is of great value to coaching science researchers, who recognize the need to consider the influence of interaction on athlete learning (Nelson & Colquhoun, 2013). There are three issues of scope within the instructional perspective, which when addressed will help to further understandings of coaching as a form of instruction. First, coach communication scholars must refocus their efforts on traditional aspects of learning, especially cognitive and behavioral learning. Coach communication scholars have done little to explain how athletes come to comprehend or implement coaches' instruction, with few scholars examining athletes' cognitive or behavioral learning (e.g., Cranmer, Gagnon, & Mazer, 2019). This focus relegates understandings of athlete learning to the emotions and feelings that they have toward their coaches and sport. Such a focus overlooks the fundamental reality that athletes must process and comprehend coaches' instructions (i.e., cognitive learning) and successfully enact these instructions during play (i.e., behavioral learning) for coaches to be effective. Moreover, cognitive and behavioral learning are at the heart of enacting sport (Kassing et al., 2004), and knowledge of coaching pedagogy rests on promoting these outcomes (Nelson & Colquhoun, 2013).

Second, athlete learning must extend beyond individual athletes' self-reports and recognize team-level outcomes and performances. Sports, especially within the United States, are often team contexts that require degrees of interdependence between athletes. Thus, learning is more than an athlete's ability to grasp and perform behaviors on his or her own. Learning in this context extends to the collective comprehension and performance of teams. Turman (2008) recognized this feature of sport as a learning environment and advocated for the integration of task cohesion as a potential learning outcome. Although this is an important step to address this issue of scope, task cohesion is perceptual in nature and does not assess athletes' actual behaviors or comprehension. Thus, there is a need for the continual development of an understanding of the team nature of sport and the roles of coaches within these learning communities.

Third, a more holistic understanding of coaching as a pedagogical practice (e.g., one that accounts for athletes' characteristics, team cultures, and sporting environments) is needed to increase the value of this perspective

(Cassidy, 2010; Nelson & Colquhoun, 2013). To date, the instructional per-spective has held a coach-centric view of learning that is consistent with the process-product paradigm of instruction (Cortez, Gayle, & Preiss, 2006). In other words, scholars disproportionately focus on coaches' use of select instructional behaviors with little regard for team environments, the content of instruction, or athletes' characteristics. This focus is somewhat justified as specific generalizable behaviors promote learning and coaching practitioners are often the applied audience of this research—meaning that focusing on variables coaches control (e.g., their behaviors) is practical. Yet, the willing-ness to ignore environmental, content, and learner characteristics excludes important variables that determine the situational effectiveness of particu-lar instructional behaviors and the possibility of athlete freewill (Nelson & Colquhoun, 2013). This exclusion is problematic given that "understanding *who is being coached* [original emphasis] … could help lead to better coaching practices, better athlete-coach relationships and, ultimately, better athletic performance" (Galipeau & Trudel, 2006, p. 91). It is logical to assume that the manner in which athletes process corrective feedback or other personality characteristics moderate the influence of coaches' instructional behaviors on learning outcomes. To date, such considerations have remained elusive but could yield novel insights.

Conclusion

The instructional perspective recognizes that coaching is an act dependent upon teaching sporting knowledge and skills through particular instructional behaviors. Its potential is indeterminable but promising. There remain great opportunities for the integration of additional instructional behaviors into the coaching context. Specifically, behaviors such as affinity seeking, humor, and self-disclosure may explain how coaches instruct their athletes, create engaging learning environments, and foster learning outcomes. Investigations of other behaviors, like coaching misbehaviors (i.e., acts that detract from learning), could shed insight regarding what coaches do that prevent ath-letes' learning (Nelson & Colquhoun, 2013). This reversed approach adds to current research by identifying additional barriers to athlete learning that coaches should avoid. Such knowledge, in combination with the established effective instructional behavior literature, could optimize coaching effective-ness. With such a promising and wide array of opportunities for continued growth, it is apparent that the instructional perspective has only begun to scratch the surface of what constitutes effective coaching.

Note

1. Brainy Quote. (2019). John Wooden quotes. *BrainyQuote.com*. Retrieved from https://www.brainyquote.com/quotes/john_wooden_621113

References

Andersen, J. F. (1979). Teacher immediacy: A predictor of teaching effectiveness. In D. Nimmo (Ed.), *Communication yearbook* (Vol. 3, pp. 543–559). New Brunswick, NJ: Transaction.

Avtgis, T. A., & Rancer, A. S. (2010). *Arguments, aggression, and conflict: New directions in theory and research.* New York, NY: Taylor & Francis.

Becker, A. J. (2009). It's not what they do, it's how they do it: Athlete experiences of great coaching. *International Journal of Sports Science & Coaching, 4,* 93–119.

Becker, A. J. (2013). Quality coaching behaviours. In P. Potrac, W. Gilbert, & J. Denison (Eds.), *Routledge handbook of sports coaching* (pp. 184–195). New York, NY: Routledge.

Becker, A. J., & Wrisberg, C. A. (2008). Effective coaching in action: Observations of legendary collegiate basketball coach Pat Summitt. *The Sport Psychologist, 22,* 197–211.

Buning, M. M., & Thompson, M. A. (2015). Coaching behaviors and athlete motivation: Female softball athletes' perspectives. *Sport Science Review, 24,* 345–370.

Camiré, M., Forneris, T., Trudel, P., & Bernard, D. (2011). Strategies for helping coaches facilitate positive youth development through sport. *Journal of Sport Psychology in Action, 2,* 92–99.

Case, R. (1998). Leader member exchange theory and sport: Possible application. *Journal of Sport Behavior, 21,* 387–395.

Cassidy, T. (2010). Understanding athlete learning and coaching practice: Utilizing 'practice theories' and 'theories of practices.' In J. Lyle & C. Cushion (Eds.), *Sports coaching: Professionalization and practice* (pp. 175–191). Edinburgh: Churchill Livingstone.

Cortez, D., Gayle, B. M., & Preiss, R. W. (2006). An overview of teacher effectiveness research: Components and processes. In B. M. Gayle, R. W. Preiss, N. Burrell, & M. Allen (Eds.), *Classroom communication and instructional process: Advances through meta-analysis* (pp. 263–277). Mahwah, NJ: Lawrence Erlbaum.

Cranmer, G. A., & Brann, M. (2015). "It makes me feel like I am an important part of this team": An exploratory study of coach confirmation. *International Journal of Sport Communication, 8,* 193–211.

Cranmer, G. A., Gagnon, R. J., & Mazer, J. P. (2019). A continued application of confirmation theory: Division-I student-athletes' responses to coach confirmation. *Communication & Sport.* Advanced online publication. Retrieved from https://journals.sagepub.com/doi/pdf/10.1177/2167479518824868

Cranmer, G. A., & Goodboy, A. K. (2015). Power play: Coach power use and athletes' communicative evaluations and responses. *Western Journal of Communication*, 79, 614–633.

Cranmer, G. A., & Spinda, J. (2017). *Coaches' use of confirmation during the preparation for a Division-I football game.* Paper submitted to the annual meeting of the National Communication Association, Dallas, TX.

Day, D. (2013). Historical perspectives on coaching. In P. Potrac, W. Gilbert, & J. Denison (Eds.), *Routledge handbook of sports coaching* (pp. 5–15). London: Routledge.

Evans, B. M., Eys, M. A., & Bruner, M. W. (2012). Seeing the "we" in "me" sports: The need to consider individual sport team environments. *Canadian Psychology*, 53, 301–308.

French, J. R. P., & Raven, B. (1959). The bases for social power. In D. Cartwright (Ed.), *Studies in social power* (pp. 150–167). Ann Arbor, MI: University of Michigan Press.

Frymier, A. B., & Shulman, G. M. (1995). "What's in it for me?": Increasing content relevance to enhance students' motivation. *Communication Education*, 44, 40–50.

Gable, D. (1999). *Coaching wrestling successfully.* Champaign, IL: Human Kinetics.

Galipeau, J., & Trudel, P. (2006). Athlete learning in a community of practice: Is there a role for the coach? In R. L. Jones (Ed.), *The sports coach as educator: Reconceptualizing sports coaching* (pp. 77–94). London: Routledge.

Goodboy, A. K. (2011). Instructional dissent in the college classroom. *Communication Education*, 60, 296–313.

Gorham, J. (1988). The relationship between verbal teacher immediacy behaviors and student learning. *Communication Education*, 37, 40–53.

Heath, S. B., & McLaughlin, M. W. (1994). The best of both worlds: Connecting schools and community youth organizations for all-day, all-year learning. *Educational Administration Quarterly*, 30, 278–300.

Infante, D. A. (1987). Aggressiveness. In J. C. McCroskey & J. A. Daly (Eds.), *Personality and interpersonal communication* (pp. 157–197). Newbury Park, CA: Sage.

Infante, D. A., & Rancer, A. S. (1996). Argumentativeness and verbal aggressiveness: A review of recent theory and research. In B. R. Burleson (Ed.), *Communication yearbook* (Vol. 19, pp. 319–351). Mahwah, NJ: Erlbaum.

Infante, D. A., & Wigley, C. J. (1986). Verbal aggressiveness: An interpersonal model and measure. *Communication Monographs*, 53, 61–69.

Jenkins, S. (2010). Coaching philosophy. In J. Lyle & C. Cushion (Eds.), *Sports coaching: Professionalization and practice* (pp. 233–242). Edinburgh: Churchill Livingstone.

Jones, R. L. (2006). *The sports coach as educator: Reconceptualizing sports coaching.* New York, NY: Routledge.

Kassing, J. W., Billings, A. C., Brown, R. S., Halone, K. K., Harrison, K., Krizek, B., … & Turman, P. D. (2004). Communication in the community of sport: The process of enacting, (re)producing, consuming, and organizing sport. In P. J. Kalbfleisch (Ed.), *Communication yearbook* (Vol. 28, pp. 373–409). New York, NY: Routledge.

Kassing, J. W., & Infante, D. A. (1999). Aggressive communication in the coach-athlete relationship. *Communication Research Reports*, 16, 110–120.

Kassing, J. W., & Sanderson, J. (2010). Trash talk and beyond: Aggressive communication in the context of sport. In T. A. Avtgis & A. S. Rancer (Eds.), *Arguments, aggression, and conflict: New directions in theory and research* (pp. 253–266). New York, NY: Routledge.

Kearney, P., & Plax, T. G. (1997). Item desirability bias and the BAT checklist: A reply to Waltman and Burleson. *Communication Education, 46*, 95–99.

Kearney, P., Plax, T. G., Richmond, V. P., & McCroskey, J. C. (1984). Power in the classroom IV: Alternatives to discipline. *Communication yearbook* (Vol. 8, pp. 724–746). Los Angeles, CA: Sage.

Martin, M. M., Rocca, K. A., Cayanus, J. L., & Weber, K. (2009). Relationship between coaches' use of behavior alteration techniques and verbal aggression on athletes' motivation and affect. *Journal of Sport Behavior, 32*, 227–241.

Mazer, J. P., Barnes, K., Grevious, A., & Boger, C. (2013). Coach verbal aggression: A case study examining effects on athlete motivation and perceptions of coach credibility. *International Journal of Sport Communication, 6*, 203–213.

McCroskey, J. C., & Richmond, V. P. (1983). Power in the classroom I: Teacher and student perceptions. *Communication Education, 32*, 175–184.

Meân, L. J. (2013). The communicative complexity of youth sport: Maintaining benefits, managing discourses, and challenging identities. In P. M. Pedersen (Ed.), *Routledge handbook of sport communication* (pp. 338–349). New York, NY: Routledge.

Mehrabian, A. (1969). Attitudes inferred from non-immediacy of verbal communication. *Journal of Verbal Learning and Verbal Behavior, 6*, 294–295.

Nelson, L., & Colquhoun, D. (2013). Athlete (non)learning: Is it time for an interdisciplinary understanding? In P. Potrac, W. Gilbert, & J. Denison (Eds.), *Routledge handbook of sports coaching* (pp. 284–295). London: Routledge.

Nussbaum, J. (1992). Effective teacher behaviors. *Communication Education, 41*, 167–180.

Richmond, V. P. (1990). Communication in the classroom: Power and motivation. *Communication Education, 39*, 181–195.

Richmond, V. P., & McCroskey, J. C. (1984). Power in the classroom II: Power and learning. *Communication Education, 33*, 125–136.

Rocca, K. A., Martin, M. M., & Toale, M. C. (1998). Players' perceptions of their coaches' immediacy, assertiveness, and responsiveness. *Communication Research Reports, 15*, 445–450.

Sagar, S. S., & Jowett, S. (2012). Communicative acts in coach-athlete interactions: When losing competitions when making mistakes in training. *Western Journal of Communication, 76*, 148–174.

Simonds, C. J. (1997). Classroom understanding: An expanded notion of teacher clarity. *Communication Research Reports, 14*, 279–290.

Sprague, J. (2002). Communication education: The spiral continues. *Communication Education, 51*, 337–354.

Staton, A. Q. (1989). The interface of communication and instruction: Conceptual considerations and programmatic manifestations. *Communication Education, 38*, 364–371.

Titsworth, S., & Mazer, J. P. (2010). Clarity in teaching and learning: Conundrums, consequences, and opportunities. In D. L. Fassett & J. T. Warren (Eds.), *The Sage handbook of communication and instruction* (pp. 241–261). Los Angeles, CA: Sage.

Turman, P. D. (2003a). Athletic coaching from an instructional communication perspective: The influence of coach experience of high school wrestlers' preferences and perceptions of coaching behaviors across a season. *Communication Education, 23,* 73–86.

Turman, P. D. (2003b). Coaches and cohesion: The impact of coaching techniques on team cohesion in the small group sport setting. *Journal of Sport Behavior, 26,* 86–104.

Turman, P. D. (2006). Athletes' perception of coach power use and the association between playing status and sport satisfaction. *Communication Research Reports, 23,* 273–282.

Turman, P. D. (2008). Coaches' immediacy behaviors as predictors of athletes' perceptions of satisfaction and team cohesion. *Western Journal of Communication, 72,* 162–179.

Turman, P. D., & Schrodt, P. (2004). New avenues for instructional communication research: Relationships among coaches' leadership behaviors and athletes' affective learning. *Communication Research Reports, 21,* 130–143.

Van Natta, D. II. (2013, April 3). Video shows Mike Rice's ire. *ESPN.com.* Retrieved from http://www.espn.com/espn/otl/story/_/id/9125796/practice-video-shows-rutgers-basketball-coach-mike-rice-berated-pushed-used-slurs-players

Waldeck, J. H., Kearney, P., & Plax, T. G. (2001). Instructional and developmental communication theory and research in the 1990s: Extending the agenda for the 21st century. In W. B. Gudykunst (Ed.), *Communication yearbook* (Vol. 25, pp. 207–229). Newbury Park, CA: Sage.

Webster, C. A. (2009). Expert teachers' instructional communication in golf. *International Journal of Sport Communication, 2,* 205–222.

Witt, P. L. (2012). The future of communication education. *Communication Education, 61,* 1–3.

Witt, P. L., Schrodt, P., & Turman, P. D. (2010). Instructor immediacy: Creating connections conducive to classroom learning. In D. L. Fassett & J. T. Warren (Eds.), *The Sage handbook of communication and instruction* (pp. 201–219). Los Angeles, CA: Sage.

· 4 ·

THE ORGANIZATIONAL PERSPECTIVE: COACHES AS MANAGERS

Coaching is people management-getting people to do what you want them to do and like doing it.—Vince Lombardi[1]

Organizing the sporting environment and team structures are central communicative processes of coaching (Kassing et al., 2004). The structural aspects of sport, such as scheduling, assigning tasks and roles, or shaping team culture, are largely within the purview of coaches. As such, coaches are a type of organizational manager, who oversee the functioning of sporting teams and environments that determine athletes' development and performance (Chelladurai, 2001; Quarterman, 2003). Communication scholars argue how sport is structured determines the effectiveness of coaches, including athletes' assumption of roles, psychological orientations, relationships with others, and team performance (Meân, 2013). Scholars who acknowledge and focus on the managerial nature of coaching operate from an organizational perspective.

The organizational perspective forwards that coaching is a process through which coaches share direction and vision with athletes. Within this process, coaches act as managers, who are responsible for their teams' performances and use their authority to develop and direct athletes toward the accomplishment of team goals. Coaches accomplish these aims via verbal and nonverbal communication that facilitate the maintenance and functioning of sports teams. In contrast, athletes are subordinates, who receive information and are charged to bring coaching to fruition on the field of play. Scholars who operate from the organizational perspective largely focus on coaches' leadership and athletes' roles in the functioning of sports teams. Thus, effective coaching occurs via the successful distribution of organizational resources, provision of information or feedback, cultivation of desirable team dynamics, and team performance (Cranmer, 2017; Kassing & Matthews, 2017).

The solidification of the organizational perspective is rooted in three arguments. First, sports teams are by definition organizations (Quarterman, 2003). Organizations are comprised of a *collection of individuals*. Within sports teams, these individuals include athletes, coaches, athletic trainers, and staff. These individuals share *common goals*. The shared goal of sport teams is usually to win games and ultimately a championship (e.g., conference, state, or national). There are numerous ways to contribute to the accomplishment of team goals, which leads to the *specialization of roles* amongst members, who focus on a limited range of tasks. The division of tasks and roles among athletes is evident in the differentiation of positions associated with phenotypes and abilities. Specialization is also observable in the roles of coaches, athletic trainers, and support staff who each provide specific services within the team structure. The specialization of roles becomes functional through *coordination*, which combines the specialized efforts of members in pursuit of team goals. Coordination is apparent in team strategies, plays, or the interplay between athletes during practices and training. Finally, organizational members are distinguished from nonmembers by physical and psychological *barriers*. These barriers include clothing (e.g., official uniforms or team apparel), access to physical spaces (e.g., training facilities, locker rooms, sidelines, or dugouts), public documents (e.g., team websites or rosters), and psychological understandings of team membership.

Second, there are parallels between athlete-coach and supervisor-subordinate relationships. Supervisor-subordinate relationships, regardless of whether officially labeled as such, naturally occur within collectives that have an explicit purpose, including sports teams. The supervisor-subordinate relationship features communicative patterns "limited to those exchanges of information and influence between organizational members, at least one of whom has formal (as defined by official organizational sources) authority to direct and evaluate the activities of other organizational members" (Jablin, 1979, p. 1202). Supervisors share job instructions and rationale, detail organizational policies and practices, provide performance feedback, and set organizational goals for subordinates. Likewise, coaches communicate information and feedback about sporting skills (e.g., proper form, footwork, and position-ing), outline how teams are to function (e.g., explaining strategies and team policies), and set individual or team goals. In contrast, subordinates mostly share information about themselves or coworkers, provide feedback about organizational policies and practices, and inquire for more information about completing tasks. Similarly, athletes' communication to coaches manifests in self-disclosures about experienced difficulties, the solicitation of coach assis-tance, and dissent about team policies, procedures, and practices.

Third, the processes that underlie supervising an organization apply to coaching. Supervisors are tasked with selecting subordinates, integrating those individuals into their work groups and tasks, managing the relation-ships between organizational members, and shaping working conditions and policies. These obligations require supervisors to have a wide variety of cog-nitive and communicative skills to ensure the success of their subordinates. Likewise, coaches perform similar functions for sport teams, including deter-mining team membership, assigning roles, structuring sporting environments, and setting team cultures. To accomplish this diverse array of tasks effectively, coaches must possess professional, interpersonal, and intrapersonal knowledge and implement this knowledge accordingly (Côté & Gilbert, 2009).

Although the organizational perspective has utility across levels of athletics (Kassing & Matthews, 2017), it is most applicable to teams that are large, highly structured, and extremely competitive in nature (e.g., travel, all-star, varsi-ty-level high school, collegiate, and professional teams), as well as situations in which authority of coaches is exacerbated or winning is a predominate concern (e.g., during playoffs). Indeed, most of the applications of the organizational perspective consider the experiences of collegiate coaches and student-athletes. Large, hierarchical structures increase the power distances between athletes and coaches and require more elaborate and developed systems of communicat-ing. As levels of hierarchy increase, communication within sport teams more closely mirrors patterns observed within traditional workplaces, including the prevalence of top-down communication and the delegation of tasks.

Moreover, a team's emphasis on task completion and winning determines the applicability of the organizational perspective. At many competitive levels of athletics (e.g., varsity high school, AAU, college, or professional), coaches are paid with the expectation that they will lead their teams to victory. If they fail to do so, they are terminated. The focus on task completion alters how teams are organized, as other objectives such as fostering interpersonal relationships with athletes, developing lesser skilled athletes, or promoting prosocial climates can become secondary (Lockwood & Perlman, 2008). As such, coaching in these environments becomes a managerial practice focused on the outcomes of sporting events.

Despite the utility of the organizational perspective, there are some stark differences between traditional organizations and sports teams. First, the power dynamics between athletes and coaches are exacerbated by the nature of sport. Sport is a physical endeavor and, as such, coaches have the ability to physically punish athletes (e.g., make them run laps) and communicate more aggressively than would be common in workplaces. Additionally, coaches who maintain success build social capital within their communities and can become beyond reproach. This social capital is a means of leveraging compliance from athletes and reinforcing one's authority. Finally, sport is an activity that mostly occurs during youth and adolescence, which means that there are often significant age differences between athletes and coaches (Atkinson, 2009). This age disparity is an additional source of influence of which coaches must be aware and careful to manage appropriately. Together, these dynamics give coaches more control than traditional supervisors possess but also present challenges, as teams are comprised of individuals in important stages of development.

Another difference is that sports teams experience drastic alterations in their membership because of systemic policies that do not apply in traditional work settings. Membership among sports teams are subject to frequent changes due to restrictions on eligibility. For example, youth athletics are restricted by age, size, or a combination of the two. Similarly, high school and college athletes are restricted via years of eligibility. The limits on participation ensure continual turnover. Coaches must adapt to these unstable social dynamics by planning for such transitions, including preparing athletes who will remain with the team for changing roles and social climates. Among travel and all-star teams, coaches may transition with athletes to new teams or leagues but these transitions may still involve alterations in team membership.

The compensation models within most levels of athletics differs extensively from traditional organizations; arguably, because sport is a non-utilitarian activity that occurs for its own sake. With the exception of professional sports, athletes seldom receive financial compensation for their participation. Division-I and II collegiate student-athletes receive indirect compensation in the form of tuition, a stipend for room and board, and the cost of attendance. The overwhelming majority of athletes, however, operate within the bounds of pure amateurism and receive no forms of financial compensation for participation. The reward structures of most competitive sports, thus, relies on alternative forms of compensation to motivate performance and team membership, including intrinsic satisfaction or extrinsic rewards (e.g., coaches' praise or playing time). Playing time is a unique form of compensation in that it is limited and a form of physical labor. As such, most coaches must rely on non-monetary means of compensating athletes to keep teams functioning well.

Sport teams are also structured so that individuals are differentiated based upon their roles and abilities, which is reflected in the starter/reserve labels. These differentiations determine which members of teams participate, and to what extent, during competitions. For example, independent sports (e.g., wrestling or cross country) have limits placed on the number of competitors and substitutions mid-competition are not possible (i.e., only starters get to compete). In interdependent sports, during which substitutions are possible (e.g., soccer, football), playing time is a limited and shared resource. In contrast, employees do not wait for coworkers to fail or become incapacitated before assisting in their organization's efforts and goals; all employed individuals have objectives to complete as part of their employment. Overall, sports teams are unique organizations in which coaches manage a variety of social dynamics, including balancing the development of individual athletes and team performance, managing the social complications that accompany high rates of turnover and face-threatening environments, and finding means to motivate and incentivize effort—often without direct financial compensation. To complicate the accomplishment of these organizational objectives, coaches must navigate the social boundaries and dynamics that accompany their positions, such as adult-minor, educator-student, or parent-child relationships.

Organizational Perspective

The organizational perspective has only recently been articulated (Cranmer & Myers, 2015; Kassing & Matthews, 2017). This perspective relies on literature from organizational communication, business management, and industrial relations to provide theories, frameworks, and variables from which coaching can be understood. Communication scholars who utilize the organizational perspective seek to understand the communicative processes that undergird managing sport teams and directing athletes toward task accomplishment (Kassing et al., 2004). Across literature, three processes are central to team functioning: socializing athletes into teams, enacting leadership, and managing athlete dissent.

Socializing Athletes Into Their Teams

Socialization into sports teams encompasses athletes' participative decision-making, learning of sporting roles, and social integration into their teams. With few exceptions, non-communication scholars focus on sport participation as a function of demographic characteristics (e.g., sex, race, socio-economic status, or family size) or the influence of agents of socialization including parents, siblings, peers, coaches, schools, and media (Coakley, 1993; McPherson, 1981). Communication scholars, however, focus on athletes' adjustment to specific teams, and contend that effective socialization requires the adoption of needed knowledge, attitudes, behaviors, and values (Cranmer, 2017, 2018). These socialization resources are obtained through interactions that convey useful information or buffer against the stress and uncertainty of transitioning into a new team or role. Athletes' socialization can be understood along a series of events that create uncertainty or through specific transitions between levels of athletics and teams (Carodine, Almond, & Gratto, 2001; Marx, Huffmon, & Doyle, 2008; Wylleman & Lavallee, 2004). Cranmer and colleagues advocated for Jablin's (2001) model of assimilation as an initial framework for understanding athlete socialization.

Athlete socialization begins prior to joining a new team, during a period known as *anticipatory socialization*. For example, the anticipatory socialization of collegiate student-athletes includes all of their interactions and experiences that occurred prior to beginning their collegiate careers (Cranmer & Myers, 2017). During this period, various stakeholders—such as parents, siblings, peers, media, teammates, or educational institutions—help develop athletes' interests and attitudes in sport, motivation for participation, specific sporting behaviors, and expectations for joining specific teams. Coaches participate in this process by preparing athletes to join their teams or communicating information that can be utilized when joining another team. Anticipatory socialization often influences athlete adjustment to teams through brief but influential messages that individuals retain and use to make sense of novel situations and relationships, evaluate their own behavior, and guide interactions during times of uncertainty—known as *memorable messages* (Knapp, Stohl, & Reardon, 1981). Comparatively, coaches are the most common sources of athletes' memorable messages about sport (Cranmer & Myers, 2017).

Memorable messages serve as socialization resources that provide information regarding the characteristics needed to be an athlete or the experiences that come with participation in particular levels of athletics (Cranmer &

Myers, 2017; Kassing & Pappas, 2007; Starcher, 2015). Commonly described characteristics include working hard (e.g., trying one's best, not giving up, and practicing), having character (e.g., loyalty, sportsmanship, or responsibility), and enjoying sport participation (Cranmer & Myers, 2017; Kassing & Pappas, 2007). Similar memorable messages have been observed across a variety of athlete populations (e.g., youth, high school, and college athletes), which provides evidence that coaches utilize scripts or rely on meta-narratives to socialize athletes. In contrast, messages about athletic experiences are tailored for specific teams, including the role of athletes within given communities (e.g., being a role model), the tribulations of college athletics (e.g., traveling schedules), and the significance of being part of a particular university (e.g., finding a new home) (see Table 4.1 for examples of these messages).

Athletes use the information that they obtain during anticipatory socialization to learn about their future roles and prepare themselves for upcoming opportunities and challenges. Cranmer (2017) surveyed 118 Division-I student-athletes to determine how memorable messages aid socialization. He found that during anticipatory socialization, memorable messages function to shape athletes' mindsets by providing motivation, confidence, and optimism, or reframing sport as a means of self-improvement and opportunity. Messages that emphasized the desirable characteristics of athletes are especially useful in this regard—likely, because they provide validated templates to follow.

Table 4.1. *Socialization Messages*

Messages	Examples
Athlete Characteristics	<ul><li>"Always compete in everything you do", Female, Volleyball Player</li><li>"Practice makes perfect", Male, Swimmer</li><li>"Pain is temporary", Male, Wrestler</li><li>"Hard work beats talent when talent doesn't work hard", Male, Soccer Player</li></ul>
Athletic Experiences	<ul><li>"Being an athlete at a Division-I school is one of the best things in life. The memories that will be made will be some of the best you will have. You wouldn't trade this time of your life for anything.", Male, Swimmer</li><li>"Take pride in being a Mountaineer, this is a special place. Once a Mountaineer, always a Mountaineer", Female, Tennis Player</li><li>"This place will be my home away from home", Female, Rifle Team</li><li>"You will not have friends outside of your sport", Female, Rower</li></ul>

Note. These messages were identified within Cranmer and Myers (2017).

Memorable messages also set expectations for college experiences by encouraging the prioritization of education, preparing athletes for increased time demands, and anticipating new relationships with coaches and teammates. In this regard, these messages help athletes fill initial voids of information about future experiences. Finally, memorable messages aid in participative decision-making, including whether to play collegiate athletics and which university to attend. Together, this research confirms the importance of communication with coaches during socialization, as these interactions become initial sources of organizational knowledge.

Another important process within anticipatory socialization is recruiting, which occurs most often within elite athletics (e.g., Amateur Athletic Union, national teams, or collegiate teams). For instance, recruiting is extremely salient within collegiate athletics because talented student-athletes are rare and highly coveted (Fondren, 2010; Perrelle, 2008). During recruiting, athletes and coaches assess their mutual fit and engage in impression management while negotiating future team membership. The recruiting process may include attending training camps, participating in interviews, taking facilities tours, or communicating with coaches (Cranmer, Yeargin, & Spinda, 2019; Kilger & Jonsson, 2017). When selecting a university, student-athletes mostly consider team facilities, perceived career opportunities (e.g., pathway to play professionally), and relationships with coaches, whereas coaches seek talented athletes who fit a desired style of play or possess a needed skillset (Doyle & Gaeth, 1990; Klenosky, Templin, & Troutman, 2001; Magnusen, Kim, Perrewe, & Ferris, 2014). Unfortunately, given the demands for talented athletes, recruiting is often deceptive and features unethical behaviors (e.g., the provision of drugs, alcohol, sex, or payments to recruits), the admonishing of other universities, and misleading information that inflates athletes' expectations (Fondren, 2010; Perrelle, 2008). These types of behaviors are evident in numerous pay-for-play (e.g., the Federal Bureau of Investigation's Adidas probe) and recruiting scandals (e.g., those during Hugh Freeze's tenure at Ole Miss). Coaches exacerbate the inaccuracy of recruiting by providing limited insight into daily routines, de-emphasizing the importance of academics, and avoiding the discussion of the detrimental aspects of becoming a public figure (Cranmer et al., 2019). Disparities between student-athletes' expectations and their eventual experiences have enduring consequences for athletes, teams, and coaches.

Once athletes join their new teams, they begin a new period of socialization known as *entry*. This period centers on athletes' initial efforts to learn their tasks and roles, as well as socially integrate among their teammates (Benson & Eys, 2018). During entry, athletes often consult the information they obtained during anticipatory socialization. This information is most useful when it is accurate or shared by teammates, which assists in the formation of relationships with others and eases the social integration into teams. Yet, dissimilarity causes friction between teammates who possess different expectations and standards for behavior (Cranmer, 2017). Unfortunately, athletes' experiences with new teams commonly fall short of their initial expectations, which creates uncertainty and stress. To resolve this uncertainty and stress, athletes must acquire social and task-related resources that allow them to adapt to their environment, teams, and tasks. Although known as *unfreezing* within organizational literature (Jablin, 2001), within sport, this process has been termed *derecruitment* by former college football coach Urban Meyer (Feldman, 2013). Meyer recognized that coaches inflate athletes' expectations for future membership (e.g., immediate roles or impact on the team) and perceptions of their abilities as part of their recruiting pitches. The misled athletes then join their teams with attitudes, motivations, and expectations that go unfulfilled. The success of their continued membership requires undoing the sales pitches from the recruiting process and shaping athletes for their new realities. Ideally, coaches who act ethically would reduce the need for such a process but unfreezing occurs for most individuals who join new task-oriented groups.

Coaches promote socialization during entry by structuring the sporting environment to meet the demands or conditions of their sport. For instance, socialization can be encouraged via formalized orientations for new team members, mentoring programs that pair newcomers with veterans, organizational documents that outline modes of behavior or assessment (e.g., playbooks, coaching philosophies, or team manuals), or team building exercises (e.g., retreats or ropes courses) (Kramer, 2010). Another structural means of socializing athletes is to offer support staff to help athletes with sports, non-sporting roles (e.g., student), or life. These staff members serve as counselors or sources of support throughout athletes' careers. For example, Cranmer et al. (2019) found that Division-I football players frequently consulted a staffer, who was tasked with athletes' professional and personal development. One player remarked about this staffer:

He is someone I go to when things get frustrating or I don't know what's going on.…
Like, if I think I should be playing more or I don't understand why coaches are treat-
ing me a particular way. He gives good advice on how to approach those types of
situations. Plus, he has been there. He went through it. And now he is here for us and
in a way that [goes] beyond just making sure that we play well. (p. 82)

The effectiveness of this individual was associated with his own success as a
collegiate and professional athlete 40 years prior. Coaches, thus, have control
over team programs and policies and should structure them to help integrate
athletes into their teams.

Athletes also actively engage in self-socialization by seeking information via social exchanges with coaches or teammates. For instance, Division-I student-athletes acquire organizational knowledge through social
exchanges of organizational resources with head coaches, assistant coaches,
and teammates (Cranmer, 2018). These interactions are complex, as multiple agents shape athletes' socialization in unique ways. Head coaches,
surprisingly, were found to have little-to-no direct influence on athletes'
organizational knowledge, with understandings of team goals and values
serving as a notable exception. Assistant coaches and teammates, however,
accounted for understandings of team history, politics, goals, and values.
These findings indicate that mid-level management and lateral interactions
with teammates are important sources of adjustment to the social and cultural elements of teams. In contrast, head coaches fulfill a managerial role,
and it is through their selection of assistants and control of team culture that
they influence socialization.

The entry period continues until athletes view themselves as full members
of their teams (i.e., a psychological state), at which point they begin a period
of *metamorphosis*. Uncertainty and stress continue to define this period, but
are subsequently associated with specific events that require continued adjustment, such as athlete or coach turnover, incoming cohorts of new athletes,
conference realignment, or other forms of institutional change. Throughout
entry and metamorphosis, well-socialized members are identifiable through
their organizational knowledge, successful performances, and acceptance of
team culture. Other indicators of socialization may include desirable organizational attitudes and behaviors such as commitment, satisfaction, or citizen-
ship behaviors. Athletes who are not successfully socialized experience negative emotions, poor relationships with coaches and teammates, and burnout
(Coakley, 1993). These athletes are likely observable through displays of disinterest, resistance to coaching, or decisions to cease membership on a team,

which may help explain the prevalence of quitting in high school sports and transfers within collegiate athletics.

Upon termination of their membership within a team—whether planned or unplanned, self or other-initiated—athletes begin the final period of socialization, known as *exit*. During this period, athletes announce and subsequently adjust to leaving their teams. Their adjustment is explored across numerous psychological and social realities, including the need to form new social relationships and develop an identity that does not include active sport participation. Coaches contribute to the socialization of athletes through creating welcoming and transparent cultures, instituting clear policies and procedures, hiring competent individuals (e.g., assistant coaches, athletes, or staffs), and ensuring that resources are available to help athletes cope with or overcome uncertainties and stress.

Enacting Leadership

Leadership explores the process of influence through which one directs another's behavior toward the accomplishment of an objective (Hackman & Johnson, 2009). Coaches are leaders, who must influence athletes' behaviors toward the pursuit of team goals. Leadership is understood through numerous frameworks, such as trait, behavioral, contingency, and interactional theories. Given the organizational contexts from which these theories arose, all are appropriate for the organizational perspective. However, interactional leadership theories are especially relevant from a communicative perspective because these frameworks emphasize the importance of relationships and communication within the process of leadership. One such theory—Leader-Member Exchange theory—illustrates this approach within coach communication literature.

Leader-Member Exchange theory (LMX) (Dansereau, Graen, & Haga, 1975) posits that leadership is a function of the relationships that occur between leaders (i.e., coaches) and followers (i.e., athletes). LMX recognizes that athlete-coach relationships are dyadic—meaning coaches form distinguishable relationships with individual athletes. More simply, within a single team, there are multiple relationships between individual athletes and their coaches, and these relationships vary in quality. The differentiated relationships occur because coaches have finite resources and need to strategically invest those resources in an effective and efficient manner to accomplish their aims. Relationships of high quality—referred to as high-LMX or in-group relationships—are characterized by mutual trust, affect, respect, influence, and professionalism. Relationships of a poor quality—referred to as low-LMX or out-group relationships—are characterized by the absence of these qualities (Graen & Uhl-Bien, 1995).

The quality of athletes' LMX relationships are of consequence for their subsequent attitudes, experiences, and performances. Within traditional organizations, those with in-group relationships receive more awards, positive appraisals, and support from leaders; possess more power and influence among collectives; and are more productive and upwardly mobile than subordinates with out-group relationships (Gerstner & Day, 1997; Graen & Uhl-Bien, 1995). Athletes with in-group relationships report similar benefits. For instance, high school athletes gain voice in their team's functioning through forming quality LMX with coaches, which opens reciprocal lines of communication (Cranmer & Myers, 2015) and creates channels to express disagreement with team policies (Cranmer & Buckner, 2017). Likewise, in-group relationships facilitate athletes' integration into team cultures (Cranmer, 2018) and their reception of developmental resources, such as confirmation (Cranmer, Arnson, Moore, Scott, & Peed, 2019). These findings indicate that athletes' roles within team functioning are partially determined by coaches' use of leadership and distribution of resources.

LMX theory also recognizes that coaches' leadership is embedded within larger team structures (Graen & Uhl-Bien, 1995). As such, in-group relationships extend to how athletes relate to their teammates. Specifically, athletes with in-group relationships report more cohesive and cooperative communication with their teammates (Cranmer & Myers, 2015). These findings suggest that athletes observe and mirror coaches' leadership efforts during subsequent interactions with teammates, and attempt to aid those with in-group relationships. It is also possible that the organizational resources that those with in-group relationships possess make them attractive nodes from which teammates seek information and support. Collectively, LMX research identifies a variety of benefits for athletes' psychological, social, and affective sporting experiences.

Given these benefits, scholars have sought to understand the formation of LMX relationships. An initial determinant of in-group relationships was argued to be athletes' starting status (Case, 1998). Although starting status reveals little about an athlete's physical skills (e.g., 40-yard dash or bench press) or mental acuity (e.g., knowledge of the playbook), it indicates which athletes coaches believe are best positioned to assist in a team's pursuit of victory. LMX theory asserts that given the importance of winning within sports, coaches dedicate their attention, effort, and time to athletes who are likely to contribute to a team's performance (Cranmer & Myers, 2015). Across multiple studies, such notions have garnered support, as starting athletes consistently report greater LMX with coaches (Case, 1998; Cranmer, 2016; Cranmer & Myers, 2015). Among high school athletes, starting status accounts for as much as 9–12% of LMX with head coaches (Cranmer, 2016). This evidence demonstrates that a team's organizational goals shape coaches' enactment of leadership. Moreover, the desire to win serves as a barrier to forming quality relationships with less talented athletes.

Despite early assertions about the preeminence of athletic ability, multiple investigations indicate that coaches' use of prosocial and interpersonal communication predict more variance within LMX than athletes' starting status (Cranmer, 2016; Cranmer et al., 2018). For instance, supportive communication, especially that which demonstrates concern or builds self-esteem, facilitates LMX formation. Such support develops trust and opens lines of communication between athletes and coaches (Cranmer, 2016). As such, coaches can utilize communication to leverage influence and exert leadership. The interpersonal mechanisms of LMX have yet to be identified but may be guided by additional considerations for athletes' ancillary roles (e.g., captain status), relational dynamics (e.g., homophily), or individual dispositions (e.g., personality and interpersonal skills). Together, LMX research underscores that coaches' leadership is derived from their relationships with athletes and that communication allows these relationships to form.

Managing Dissent

Within all organizations, individuals experience dissatisfaction and disagreement with how their organizations function (Kassing, 2011). *Dissent* refers to expressions of disagreement with organizational policies, procedures, and practices (Kassing, 1997). Despite sporting cultures of top-down communication that contradict the notion of athlete dissent, dissent is a ubiquitous phenomenon among sport teams. Coaches, who are responsible for keeping teams functioning properly, must manage athletes' disagreement. Those coaches who do not properly address athletes' concerns may inspire absenteeism, quitting, resistance to coaching, and behaviors that detract from team climates (Kassing & Anderson, 2014).

Dissent begins when athletes experience *triggering events*, which fosters feelings of discomfort or distance from a team. Triggering events are contextual and arise from the policies, procedures, or practices of a given coach or team. Given coaches oversee and are responsible for the structure and rules by which teams function, triggering events are commonly within their purview. Based upon the reports of 262 high school athletes, Cranmer, Buckner, Pham, and Jordan (2018) identified common triggers of athlete dissent. They found that athletes most commonly voiced dissent in response to policies, procedures, or practices that are perceived to be *detrimental to a team's performance*, such as playing time or position assignments, failing to implement the correct strategy, or selecting inefficient training techniques. Issues of power and social climates, such as impediments to *team functioning* (e.g., parental influence, demonstrations of favoritism, or not exercising authority when needed) or *communication climates and culture* (e.g., verbally aggressive coaching, gossiping between teammates, and environments that stifle expression) were also common triggers of dissent. Finally, athletes dissented in response to the *logistical requirements* of team membership, including financial burdens, scheduling, time demands, and restrictions on physical appearance. Knowledge of these triggering events may help address dissent preemptively, as uncertainty and unmet expectations are factors in triggering dissent (Kassing, 2011). Coaching documents (e.g., coaching philosophies, player contracts, or parent handbooks) may clearly establish policies, procedures, and practices and eliminate dissent before it arises. If coaches enforce these standards consistently, they may prevent potential misunderstandings and save the time needed to manage excessive dissent. Although these strategies are helpful, it would be naïve—and counterproductive—to believe that all disagreements are preventable. Accordingly, dissent research focuses on maximizing the effectiveness of dissent.

Athletes may dissent to three potential audiences: coaches (*upward dissent*), teammates (*lateral dissent*), and individuals external to their teams (*displaced dissent*) (Kassing & Anderson, 2014). Managing dissent effectively requires that it be expressed directly to coaches, who are best positioned to address disagreements. Coaches resolve dissent through altering *or* justifying a team policy, procedure, or practice. When disagreement is warranted and alternatives are available, dissent can be a mechanism of innovation that allows coaches to improve their skills and team environments. However, athletes may be ignorant of coaches' justifications for team policies and procedures, including league or institutional policies that govern how teams function. Coaches can resolve dissent by sharing the justification for the status quo. With additional information, athletes may come to accept that with which they initially disagreed. Thus, it is noteworthy that alterations to team policies, procedures, or practices are not necessitated merely because dissent is expressed.

To ensure upward dissent, coaches must cultivate open environments by creating formal structures for feedback (e.g., grievance policies, suggestion boxes, or team councils), fostering positive interactions, and enacting a democratic leadership style (Kassing & Anderson, 2014). Another tactic is appointing starters or captains as conduits of team disagreement, as these individuals are more empowered to engage in upward dissent (Cranmer & Buckner, 2017). For instance, Dabo Swinney (Clemson University's football coach) instituted the Swinney Council—a group of appointed team leaders who provide a weekly report to coaches and administrators regarding team concerns or issues. Athletes' relationships with teammates, among other informal social structures, are also important for promoting upward dissent. High school athletes who have socially cohesive relationships with teammates engage in more upward dissent, which indicates a reliance on coalition building (Cranmer & Buckner, 2017). Coalition building is especially important when large power disparities exist between dissenters and their superiors—like those between athletes and coaches (Kassing, 2002). By facilitating connections between teammates, coaches provide athletes with the social resources needed to voice their concerns and overcome power disparities.

Although coaches are best positioned to address dissent, upward communication runs contrary to traditional, top-down models of athlete-coach interaction. As such, athletes often dissent to teammates, family, and friends. These individuals are ineffective audiences of dissent because they cannot address athletes' concerns. Further, by habitually dissenting to teammates, athletes may cultivate a milieu that reinforces perceptions of inequity, exacerbates dissatisfaction, and hinders team functioning. Thus, coaches should discourage those forms of dissent and remove the social conditions that promote them. One key social condition that strongly predicts lateral dissent is a coach's approachability. In short, if athletes do not view their coaches as approachable, they express dissent to teammates or others (Cranmer & Buckner, 2017; Kassing & Anderson, 2014). Coaching effectiveness, therefore, requires building lines of communication that welcome athlete concerns.

Coaches may also optimize athlete dissent by encouraging the use of specific strategies that are better suited to resolve disagreements. Eleven types of dissent messages have been identified (Garner, 2009). These messaging strategies attach the expressions of disagreement to descriptions of emotions (*venting*), demands for compliance (*pressure*), offers of quid-pro-quo (*exchange*), appeals to morals or ethics (*inspiration*), efforts to make the receiver of dissent feel important (*ingratiation*), reasons for disagreement (*direct-factual appeal*), resolutions for disagreement (*solution presentation*), references to the support of others (*coalitions*), or jokes and witty remarks (*humor*). Additionally, dissent expressions may be repeated (*repetition*) or expressed to the superior of a coach (*circumvention*). These message strategies are used independently or conjointly. Evidence indicates that athletes mostly rely upon solution presentation messages, followed by direct-factual appeals, and subsequently inspiration and coalitions (Cranmer et al., 2018). This selection of dissent messages demonstrates the need for rational approaches to dissent resolution and the negotiation of power imbalances between athletes and coaches. The purposeful selection of dissent messages is important, as "the success or failure of dissent is dependent on *how it is expressed* rather than *what it is about*" (Cranmer et al., 2018, p. 540). In general, solution presentation is the most appropriate and effective way to express dissent, with pressure, circumvention, and humor being especially ineffective. Coaches may encourage such message strategies by instituting policies through which realistic solutions must accompany expressions of disagreement. Collectively, coaches are best able to address athletes' disagreements when they are addressed directly and civilly, understand why disagreement has occurred, and are presented with potential resolutions to consider.

The Future of the Organizational Perspective

There remains many opportunities to advance the organizational perspective. The processes discussed within this chapter may serve as the foundation for future scholarship but there are considerable shortcomings of scope within this literature. To date, head coaches and their influence are the focal point of a majority of organizational research, which replicates patterns of managerial bias and restricts understandings of the reciprocal nature of human interaction within sport teams. The organizational perspective of coaching utilizes classical management approaches that are defined by top-down patterns of communication. In reality, athlete-coach relationships are to some extent reciprocal—although rarely symmetrical. Athletes are capable of upward influence and serve important roles within the highlighted organizational processes that determine team functioning, including self-socialization, self-leadership, and autonomy within dissent expression. Incorporating athletes' experiences and viewpoints within these processes yields more intricate and meaningful insight into the realities of coaching (e.g., student-athletes' emotional labor; Romo, 2017).

Sports teams are also more complex in their structure and functioning than current research models report. Teams are comprised of a multitude of individuals, who span athletes, coaches, and staff members. Despite differing roles and levels of formal authority, these various stakeholders influence organizational processes and athletes' experiences and attitudes. However, coach researchers often examine head coaches in isolation and rarely consider the importance of other stakeholders within organizational processes. An emergent collection of studies has considered athletes' relationships within multiple organizational members, simultaneously (Cranmer, 2018; Cranmer & Buckner, 2017). These studies contradict earlier theorizing regarding the importance of head coaches in determining athletes' organizational experiences. It appears that despite their authority, head coaches of large, competitive teams (i.e., ideal contexts for the application of the organizational perspective) have less face-to-face interaction with athletes. Thus, organizational members who are lower in team hierarchy are the main contact points for information, support, and influence. These patterns highlight the need for a shift toward viewing head coaches as top-level management, who delegate to assistant coaches and athletes of elevated statuses (e.g., captains or starters). These individuals act as mid-level management, who have direct contact with athletes and shape their experiences. Such an approach would better encompass the actual structure and functioning of many high-level sports teams.

Further, there is a need to recognize that sports teams are embedded within larger social communities, such as towns, regions, or states. Within these communities, parents, relatives, and friends of athletes are important stakeholders who may provide tangible (e.g., funding and transportation) and emotional support, as well as influence athletes' decision-making and sporting experiences (Erdner & Wright, 2018). Sports teams are also often under the oversight of athletic departments, academic institutions, and/or athletic conferences and leagues. These institutions serve as regulatory bodies that set rules and guidelines for how teams and coaches interact with athletes, including the timing, length, and sometimes modes of interaction. To date, the organizational perspective has yet to encompass the stakeholders who are not on the field of play. An open systems approach that recognizes coaches' engagement with numerous stakeholders and the management of their competing interests would further the understanding of effective coaching practices (Washington & Reade, 2013). Such information will optimize sporting stakeholders' contributions and minimize distractions by fostering cooperation, appropriate degrees of investment, and professional relationships.

Conclusion

The organizational perspective is beneficial for understanding how coaches act as managers within sport and guide the efforts of their teams. This perspective provides the tools to consider issues of formal authority and team structures, as well as the flow of information about a host of task-related issues. The development of this perspective could benefit from further explorations of the role of communication within organizational processes. For instance, the negotiation of team membership is essential to coaching, as talent selection and turnover are ubiquitous within sport. Given such dynamics, understanding the processes through which individuals are selected for and transition out of sport are as important as the socialization of new athletes. Other processes like those that encompass managing the concerns of internal and external stakeholders (e.g., team building and community relations) should also be considered. These processes speak to issues of power and the interplay between various and potentially competing interests. With the inclusion of additional processes, the organizational perspective would offer a more representative viewpoint of coaches as managers and teams as organizations.

Note

1. Brainy Quotes. (2019). Vince Lombardi quotes. *BrainyQuotes.com*. Retrieved from https://www.brainyquote.com/authors/vince_lombardi

References

Atkinson, J. L. (2009). Age matters in sport communication. *The Electronic Journal of Communication, 19*. Online Journal. Retrieved from http://www.cios.org/EJCPUBLIC/019/2/019341.html

Benson, A. J., & Eys, M. A. (2018). Understanding the consequence of newcomer integration processes: The sport teams socialization tactics questionnaire. *Journal of Sport & Exercise Psychology, 39*, 13–28. doi:10.1123/jsep.2016-0182.

Carodine, K., Almond, K. F., & Gratto, K. K. (2001). College student athlete success both in and out of the classroom. *New Directions for Student Services, 2001*, 19–33.

Case, R. (1998). Leader member exchange theory and sport: Possible applications. *Journal of Sport Behavior, 21*, 387–396.

Chelladurai, P. (2001). *Managing organizations for and physical activity: A systems perspective.* Scottsdale, AZ: Holcomb Hathaway.

Coakley, J. (1993). Sport and socialization. *Exercise and Sport Sciences Reviews, 21*, 169–200.

Côté, J., & Gilbert, W. (2009). An integrative definition of coaching effectiveness and expertise. *International Journal of Sports Science & Coaching, 4*, 307–323.

Cranmer, G. A. (2016). A continuation of sport teams from an organizational perspective: Predictors of athlete-coach leader-member exchange. *Communication & Sport, 4*, 43–61.

Cranmer, G. A. (2017). A communicative approach to sport socialization: The functions of memorable messages during Division-I student-athletes' socialization. *International Journal of Sport Communication, 10*, 233–257.

Cranmer, G. A. (2018). An application of socialization resources theory: Collegiate student-athletes' team socialization as a function of their social exchanges with coaches and teammates. *Communication & Sport, 6*, 349–367.

Cranmer, G. A., Arnson, E., Moore, A., Scott, A., & Peed, J. (2019). High school athletes' reports of confirmation as a function of starting status and leader-member exchange. *Communication & Sport, 7*, 510–528. doi:10.1177/2167479518783838

Cranmer, G. A., & Buckner, M. (2017). High school athletes' relationships with head coaches and teammates as predictors of their expressions of upward and lateral dissent. *Communication Studies, 68*, 37–55.

Cranmer, G. A., Buckner, M., Pham, N., & Jordan, B. (2018). "I disagree": An exploration of triggering events, messages, and effectiveness of athletes' dissent. *Communication & Sport, 5*, 523–546.

Cranmer, G. A., & Myers, S. A. (2015). Sports teams as organizations: A leader-member exchange perspective of player communication with coaches and teammates. *Communication & Sport, 3*, 100–118.

Cranmer, G. A., & Myers, S. A. (2017). Exploring Division-I student-athletes' memorable messages from their anticipatory socialization. *Communication Quarterly, 65*, 125–143.

Cranmer, G. A., Yeargin, R., & Spinda, J. (2019). Life after signing: The recruiting process as a resource of college football players' socialization. In T. L. Rentner & D. P. Burns (Eds.), *Case studies in sport communication: You make the call* (pp. 77–84). New York, NY: Routledge.

Dansereau, F., Graen, G., & Haga, W. J. (1975). A vertical dyad linkage approach to leadership within formal organizations: A longitudinal investigation of the role making process. *Organizational Behavior and Human Performance, 13*, 46–78.

Doyle, C. A., & Gaeth, G. J. (1990). Assessing the institutional choice process of student-athletes. *Research Quarterly, 61*, 85–92.

Erdner, S. M., & Wright, C. N. (2018). The relationship between family communication patterns and the self-efficacy of student-athletes. *Communication & Sport, 6*, 368–389.

Feldman, B. (2013, February 7). Coach vents about the hypocrisy of the de-recruiting process. *CBSsports.com*. Retrieved from https://www.cbssports.com/college-football/news/coach-vents-about-the-hypocrisy-of-the-de-recruiting-process/

Fondren, K. M. (2010). Sport and stigma: College football recruiting and institutional identity of Ole Miss. *Journal of Issues in Intercollegiate Athletics, 3*, 154–175.

Garner, J. T. (2009). When things go wrong at work: An exploration of organizational dissent messages. *Communication Studies, 60*, 197–218.

Gerstner, C. R., & Day, D. V. (1997). Meta-analytic review of leader–member exchange theory: Correlates and construct issues. *Journal of Applied Psychology, 82*, 827–844.

Graen, G. B., & Uhl-Bien, M. (1995). Relationship-based approach to leadership: Development of leader-member exchange (LMX) theory of leadership over 25 years: Applying a multi-level multi-domain perspective. *The Leadership Quarterly, 6*, 219–247.

Hackman, M. Z., & Johnson, C. E. (2009). *Leadership: A communicative perspective* (5th ed.). Long Grove, IL: Waveland.

Jablin, F. M. (1979). Superior–subordinate communication: The state of the art. *Psychological Bulletin, 86*, 1201–1222.

Jablin, F. M. (2001). Organizational entry, assimilation, and disengagement/exit. In F. M. Jablin & L. L. Putnam (Eds.), *The new handbook of organizational communication: Advances in theory, research, and methods* (pp. 732–818). Thousand Oaks, CA: Sage.

Kassing, J. W. (1997). Articulating, antagonizing, and displacing: A model of employee dissent. *Communication Studies, 48*, 311–332.

Kassing, J. W. (2002). Speaking up: Identifying employees' upward dissent strategies. *Management Communication Quarterly, 16*, 187–209.

Kassing, J. W. (2011). *Dissent in organizations*. Malden, MA: Polity.

Kassing, J. W., & Anderson, R. L. (2014). Contradicting coach or grumbling to teammates: Exploring dissent expression in the coach–athlete relationship. *Communication & Sport, 2*, 172–185.

Kassing, J. W., Billings, A. C., Brown, R. S., Halone, K. K., Harrison, K., Krizek, B., … Turman, P. D. (2004). Communication in the community of sport: The process of enacting, (re)producing, consuming, and organizing sport. In P. J. Kalbfleisch (Ed.), *Communication yearbook* (Vol. 28, pp. 373–409). Mahwah, NJ: Erlbaum.

Kassing, J. W., & Matthews, R. (2017). Sport and organizational communication. In A. C. Billings (Ed.), *Defining sport communication* (pp. 137–149). New York, NY: Routledge.

Kassing, J. W., & Pappas, M. E. (2007). "Champions are built in the off season": An exploration of high school coaches' memorable messages. *Human Communication, 10*, 537–546.

Kilger, M., & Jonsson, R. (2017). Talent production in interaction: Performance appraisal interviews in talent selection camps. *Communication & Sport, 5*, 110–129.

Klenosky, D. B., Templin, T. J., & Troutman, J. A. (2001). Recruiting student athletes: A means-end investigation of school-choice decision making. *Journal of Sport Management, 15*, 96–106.

Knapp, M. L., Stohl, C., & Reardon, K. K. (1981). Memorable messages. *Journal of Communication, 31*, 27–41.

Kramer, M. W. (2010). *Organizational socialization: Joining and leaving organizations.* Malden, MA: Polity.

Lockwood, P., & Perlman, D. (2008). Enhancing the youth sport experience: A re-examination of methods, coaching style, and motivational climate. *The Journal of Youth Sports, 4,* 30–34.

Magnusen, M. J., Kim, Y., Perrewe, P. L., & Ferris, G. R. (2014). A critical review and synthesis of student-athlete college choice factors: Recruiting effectiveness in NCAA sports. *International Journal of Sports Science & Coaching, 9,* 1265–1286.

Marx, J., Huffmon, S., & Doyle, A. (2008). The student-athlete model and the socialization of intercollegiate athletes. *Online Journal of Sport Psychology, 10.* Retrieved from https://www.athleticinsight.com/Vol10Iss1/StudentAthleteModel.htm

McPherson, B. D. (1981). Socialization into and through sport involvement. In G. R. F. Luschen & G. H. Sage (Eds.), *Handbook of social science of sport* (pp. 246–273). Champaign, IL: Stipes.

Meân, L. J. (2013). The communicative complexity of youth sport: Maintaining benefits, managing discourses, and challenging identities. In P. M. Pedersen (Ed.), *Routledge handbook of sport communication* (pp. 338–349). New York, NY: Routledge.

Perrelle, J. (2008). An opportunity for reform—Tennessee Secondary School Athletic Association v. Brentwood Academy and NCAA recruiting. *Brooklyn Law Review, 74,* 1213–1252.

Quarterman, J. Q. (2003). Managing and leading sport organizations. In J. B. Parks & J. Q. Quarterman (Eds.), *Contemporary sport management* (2nd ed., pp. 149–164). Champaign, IL: Human Kinetics.

Romo, L. K. (2017). College student-athletes' communicative negotiation of emotional labor. *Communication & Sport, 5,* 492–509.

Starcher, S. C. (2015). Memorable messages from fathers to children through sports: Perspectives from sons and daughters. *Communication Quarterly, 63,* 204–220.

Washington, M., & Reade, I. (2013). Coach: The open systems' manager. In P. Protrac, W. Gilbert, & J. Denison (Eds.), *The Routledge handbook of sports coaching* (pp. 297–306). New York, NY: Routledge.

Wylleman, P., & Lavallee, D. (2004). A developmental perspective on transitions faced by athletes. In M. R. Weiss (Ed.), *Developmental sport and exercise psychology: A lifespan perspective* (pp. 507–527). Morgantown, WV: Fitness Information Technology.

· 5 ·

THE GROUP PERSPECTIVE: COACHES AS GROUP MEMBERS

[When coaching] make sure that team members know they are working with you, not for you.—John Wooden[1]

Coaching is a process that occurs within social collectives comprised of coaches, staff, and athletes (Carron, Hausenblas, & Eys, 2005). Within these collectives, coaches oversee the web of interactions between athletes and themselves, as well as those between teammates. Coaching is inherently a group context that requires attention to social climates, calculated efforts to build team cultures, and the negotiation of athletes' roles and team strategies toward task accomplishment (Myers & Anderson, 2008). The quality of team social dynamics may inspire innovation and collaboration, or deter teamwork and promote hostility between team members (Carron et al., 2005). Thus, the social climates of sports teams influence how teams approach their goals and, ultimately, whether they are successful. Effective coaches ensure members of their teams work together by creating social environments that assist in the accomplishment of shared tasks and goals. As such, it is unsurprising that the teams of effective coaches offer a sense of family or belonging among members (Becker, 2009; Cranmer & Brann, 2015; Cranmer & Myers, 2017). Coach communication scholars who acknowledge and focus on coaches' roles within these collectives operate from a group perspective.

The group perspective recognizes that coaches and athletes are co-members of a shared collective, and that coaching is an act rooted within managing the social dynamics that accompany such collectives. Although coaches and athletes share experiences and are members of the same team, coaches are differentiated by their formal positions and task of overseeing teams. This oversight requires coaches to structure the sporting environment to assist athletes in adjusting to group norms, making decisions, negotiating roles, resolving conflict, and forming relationships (Anderson, Riddle, & Martin, 1999; Myers & Anderson, 2008; O'Hair & Wiemann, 2004). It is through verbal and nonverbal communication that coaches establish and maintain the relational climates of teams. In contrast, athletes comprise the bulk of group members on a team, and forge relationships with each other and their coaches. Additionally, athletes participate in the negotiation of informal, and sometimes formal, roles, as they seek to accomplish goals. Within this perspective, the performance and development of athletes are fostered through social dynamics that maximize the collaborative efforts of teams toward shared and individual goals (Turman, 2003b, 2017). Thus, effective coaching is evident via social climates, team cultures and norms, athletes' social networks, cohesion, and team performances.

The group perspective of coaching forwards that sports teams are by definition groups based upon three features. A central feature of a group is the number of participants engaging in interaction. All group scholars agree that a group consists of at least three people (Myers & Anderson, 2008; O'Hair & Wiemann, 2004). However, opinions regarding the size of groups vary extensively, with some scholars suggesting that the group perspective ceases functionality when groups reach 15 (Myers & Anderson, 2008) or 20 members (O'Hair & Wiemann, 2004). The number of individuals within interactions renders group communication more complex than dyadic interactions that come to define the instructional and interpersonal perspectives of coaching. Within group contexts, athletes form relationships with each other and coaches, and come to consider the relationships that others have during their interactions (O'Hair & Wiemann, 2004). As groups increase in size, interactions become complex, formalized, less intimate, and take longer (O'Hair & Wiemann, 2004). Coaches must be aware of these dynamics and be wary of cliques and coalitions that occur naturally within group settings.

The second feature of a group is that members share goals, as groups often exist to accomplish tasks too complicated for a single individual. The primary goal of a sports team is to win games (Myers & Anderson, 2008), but a variety of additional goals may be considered by coaches or athletes. For example, coaches' goals may include teaching sporting skills or creating cooperative sporting environments, whereas athletes may desire to improve their skills or form a sense of belonging among their teammates. Forming and maintaining a group requires the balancing of relational dynamics that occur between members while also seeking task accomplishment. The responsibility to guide teams towards the accomplishment of tasks becomes increasingly complex when athletes prioritize their individual goals (e.g., a desired number of points scored), which may impede team goals. Team norms and cultures guide how athletes work together regarding what tasks are prioritized and how these tasks are achieved.

The third feature is that groups require interdependence between members for the accomplishment of team goals. Interdependence is especially evident in team sports, which by their very nature require the coordination of a variety of skillsets and phenotypes to accomplish team goals. Such interdependence is evident in positions and the interplay between athletes during the execution of strategy. However, even independent sports (e.g., wrestling, swimming, or track and field) require athletes with a variety of skillsets and physical features to contribute to a team's efforts, as team outcomes require the success of multiple athletes during competition. Further, individual performances within independent sports are influenced by the interplay between teammates that come to define practices and training sessions. Likewise, there is interdependence between athletes and coaches, who must work together in a coordinated manner. For example, coaches strategize athletes' efforts before and during competitions, with interdependent sports providing periods for communication (e.g., timeouts and quarters or halftimes) and independent sports featuring opportunities to communicate during competition (e.g., as seen in wrestling or boxing). Promoting cooperation amongst teams can be difficult, as groups feature multiple individuals with varying interests, personalities, and goals. Due to these features, relationships within the group context are complex and easily strained. Successful interdependence requires that coaches create social climates to encourage cooperation and minimize discord among team members.

At times, differentiating between the group and organizational perspectives is challenging, as there is considerable conceptual overlap between these two perspectives. Both perspectives recognize that coaches are embedded within social collectives, seek to accomplish shared goals, and address levels of interdependence or coordination among teams. Moreover, many communicative processes may be explored from either group or organizational perspectives, including socialization, leadership, or turnover. Some argue that the distinctions between the scholars who operate within these perspectives are rooted in their scholarly traditions or a consequence of their expertise— rather than the product of conceptual distinctions between groups and organizations. Yet, there are nuanced differences that, although seldom explicitly recognized, are important for determining the bounds of each perspective.

The group perspective is ideal for understanding informal interactions and social climates within small collectives that feature limited forms of hierarchy and are temporary. The number of individuals that the group perspective can accommodate is restricted, as it is most useful for examining collectives of five-to-seven members (Cragan & Wright, 1999) but inadequate for larger groups (15+ members) (Myers & Anderson, 2008; O'Hair & Wiemann, 2004). The group perspective is intended for collectives with relatively flat hierarchies and that feature informal communication, as group roles, norms, and networks are negotiated between members (O'Hair & Wiemann, 2004). As such, group scholars come to emphasize the shared social climates and experiences of athletes, especially regarding coaches' roles within collective dynamics. The organizational perspective, however, is best for understanding large competitive teams, which feature complex and structured hierarchies that increase power distances between communicators (Cranmer, 2015). Within the organizational perspective, coaches' formalized prescriptions are passed down to subordinates in the form of directives regarding what tasks are to be completed, by whom, and how, as well as what constitutes acceptable forms of behavior. These nuanced differences are evident in group scholars' focus on the shared experiences of athletes and organizational scholars' emphasis on interactions that span hierarchical differences.

Such distinctions underscore several contexts in which the group perspective is especially relevant. Small teams (e.g., golf or cross country) or sub-groups within teams (e.g., position groups) are ideal contexts for applying the group perspective. These groups feature a small number of athletes, limited hierarchy, and denser social connections—conditions apt for utilizing the group perspective. Moreover, team sports that feature smaller rosters (e.g., basketball) may benefit greatly from the incorporation of the group perspective. Within such sports, the cohesiveness among athletes is important for determining productivity. For instance, in examinations of basketball and club soccer teams, task cohesion explained as much as 30–45% variance of team success (Carron, Bray, & Eys, 2002). Finally, this perspective may be a useful framework for examining less structured and more process focused sports leagues, such as adult recreational leagues. Such groups focus on providing opportunities for participants to socialize, be active, and have fun. These groups also feature flatter-hierarchies, are self-organized, and emphasize the social networks between participants (Okamoto, 2016). Together, these sporting contexts offer several collectives in which relational dynamics come to define participants' experiences.

Sports teams are notably different from other types of groups, such as social, service, religious, or learning groups (Myers & Anderson, 2008). The nature of the group outcome for a sports team (i.e., winning) is fairly objective, public, and comparative. In contrast, social and service groups seldom have goals that can be objectively evaluated, learning groups rarely operate in the public sphere, and none of these groups' outcomes are determined through direct comparison with others. The role of competition and sizable audiences provides opportunities for athletes to experience collective face threats or shared glory, which intensify either discord or collegiality among athletes. Put differently, losing or poor performances can threaten the identity of athletes or be sources of embarrassment, and outside observers exacerbate these potential realities. Moreover, the internal competition for positions and limitations on playing time are additional face threats. These conditions create heightened possibilities for athletes to experience detrimental emotions or strained relationships with teammates. In contrast, the successful performance of a team may be a source of group identity, pride, and enjoyment. Coaches are tasked with managing the emotional regulation of athletes after both successes and failures (Turman, 2005).

An additional feature of sport is that it includes a host of measures and opportunities for individual assessment and goal setting. Sport commonly quantifies the performance of individuals in a way that other groups do not (e.g., runs scored, goals, touchdowns, tackles, points, rebounds, or time). These opportunities reify the importance of individual accomplishment and goal setting within the team structure, which are prioritized within modern sport (Billings, Butterworth, & Turman, 2018). As such, sports, especially independent sports, provide benchmarks for the individual goals of athletes and the collective goals of their teams. These goals may be mutually enforcing, as individual success of athletes may contribute to team performance. However, this is not always the case, as athletes may contradict team strategy or efforts to improve individual performance. Coaches must balance individual and team goals, and use individual goals to motivate athletes toward team efforts.

Sport also restricts the participation of group members through limiting the number of contributors toward a team effort. For instance, only five players are on the court in basketball at a time; likewise, a cross country team fields seven runners for a race. Teams, however, are often comprised of more members than are officially allowed to play at one time, which ensures that some athletes will not directly contribute to team performance. Coaches are responsible for determining which athletes participate and which serve secondary roles. These practices offer an additional source of tension within a team's social dynamics, as athletes compete against teammates for desired roles and playing time. The labeling and ranking of athletes within teams can create hostility within teammate or athlete-coach relationships, as assignment to secondary roles may inspire negative emotional reactions (e.g., jealousy, distrust, and anger). In contrast, members of other types of groups are seldom restricted in their ability to contribute by formal rules or policies. Instead, decisions to distribute work are made informally by group members and are based upon individuals' abilities, willingness to participate, and personality.

Other aspects that make sporting teams unique groups (e.g., physicality and degrees of interdependence) vary as a function of the sport in question. These factors, however, shape team social dynamics, norms, and cultures. For instance, in highly physical sports that have hegemonic cultures (e.g., football or wrestling), greater degrees of rough housing, verbal aggression, and teasing may be deemed normative within athlete-coach and teammate interactions (Cranmer & Spinda, 2017; Turman, 2003b). Messner (1992) explored such teams in *Power at Play*, in which he linked these team cultures to hostile interactions between athletes, the neglect of athlete well-being, and deviant behaviors directed at opponents and non-participants. The environments in which athletes play is certainly a determining factor in their sporting experiences, including how they come to be socialized into and via sport. Collectively, sports teams are a distinct type of group because of the various social processes that require levels of competition and cooperation within and between teams.

Group Perspective

Some of the earliest coach communication research featured elements of the group perspective (Turman, 2001, 2003b, 2008). Yet, this perspective is one of the least developed within coaching literature; potentially because of the similarity to the organizational perspective, which has grown considerably (see Chapter 4). Scholars who operate from the group perspective often rely on literature from group communication, leadership studies, or sport management and psychology. These scholars seek to understand how coaches manage the social dynamics and climates of their teams, as they guide athletes toward the accomplishment of goals. Within the group perspective, scholars consider how coaches relate to their teams as collectives. This focus is evident in three bodies of research that consider coaches' use of regret messages during team addresses, coaching styles, and team building.

Regret Messages

Coaches are responsible for coordinating group efforts and goals through the fostering team climates. One salient example of these efforts is coaches' use of team addresses—also known as locker room speeches. These addresses occur pre-game, mid-game, or post-game, and serve as periods through which teams gather in solidarity to heed the words of their coaches (Gallmeier, 1987). These types of addresses are romanticized within popular sporting culture as important moments that solidify teams and determine performances (e.g., Herb Brooks' pregame speech during the 1980 Olympic match versus the Soviet Union or Knute Rockne's halftime speech, known as "Win one for the Gipper"). Although Maisel (2003) questioned the actual effectiveness of iconic locker room speeches, researchers have suggested team addresses can focus athletes on particular objectives, outline desired approaches for meeting those objectives, and regulate athletes' emotions and motivation (Gallmeier, 1987). As such, team addresses are an important communicative interaction and define how coaches interact with groups of athletes.

Communication scholars recognize that coaches use their pre-game, half-time, and post-game speeches to motivate athletes, especially via the use of regret messages that speak to the importance of winning. These messages address athletes' feelings of regret or guilt, whether anticipated or real, and are intended to encourage performance (Landman, 1993). Simply, athletes are motivated to work together to accomplish tasks to avoid feelings of regret or guilt. However, feelings of regret can be psychologically harmful for young and developing individuals. For instance, regret inducing messages may contribute to athletes' experiences of stress, detrimental emotions (e.g., sorrow, disappointment, or frustration), and decisions to cease playing sports (Turman, 2005). Regret inducing messages are especially relevant within the group perspective, as these appeals guide groups toward shared tasks and frequently include appeals referring to the connections between athletes or external stakeholders. With this in mind, Turman (2005) sought to understand how coaches manage feelings of regret among their teams through identifying *what coaches say* and *when they say it* during team addresses.

These efforts demonstrate that coaches utilize six types of regret messages during team addresses—of which multiple types speak to the connection between athletic performances and group experiences (Turman, 2005, 2007). The first type of regret message (known as *accountability regret*) assigns blame for previous collective performance and connects these shortcomings with teams' future outcomes. By doing so, these messages guide team performance and recognize the links between particular sporting circumstances and the accomplishment of team goals. For example, a coach may blame a team's deficit on a lack of field position or failed execution, and can assert that the team will need to change this feature to win. A second type of regret message (known as *collective failure regret*) connects athletes' individual performances with the disappointment of coaches and teammates. This type of regret message utilizes the emotional states of fellow group members to hold individuals accountable for their performances. For example, a coach may tell athletes that their teammates are counting on them to execute a particular skill or strategy and their failure to do so would let their teammates down. A third type of regret message (known as *social significance regret*) acknowledges the social implications of games to surrounding communities as sources of potential regret. This type of regret message recognizes the public contexts in which sport teams attempt to accomplish shared tasks and that these events hold meaning to external stakeholders. This type of message is evident in coaches' calls to perform for the pride of a local community (e.g., town or state).

Other forms of anticipatory regret messages highlight the individual consequences of poor performances. A fourth type of regret message (known as *individual performance* regret) increases athletes' awareness of the potential regret that they might feel after a poor individual performance. This type of message is able to leverage athletes' individual goals, as well as use their identification and commitment to a team, to motivate them. For instance, coaches may emphasize the disappointment, frustration, or sadness that athletes will feel in the wake of defeat, if they do not put forth a maximum effort and level of enthusiasm. A fifth type of regret message (known as *future regret*) emphasizes the long-term implications of regret resulting from poor performances, including reflecting on failures for the rest of one's life. This type of regret message recognizes the role of athletics as a source of identity and the potential enduring implications of sporting experiences as one ages. For example, coaches might suggest that athletes will regret poor performances into adulthood when they reminisce on their sporting careers.

In contrast with the first five types of regret messages, a sixth type of message seeks to mitigate potential feelings of regret (known as *regret reduction*). These types of regret messages underscore that the use of regret as a motivational mechanism during team addresses is only productive in the context of potential or anticipatory regret. Attempting to utilize guilt for past regrets is a dangerous proposition for coaches, as athletes are unable to undo the past reality and may engage in emotional regulation that renders them angry or avoidant of future sport participation (Gavanski & Wells, 1989). Thus, regret reduction keeps athletes engaged and motivated after defeats or poor performances. For example, coaches may suggest athletes tried their best, should be proud of their efforts, or have nothing to be ashamed of in defeat.

Collectively, regret messages demonstrate that coaches use a variety of tools to inspire feelings of potential regret, especially those that touch upon commitments to fellow group members and goals. The prominence of individual goals and accountability to groups are leveraged toward motivating performance within these messages. In combination with regret reduction, these messages reveal that coaches utilize team addresses to regulate their teams' emotions and motivational states. In particular, coaches seek to keep athletes grounded before or after success and build them up after defeats. Put differently, coaches must guide their teams to ensure future performances are not hindered by emotions stemming from past outcomes.

Coaches implement regret inducing messages strategically to maximize team functionality. In this effort, coaches of high school sports teams consider the context of their team addresses (e.g., pre-game or post-game), the success of their teams, and timing within their season (Turman, 2005, 2007). Before games, coaches emphasize the potential of future regret due to not competing well or disappointing those outside of their teams (e.g., family members). This selection of messages creates both intrinsic and extrinsic sources of regret and focuses athletes on impending sporting events. More concerning, during team addresses prior to post-season events, coaches heavily rely on social significance and future regret inducing messages. Simply, as games become more noteworthy for divisional, conference, state, or national standings, coaches increase the pressure on athletes by accentuating the implications for athletes' communities and their long-term wellbeing. These messages distinguish post-season play as especially important but likely exacerbate negative reactions to defeat. Mid-game addresses (e.g., halftime breaks) are utilized to strategize and adjust styles of play. When trailing on the scoreboard, coaches foster regret through connecting athletes' performances with team shortcomings and the disappointment felt by coaches and teammates. These observations demonstrate the value of the group perspective, as coaches' attempts to regulate the emotions and efforts of their players through emphasizing the connections between individual performance and teammates' experiences. Post-game addresses, especially after a loss, are periods for reducing athletes' feelings of regret. Put differently, after building the anticipation of regret before and during games, coaches downplay regret experiences to keep athletes engaged and focused on future endeavors.

Overall, regret message research indicates that coaches utilize a variety of strategies that utilize potential negative affective states to motivate athletes to perform well. Although the experience of potential regret may be an effective motivator—a concept that has yet to be validated within sport—the use of regret reduction after losses indicates that coaches must carefully manage the psychological states of athletes with a longitudinal approach. In other words, coaches must meticulously manage the tensions of inducing anticipations of future regret while attempting to reduce such regret when it occurs after poor performances. Such dynamics highlights the importance of altering team social climates and utilizing group interactions to guide performances.

Coaching Styles

Within teams, coaches are leaders among groups of athletes (Horn, 2002). Leadership is a central process of group functioning, as members are influenced toward task accomplishment (Myers & Anderson, 2008; O'Hair & Wiemann, 2004). The group perspective acknowledges leadership manifests within general coaching styles, which encompass how coaches relate to their teams. One framework for understanding leadership from a group perspective is the Multidimensional Leadership Model (MDLM) (Chelladurai & Saleh,

1978, 1980). This model suggests that leadership is a set of general behaviors that coaches enact toward their teams, which are viewed as collectives. Put differently, coaches maintain particular and general styles of coaching throughout interactions, which is in direct contrast to the dyadic focus of LMX theory (Dansereau, Graen, & Haga, 1975); (see Chapter 4).

MDLM is a theory that explains coaches' leadership via five distinct styles of coaching. These coaching styles address team climates and group processes. For instance, two of these coaching styles address team decision-making, which is central to group functioning and task accomplishment. Decision-making encompasses the "... process of problem diagnosis, solution selection, or solution implementation," and is accomplished through communicative exchanges between athletes and coaches (Myers & Anderson, 2008, p. 130). These efforts direct the generation of ideas, focus group members on the implementation of one of those ideas, and guide the interplay between group members. Coaches' leadership styles toward decision-making influence how athletes come to understand and participate in team functioning. Coaches may enact *democratic behaviors*, which invite athletes to collaborate in team decision-making, including in decisions regarding team goals, strategies, and practice methods. In contrast, coaches may also utilize *autocratic behaviors*, which disinvite athletes from participating in team decision-making. Autocratic behaviors reinforce coaches' authority and create distance between athletes and coaches. Together, these styles determine the level of cooperation and reciprocity between athletes and coaches within the decision-making process, which may range from coaches making decisions alone to decisions being entirely delegated to athletes. The manner in which teams come to collective decisions is largely at the discretion of coaches.

MDLM forwards an additional two coaching styles that address the motivational climates of teams. Motivating participation in a group's efforts to accomplish its goals is a central function of leadership (Myers & Anderson, 2008). Within the MDLM, motivational climates are established via the use of *positive feedback*, which includes expressions of appreciation or recognition for athletes' accomplishments and efforts. Positive reinforcement denotes warmth, regard, and assists in promoting prosocial team environments. Similarly, coaches' leadership styles may include the provision of *social support*, which consists of the behaviors that meet the interpersonal needs of athletes. This set of behaviors individualize interactions to the circumstances and personalities of a given team. Together, these coaching styles foster motivational climates that keep athletes engaged.

Another coaching style addresses the accomplishment of team goals. Coaches can further contribute to these efforts through the degree to which they engage in *training and instruction*, which include the behaviors meant to help athletes develop their knowledge and sporting abilities. This style directly addresses the creation of team skills and abilities, with teams' collective goals in mind. Although some argue that these leadership styles serve either prosocial (i.e., positive feedback, social support, training and instruction, and democratic behaviors) or antisocial functions (i.e., autocratic behaviors) (Horn, 2002; Turman & Schrodt, 2004), coaches utilize combinations of some or all of these styles.

The MDLM is readily adaptable and a useful framework for behavioral and contingency approaches to coach leadership (Turman, 2001). Behavioral leadership approaches seek to understand effective leadership as a product of *what coaches do*, whereas contingency approaches recognize that it is *when and with whom* particular behaviors are enacted that determines coaching effectiveness. The behavioral approach to leadership forwards general modes of interaction that coaches should utilize to guide teams. In particular, coaches' use of democratic behaviors, positive feedback, social support, and training and instruction are associated with fostering positive team climates that develop appreciation for sports and coaches (Turman & Schrodt, 2004). In contrast, coaches' use of autocratic behaviors hinders such team climates (Turman & Schrodt, 2004). These findings reveal that leadership styles account for athletes' internalization of positive attitudes with regard to coaching and sport participation. The conclusion of this research is that coaches must be self-aware of their default modes of interaction and attempt to promote team involvement in decision-making, motivational climates, and task achievement.

Contingency approaches to leadership build upon the behavioral approach by considering the context in which coaching styles come to exert influence over teams. Contextual aspects—such as athletes' preferences, the timing within a season, and team success—come to determine when particular leadership styles are effective. As such, contingency approaches recognize that coaches must use their intrapersonal knowledge to be aware of their own communication, as well as their interpersonal knowledge to determine the situations in which particular behaviors would be effective. Through examinations of high school wrestling teams from the Midwest, Turman (2001, 2003a) identified the contexts in which leadership styles are effective. These efforts revealed that as seasons begin, athletes desire leadership styles that provide greater degrees of positive feedback, with autocratic behaviors becoming more acceptable as seasons progress. Thus, as team dynamics are forming and the significance of competition is low, praise and encouragement help build team climates and keep athletes engaged. However, as teams solidify and competition becomes more significant, coaches are expected to take further control of team processes. Team success is also an important consideration, as successful teams desire elevated and steady amounts of training and instruction, whereas unsuccessful teams become more susceptible to autocratic behaviors. This information suggests that coaches of winning teams have more leeway to utilize autocratic decision-making and must continue to find means to develop athletes' abilities. Collectively, the MDLM scholarship underscores the importance of coaches' leadership behaviors in the group functioning of sport teams, as the manner in which teams are collectively addressed shape athletes' sporting experiences and efforts.

Team Building

A defining aspect of sports teams are the connections between athletes. Such connections offer insight into the interpersonal relationships between teammates, their shared responsibilities or objectives, and their collective performances (Bollen & Hoyle, 1990; Widmeyer, Carron, & Brawley, 1993). Coaches have a central role in building team chemistry and the bonds between athletes. Coach communication creates the relational climates in which teammate interaction occurs and sets patterns of behavior regarding the treatment of others (Turman, 2003b, 2008). Moreover, coaches set patterns of team functioning, from which athletes come to understand and negotiate their roles on a team (Benson, Eys, Surya, Dawson, & Schneider, 2013; Eys, Carron, Beauchamp, & Bray, 2005).

Team chemistry and the connections between athletes can be understood through the cohesion between teammates. *Cohesion* refers to "an individual's sense of belonging to a particular group and his or her feelings of morale associated with membership in groups" (Bollen & Hoyle, 1990, p. 482). In other words, cohesion addresses the symmetry and shared understandings of athletes' tasks and social relationships. Cohesion is an important component of team success, as the accomplishment of group goals is dependent upon athletes working together during training and competitions (Widmeyer et al., 1993). Coaches determine levels of team cohesion through a variety of communicative techniques. For instance, demonstrating favoritism or embarrassing athletes hinder cohesion, including for those who only witness such events (Turman, 2003b). More simply, mistreating one athlete has social implications throughout a team and detracts from the formation of quality and healthy connections. These realities illustrate that coaching occurs within group environments whereby athletes consider coach-teammate interactions when evaluating their own relationships with coaches and teammates (O'Hair & Wiemann, 2004). Specifically, communicative patterns that are associated with detrimental emotions (e.g., jealousy of teammates, anger, or shame) detract from athletes' sense of belonging.

Coaches may build cohesion through numerous communicative strategies, including highlighting the abilities and accomplishments of position groups or teammates, building up the quality of future opponents, participating in team prayer, encouraging social integration (e.g., team social events or study hall), or addressing teams collectively (e.g., motivational speeches). These strategies emphasize athletes' shared experiences as sources of relational development and social connection. Of particular note, building cohesion through emphasizing a common and worthwhile opponent relies upon the group dynamics of sport to reinforce collaboration between teammates. Together, cohesion-building strategies indicate that shared and positive experiences provide starting points from which athletes may get to know each other and form relationships.

Another component of building teams is the assignment and assumption of formal and informal roles. Formalized roles include those associated with specialized and sport specific roles (e.g., leadoff batter in softball or baseball) or leadership positions (e.g., captain) (Benson, Surya, & Eys, 2014). Informal roles (i.e., those not prescribed within sport), may include performing generic task roles (e.g., bring energy to the team) or creating relationships between team members. While coaches assign formal roles, athletes often seek and find informal roles via self-initiated efforts and teammate feedback (Benson et al., 2014; Eys et al., 2005). In this manner, athletes seek to contribute to their teams by utilizing existing social frameworks and relationships to create positions for themselves, such as the role of comedian, spark plug, enforcer, cancer, distractor, mentor, or leader—among others (Cope, Eys, Beauchamp, Schinke, & Bosselut, 2011). The negotiation of informal roles considers coaches' assignment of formal roles and team culture to identify unfilled niches for specific athletes. Coaches contribute to such processes through their influence on team goals and norms.

The Future of the Group Perspective

The group perspective contributes to the understanding of the complexities of coaching small teams and sub-groups of athletes. Yet, much of this perspective emphasizes dynamics or foci borrowed from the instructional or organizational perspectives. With this in mind, the scope of the group perspective can be refined in several ways. One means of further developing the group perspective is through recognizing that coaches and athletes belong to multiple groups and may be experiencing tensions that come with competing demands or roles. For instance, coaches are often parents of athletes or teachers at a given educational institution (Jowett, 2008; Jowett, Timson-Katchis, & Adams, 2007). There are tensions that exist between the purposes of these roles. Parent-coaches might be conflicted between providing one's child with opportunities versus playing the best athletes. Likewise, educators might be conflicted between keeping athletes eligible to compete versus holding them accountable for academic performances. This oversight may be rectified with the incorporation of a bona fide group framework, which acknowledges that individuals naturally and simultaneously hold membership in multiple groups (Stohl & Putnam, 1994). Often, membership in multiple groups requires negotiating the tensions and demands associated with each membership. For adults, the bona fide group framework is useful for understanding their attempts to balance work, home life, service, and social groups (Ashforth, Kreiner, & Fugate, 2000; Kramer, 2002, 2011). As such, it may also help explain how coaches' roles intersect with membership in other groups.

The dual roles of parent and coach merit specific attention. Estimates suggest that coaches are fathers of athletes at a rate greater than 90% across youth sports (Brown, 1998). Many practitioners have theorized that parents are effective coaches because of the rapport, trust, and understanding associated with the parent-child bond. Further, athletes are widely believed to benefit from being coached by parents through gaining additional resources (e.g., information, praise, or attention) and voice in team functioning. Likewise, practitioners argue that such arrangements enhance the parent-child bond through shared activities and time spent together. These colloquial assertions position the roles of parent and coach as sharing mutually enforcing objectives. Despite the popularity of these assertions, coaching science research consistently indicates that parent-coaches experience difficulty distinguishing between their dual roles, which has the capacity to create negative experiences for athletes. For example, athletes who are coached by their parents receive more hostile or abusive behaviors (Schmid, Bernstein, Shannon, Rishell, & Griffith, 2015; Weiss & Fretwell, 2005), are under greater expectations for performance (Weiss & Fretwell, 2005), and have less voice (Jowett et al., 2007). Children-athletes, thus, experience negative emotional responses to parent-coaches' yelling, expectations, and hostility (Jowett et al., 2007), and often respond with resistance to coaching efforts or rebellion at home (Jowett, 2008; Schmid et al., 2015; Weiss & Fretwell, 2005). Numerous examples of parent-coaches within popular sporting culture (e.g., Marv Marinovich) illustrate these tensions. Coach communication scholars should address how individuals manage the dual roles of parent-coach, including on the field of play and at home.

Another potential avenue of growth for the group perspective is to explore the interplay between individual and group goals. A major component of group functioning is the accomplishment of task and social goals that may be valued by a group or individuals (O'Hair & Wiemann, 2004). The interplay between individual and group goals may be one of mutual reinforcement or contradiction. *Antigroup roles* encompass when individual goals come to detract from a group's accomplishment of shared goals (O'Hair & Wiemann, 2004). As aforementioned, sport provides a host of indicators of individual success, which are becoming increasingly salient in modern sporting cultures (Billings et al., 2018) and may be more relevant to athletes competing in independent sports. It is important to understand how coaches may shape and utilize individual goals to reinforce team goals (i.e., winning), while reducing the perceived importance of individual accomplishments that are contrary to a team's style of play or strategy. These persuasive efforts would offer an alternative to regret messages and aid in the promotion of cohesive cultures. The communicative approaches and strategies that might foster such alignment, however, remain elusive. Filling the dearth of knowledge around these issues is central to overseeing sports teams as groups.

Conclusion

The group perspective of coaching offers a framework that assists in understanding the management of the complex social dynamics that define collectives, as coaches seek to lead their teams in the accomplishment of shared tasks. This perspective offers tools for how coaches may use their formal positions as leaders to address teams as collectives and inspire effective cultures. The development of this perspective could benefit from exploring the role of communication within additional group processes, including how groups construct and manage norms that guide athlete and coach behavior, as well as how individuals come to assume roles. Coaches may come to guide these processes through their team addresses and leadership styles, but the degree to which athletes participate in self-management or direction is largely unknown. To maximize group effectiveness, coaches must build team climates that facilitate and encourage task accomplishment and cooperation, and empower athletes to oversee themselves and contribute to their teams.

Note

1. AZ Quotes. (2019). John Wooden quotes. *AZQuotes.com*. Retrieved from https://www.azquotes.com/quote/535056

References

Anderson, C. M., Riddle, B. L., & Martin, M. M. (1999). Socialization processes in groups. In L. R. Frey, D. S. Gouran, & M. S. Poole (Eds.), *The handbook of group communication theory and research* (pp. 139–163). Thousand Oaks, CA: Sage.

Ashforth, B. E., Kreiner, G. E., & Fugate, M. (2000). All in a day's work: Boundaries and micro role transitions. *Academy of Management Review, 25*, 472–491.

Becker, A. J. (2009). It's not what they do, it's how they do it: Athlete experiences of great coaching. *International Journal of Sports Science & Coaching, 4*, 93–119.

Benson, A. J., Eys, M., Surya, M., Dawson, K., & Schneider, M. (2013). Athletes' perceptions of role acceptance in interdependent sport teams. *The Sport Psychologist, 27*, 269–280.

Benson, A. J., Surya, M., & Eys, M. A. (2014). The nature and transmission of roles in sport teams. *Sport, Exercise, and Performance Psychology, 3*, 228–240.

Billings, A. C., Butterworth, M. L., & Turman, P. D. (2018). *Communication and sport: Surveying the field* (3rd ed.). Los Angeles, CA: Sage.

Bollen, K. A., & Hoyle, R. H. (1990). Perceived cohesion: A conceptual and empirical examination. *Social Forces, 69*, 479–504.

Brown, E. W. (1998). Social interactions in coaching your child's team: Harmony or hassle (Part I). *Spotlight on Youth Sports, 20*(4), 1–5.

Carron, A. V., Bray, S. R., & Eys, M. A. (2002). Team cohesion and team success in sport. *Journal of Sport Sciences, 20*, 119–126.

Carron, A. V., Hausenblas, H. A., & Eys, M. A. (2005). *Group dynamics in sport*. Morgantown, WV: Fitness Information Technology.

Chelladurai, P., & Saleh, S. D. (1978). Preferred leadership in sports. *Canadian Journal of Applied Sport Sciences, 3*, 85–92.

Chelladurai, P., & Saleh, S. D. (1980). Dimensions of leader behavior in sports: Development of a leadership scale. *Journal of Sport Psychology, 2*, 34–45.

Cope, C. J., Eys, M. A., Beauchamp, M. R., Schinke, R. J., & Bosselut, G. (2011). Informal roles on sport teams. *International Journal of Sport and Exercise Psychology, 9*, 19–30.

Cragan, J. F., & Wright, D. W. (1999). *Communication in small groups: Theory, processes, skills* (5th ed.). Belmont, CA: Wadsworth.

Cranmer, G. A. (2015). *Exploring the anticipatory socialization stage of Division I student-athletes: The content, characteristics, and functions of memorable messages.* (Unpublished doctoral dissertation). West Virginia University, Morgantown, WV.

Cranmer, G. A., & Brann, M. (2015). "It makes me feel like I am an important part of this team": An exploratory study of coach confirmation. *International Journal of Sport Communication, 8*, 193–211.

Cranmer, G. A., & Myers, S. A. (2017). Exploring Division-I student-athletes' memorable messages from their anticipatory socialization. *Communication Quarterly, 65*, 125–143.

Cranmer, G. A., & Spinda, J. (2017). *Coaches' use of confirmation during the preparation for a Division-I football game.* Paper submitted to the annual meeting of the National Communication Association, Dallas, TX.

Dansereau Jr, F., Graen, G., & Haga, W. J. (1975). A vertical dyad linkage approach to leadership within formal organizations: A longitudinal investigation of the role making process. *Organizational Behavior and Human Performance, 13*, 46–78.

Eys, M. A., Carron, A. V., Beauchamp, M. R., & Bray, S. R. (2005). Athletes' perceptions of the sources of role ambiguity. *Small Group Research, 36*, 383–403.

Gallmeier, C. P. (1987). Putting on the game face: The staging of emotions in professional hockey. *Sociology of Sport Journal, 4*, 347–362.

Gavanski, I., & Wells, G. L. (1989). Counterfactual processing of normal and exceptional events. *Journal of Experimental Social Psychology, 25*, 314–325.

Horn, T. S. (2002). Coaching effectiveness in the sport domain. In T. S. Horn (Ed.), *Advances in sport psychology* (2nd ed., pp. 309–354). Champaign, IL: Human Kinetics.

Jowett, S. (2008). Outgrowing the familial coach-athlete relationship. *International Journal of Sport Psychology, 39*, 20–40.

Jowett, S., Timson-Katchis, M., & Adams, R. (2007). Too close for comfort? *International Journal of Coaching Science, 1*, 59–78.

Kramer, M. W. (2002). Communication in a community theater group: Managing multiple group roles. *Communication Studies, 53*, 151–170.

Kramer, M. W. (2011). Toward a communication model for the socialization of voluntary members. *Communication Monographs, 78*, 233–255.

Landman, J. (1993). *Regret: The persistence of the possible.* New York, NY: Oxford University Press.

Maisel, I. (2003, November 7). The art of the locker-room speech. ESPN.com. Retrieved from http://www.espn.com/college-football/columns/story?columnist=maisel_ivan&id=1656370

Messner, M. A. (1992). *Power at play: Sports and the problem of masculinity.* Boston, MA: Beacon Press.

Myers, S. A., & Anderson, C. M. (2008). *The fundamentals of small group communication.* Los Angeles, CA: Sage.

O'Hair, D., & Wiemann, M. O. (2004). *The essential guide to group communication.* Boston, MA: Bedford/St. Martin's.

Okamoto, K. E. (2016, November). *"Box me in coach:" An exploration of support within Cross-Fit.* Paper presented at the annual meeting of the National Communication Association, Philadelphia, PA.

Schmid, O. N., Bernstein, M., Shannon, V. R., Rishell, C., & Griffith, C. (2015). "It's not just your dad, it's not just your coach…" The dual-relationship in female tennis players. *The Sport Psychologist, 29,* 224–236.

Stohl, C., & Putnam, L. L. (1994). Group communication in context: Implications for the study of bona fide groups. In L. R. Frey (Ed.), *Group communication in context: Studies of natural groups* (pp. 285–292). Hillsdale, NJ: Lawrence Erlbaum.

Turman, P. D. (2001). Situational coaching styles: The impact of success and athlete maturity level on coaches' leadership styles over time. *Small Group Research, 32,* 576–594.

Turman, P. D. (2003a). Athletic coaching from an instructional communication perspective: The influence of coach experience of high school wrestlers' preferences and perceptions of coaching behaviors across a season. *Communication Education, 23,* 73–86.

Turman, P. D. (2003b). Coaches and cohesion: The impact of coaching techniques on team cohesion in the small group sport setting. *Journal of Sport Behavior, 26,* 86–104.

Turman, P. D. (2005). Coaches' use of anticipatory and counterfactual regret messages during competition. *Journal of Applied Communication Research, 33,* 116–138.

Turman, P. D. (2007). The influence of athlete sex, context, and performance on high school basketball coaches' use of regret messages during competition. *Communication Education, 56,* 333–353.

Turman, P. D. (2008). Coaches' immediacy behaviors as predictors of athletes' perceptions of satisfaction and team cohesion. *Western Journal of Communication, 72,* 162–179.

Turman, P. D. (2017). What effects do coaches' communicative messages have on their athletes/teams? In A. K. Goodboy & K. Shultz (Eds.), *Introduction to communication studies: Translating scholarship into meaningful practice* (pp. 121–128). Dubuque, IA: Kendall Hunt.

Turman, P. D., & Schrodt, P. (2004). New avenues for instructional communication research: Relationships among coaches' leadership behaviors and athletes' affective learning. *Communication Research Reports, 21,* 130–143.

Weiss, M. R., & Fretwell, S. D. (2005). The parent-coach/child-athlete relationship in youth sport: Cordial, contentious, or conundrum? *Research Quarterly for Exercise and Sport, 76,* 286–305.

Widmeyer, W. N., Carron, A. V., & Brawley, L. R. (1993). Group cohesion in sport and exercise. In R. N. Singer, M. Morphey, & L. K. Tennant (Eds.), *Handbook of research on sport psychology* (pp. 672–692). New York, NY: Macmillan.

· 6 ·

THE INTERPERSONAL PERSPECTIVE: COACHES AS RELATIONAL PARTNERS

A common mistake among those who work in sport is spending a disproportional amount of time on "x's and o's" as compared to time spent learning about people.—Mike Krzyzewski[1]

Coaching requires both formal and informal modes of communication, as well as the proper attention toward task *and* relational aspects of team functioning (Turman, 2017). Coaches' interactions with athletes commonly extend beyond the task-related prescriptions of their roles (i.e., to guide performance and teach sporting skills), as many coaches desire to form connections with and develop athletes as people. The interpersonal relationships that form between athletes and coaches are a valuable source of motivation for continued participation in sport and shape various psychological dispositions toward coaches, teams, and overall sporting experiences (Ishak, 2017; Jowett, 2017). In her examination of elite coaches, Becker (2009) noted that athletes come to value coaches who demonstrate concern and support for them beyond the realm of sport. In other words, while maintaining appropriate boundaries is necessary, athletes appreciate coaches who connect with them on an emotional and personal level. Unsurprisingly, athletes describe effective coaches as mentors, friends, or parents (Becker, 2009; Cranmer & Brann, 2015; Cranmer & Myers, 2017). Coach communication scholars who focus on the formation and consequences of athlete-coach relational dynamics operate from an interpersonal perspective.

The interpersonal perspective recognizes that coaching is a process rooted in the development of meaningful and fulfilling relationships with athletes. From this perspective, the performance and development of athletes, as well as the management of the circumstances in which sport occurs, are only possible through forming and managing quality interpersonal relationships (Jowett, 2017; Rhind & Jowett, 2012). The interpersonal perspective frames coaches as relational partners, who connect with athletes and provide them with social and emotional resources, either directly via verbal and nonverbal communication or indirectly through structuring sporting environments. In contrast, athletes are framed as developing individuals with unique psychological, social, and communicative needs, which when met better facilitate their performance and development. Thus, forming meaningful athlete-coach relationships to meet athletes' needs is a means of increasing coaching effectiveness (Cranmer & Brann, 2015; Jowett, 2017). Effectiveness within the interpersonal perspective is assessed via reports of relational quality, emotional and motivational states, as well as the psychosocial, social, and moral development of athletes.

The interpersonal perspective of coaching rests upon on three assumptions. The first assumption is that quality athlete-coach relationships are defined by many of the same characteristics as other interpersonal relationships, including friendships, familial, and romantic relationships (Jowett, 2008; Jowett & Meek, 2000; Jowett, Paull, & Pensgaard, 2005). Such characteristics include mutual respect, intimacy, trust, and affect. Healthy and high-quality athlete-coach relationships readily include such characteristics (Becker, 2009; Jowett, 2017). Without the establishment of these characteristics, the social and psychological connections between individuals are difficult to form and maintain.

The second assumption is that the quality of athlete-coach interpersonal relationships are relevant for coach effectiveness. Quality athlete-coach relationships assist in athletes' performance and development, as well as the management of sporting environments. Specifically, these relationships open lines of communication that ease the transmission of technical information or feedback and the management of team dynamics (Jowett, 2017; Turman, 2017). Put differently, coaches who are respected, liked, and trusted have more leeway to influence their athletes and teams, without encountering resistance or negative outcomes. For example, the reception of corrective feedback within public contexts, like those of team practices, often triggers face threats and produces discomfort, sorrow, or anger. However, face threats may be mitigated when a trusted and admired coach is the source of said feedback. As such, the formation of personal relationships can be leveraged to aid in athlete and team performances.

The third assumption of the interpersonal perspective is that sport is a context in desperate need of an interpersonal framework (Jowett, 2017). The need for this perspective is underscored by the ineffective and antisocial modes of communication that coaches commonly utilize, as well as the formative periods in which most athletes find themselves (Cranmer, Brann, & Anzur, 2016). It is well documented within popular media that coaches of youth and adolescent sports teams can rely on overly aggressive forms of communication, which the public wrongfully deems to be effective. Instead, empirical evidence indicates that these techniques are quite destructive (Kassing & Infante, 1999; Mazer, Barnes, Grevious, & Boger, 2013). The negative impact of such communication is exacerbated by the reality that most athletes whom partake in organized sport range from early childhood to late adolescence. Such individuals are in need of psychosocial resources to build their identities and connections with others (Atkinson, 2009).

The interpersonal perspective is the most novel of the four perspectives featured within extant literature (Jowett, 2017; Turman, 2017). As such, there is a need to define the bounds and utility of this perspective. Arguably, the interpersonal perspective has value in all contexts of coaching (Jowett, 2017). The relevance of the interpersonal perspective is not surprising because coaching is a social process and, as such, creating relationships should be valued by all who engage in or study coaching. Yet, the recognition of specific contexts or situations in which the interpersonal perspective might be especially important is a meaningful exercise. The interpersonal perspective offers unique insight when the central purpose of a sporting context is human development or social connection. Many sporting contexts, such as youth and adolescent sporting leagues, have a strong emphasis on the social, moral, and life skill development of athletes (Vella, Oades, & Crowe, 2011). Moreover, some sports leagues—such as recreational or non-competitive adult leagues—aim to provide social connection. The interpersonal perspective is uniquely equipped to assist coaches in this regard because it focuses on meeting athletes' developmental needs, including those extending beyond the task objectives of sport. The developmental focus of this perspective is evident in the central themes of addressing how athletes come to form identities, embrace societal norms, and form relationships with others.

A second context in which the interpersonal perspective is notably useful is during times of adversity for athletes. Sport is defined by degrees of stress, uncertainty, and eventual failure. On the field of play, athletes may experience slumps in performance, become injured, commit mistakes, lose games, change positions, or be replaced for a role on a team. Off the field, athletes also experience difficulties and time demands that accompany their roles in other social groups (e.g., student, son or daughter, and community member). Such difficulties are unpleasant for highly invested athletes, especially for those still emotionally developing. Athletes desire coaches to serve as sources of support during these times (Clement & Shannon, 2011; Cranmer & Brann, 2015), and they respond more favorably to difficulties when coaches communicate with them in a prosocial manner and offer guidance (Becker, 2009; Sagar & Jowett, 2012). The interpersonal perspective recognizes athletes' needs in such circumstances, including those off the field, and encourages coaches to form individualized relationships with athletes that meet said needs (Cranmer & Brann, 2015).

Despite the utility of an interpersonal approach to coaching, the athlete-coach relationship is different from other interpersonal relationships. Sport, most notably, is a task-oriented environment, within which interpersonal relationships happen to occur. Simply, a quality relationship with athletes is not the ultimate goal of most coaches. Instead, refining athletes' physical abilities and understandings of their sport are the prescribed focal points of coaches. These efforts are in preparation for competition in a highly structured, public task that occurs during specified times, operates according to codified rules, and is evaluated based upon objective and codified forms of assessment (i.e., score). Other interpersonal relationships are not accompanied by such formalized tasks that must be completed. Many of the informal tasks that might be common within other interpersonal relationships (e.g., sharing meals or disclosing information) are often optional, less structured, and not as regulated by codified prescriptions for behavior. Additionally, while interpersonal relationships may be evaluated based upon notions of what is normative, these relationships are not scored with established criteria nor compared to other relationships in an effort to declare a "winner." The distinctiveness of the athlete-coach relationship may alter the manner in which interpersonal concepts, theories, and principles apply to coaching.

The dynamics of athlete-coach relationships are differentiated further by the formalized role of coaches. Various leagues, organizations, and governing agencies prescribe the responsibilities, policies, and criteria by which coaches are regulated and evaluated (European Coaching Council, 2007; Project Play, 2018). For instance, school districts, state agencies, or sports leagues (e.g., Little League and Pop Warner) may codify and reinforce such standards. The prescriptions of these institutions guide coaches' interactions with athletes and the policies that they create among their teams. Often these prescriptions are accompanied by levels of oversight and means to hold coaches accountable, whether it be formally documenting violations, fining, or firing a coach. In this regard, the athlete-coach relationship is restricted via these prescriptions and subject to evaluation.

The social context in which coaching occurs also distinguishes it from other interpersonal relationships. The athlete-coach relationship usually occurs within a larger social collective, even for those participating in independent sports. One of the few interpersonal relationships that features shared membership in a group is the nuclear family. Yet, membership among sports teams are not based on kinship but rather a shared purpose of competition in sport. While it is common for parents to serve as coaches in youth sports (Jowett, 2008; Jowett, Timson-Katchis, & Adams, 2007; Weiss & Fretwell, 2005), the majority of athlete-coach dyads do not share kinship. For many youth athletes, coaches serve as the first source of authority and instruction to whom they are not related. As such, sports offer athletes early opportunities to understand the social dynamics that accompany balancing relationships and tasks without the affections that come to define families. Overall, in comparison to other commonly studied relationships, athlete-coach relationships are more restricted by the perceptions of normative behavior, tasks associated with sport, formalized nature of the coaching role, and group dynamics that accompany team structures. Coaches must navigate these realities carefully to form quality relationships with athletes that benefit their teams' efforts.

Interpersonal Perspective

The interpersonal perspective has grown tremendously in recent years, with calls from scholars and practitioners to promote prosocial interactions between athletes and coaches. Although the newest of the four perspectives outlined within this text, some elements of the interpersonal perspective can be traced to previously established assertions, including the importance of cultivating athletes' positive affect for coaches (Mazer et al., 2013) or the dyadic nature of athlete-coach relationships within team management (Cranmer & Myers, 2015). Yet, the interpersonal perspective prioritizes the relational dynamics between athletes and coaches, including those spanning beyond competition and performance (Turman, 2017). Coach communication researchers who operate from this perspective incorporate interpersonal communication and sport psychology concepts within their own scholarship (Cranmer & Brann, 2015; Cranmer & Sollitto, 2015). These influences are evident in the scholarly focus on interpersonal behaviors enacted by coaches and messages that seek the personal and moral development of athletes. Three lines of research are featured below: social support, confirmation, and messages of personal development.

Social Support

Coaches form relationships with athletes that include the provision of social support (Cranmer, 2016; Cranmer, Anzur, & Sollitto, 2017; Cranmer & Sollitto, 2015). *Social support* is a broad concept that links the involvement in social relationships to one's wellbeing (Cohen, 1988; Cohen & Wills, 1985). In general, the term social support is an umbrella concept, which encompasses multiple distinct phenomena, including the size of social networks, general relationship quality, perceptions of available resources, or reports of receiving support (Rees & Hardy, 2000). Communicative approaches toward support focus on two understandings of social support: enacted and received support. *Enacted support* consists of the messages and acts of support shared within human interaction, or more plainly "the things people say and do for one another" in an effort to be helpful (Goldsmith, 2004, p. 3). This understanding of social support is explicitly communicative because it focuses on acts and messages within interactions, rather than receivers' perceptions. *Received support* refers to an individual's recognition of another's attempts to do or say something in the service of being helpful (Albrecht & Adelman, 1987). Although received support rests upon the cognitive processing and sense making of another's actions, it is of value to communication scholars because the meaning of communication is receiver-oriented (Cranmer & Sollitto, 2015). Moreover, received support is a beneficial concept because "the support that counts is the behavior perceived by the subject as supportive" (Albrecht & Adelman, 1987, p. 68). Together, received and enacted support provide two frameworks from which coaches provision of social support to athletes can be understood.

Social support serves various functions for athletes. These functions include providing informational, emotional, esteem, and tangible support. *Informational support* includes the advice and information that coaches provide to athletes. This type of support is evident in the provision of corrective feedback, sporting strategy or techniques, and general life advice. *Emotional support* refers to coaches' expressions of affect, empathy, or concern for athletes. Coaches provide emotional support via expressions of concern in the wake of disappointments or adversities. *Esteem support* consists of coaches' reassurance of athletes' sense of worth and abilities. Coaches may provide esteem support to develop athletes' confidence, reduce the pressures of performance, or motivate them to participate. *Tangible support* encompasses coaches' efforts to assist athletes via the provision of goods or services. Coaches control many goods and services within the context of sport, sometimes including equipment, transportation, schedules, medical care, or specialized training.

Enacted support research focuses on the specific messages that coaches utilize to support athletes. Through surveying 102 former high school athletes, Cranmer et al. (2017) investigated the influential and enduring messages of support that are provided by coaches. This research demonstrated that enacted informational support messages guide sporting performance (e.g., how to perform skills or techniques, approach sport, or execute strategy), promote means of success (e.g., hard work, risk-taking, and resiliency), and encourage autonomy (e.g., being self-sufficient). Emotional support was enacted through messages that support athlete wellbeing (e.g., physical, social, and psychological welfare), praise them (e.g., their leadership skills, nonsporting accomplishments), express a desire to see them perform well, or minimize the negative emotions associated with poor performances and defeats. Finally, enactments of esteem support occurred via messages that emphasize athletes' capabilities to win (e.g., recognizing their past successes or potential, drawing favorable comparisons to their opponents), intangible qualities (e.g., concentration, composure, or effort), or connections and roles within a team. These messages illustrate the assumptions of the interpersonal perspective of coaching, as support addresses the sporting and non-sporting aspects of athletes' lives and responds to the unique needs and situations that athletes face. Together, research on enacted forms of social support identify supportive messages and offer coaches prescriptive knowledge regarding what to say to athletes when offering support. See Table 6.1 for examples of enacted support.

The importance of coaches' use of social support is underscored by the benefits accrued by athletes when words and actions are deemed supportive (i.e., received support). Some researchers argue that receiving support allows individuals to deal with stresses and uncertainties that accompany task-oriented environments (i.e., the buffering hypothesis), provides social resources that make prescribed behaviors easier to enact, or influences biological and cognitive reactions that cause beneficial states (Cohen, 1988; Cohen & Wills, 1985).

Table 6.1. *Coaches' Enacted Support*

Type of Support	Examples
Informational	• "If you don't play at 100% intensity at all times, then you can get injured easier"—Female, Basketball Player • "It's not hard to succeed if you put in the work"—Male, Lacrosse Player • "Stop jumping so damn much [and] keep your feet planted"—Male, Soccer Player • "You miss 100% of the shots you don't take"—Male, Hockey Player
Emotional	• "I am always here, if you need anything. Call or text me anytime you want to talk" (re: to a parental divorce)—Female, Volleyball Player • "It is my responsibility to keep you safe. I don't need you hurting yourself in an easy game" (re: an injury)—Female, Soccer Player "You are a great person, who has awesome grades. Don't let people bring you down" (re: to bullying)—Female, Cross Country Runner • "At the end of the game, it's not whether you win or lose but it's about the kind of winner or loser you were"—Female, Basketball Player
Esteem	• "You are better than any one of the girls here. You can win this whole tournament"—Female, Tennis Player • "You are capable of doing. You're a better player than that [re: film]"—Male, Football Player • "You might not be the fastest guy on the team but you make up for this with your effort every time you take the field"—Male, Lacrosse Player • "You are a role model for the younger girls. You are one of the best captains we have ever had"—Female, Track Runner

Note. These messages were identified within Cranmer et al. (2017).

Regardless of the mechanism, received support benefits athletes in numerous ways, including increasing their motivation (DeFreese & Smith, 2013), self-confidence (Rees & Freeman, 2007), and performance (Rees, Hardy, & Freeman, 2007; Rees, Ingledew, & Hardy, 1999), as well as decreasing burn out (DeFreese & Smith, 2013) and recovery periods from injuries (Lu & Hsu, 2013).

Coaches' use of social support also influences athletes' relationships with coaches and teammates, as well as their evaluations of sporting experiences. In particular, the reception of emotional and esteem support from coaches promotes closer relationships with coaches and teammates (Cranmer, 2016; Cranmer & Sollitto, 2015; Westre & Weiss, 1991). Subsequently, the formation of these high-quality relationships improves athletes' satisfaction with their participation in sport (i.e., a mediated effect) (Cranmer & Sollitto, 2015), which demonstrates holistic evaluations of sport are shaped by athletes' interactions and relationships. Coaches who recognize and meet athletes' needs for support with demonstrations of concern and attempts to build esteem may improve their effectiveness. This is not to say informational and tangible support are not important, but these types of support may be expected as part of coaches' formal roles. To summarize, social support is a type of communication that—through meeting the needs of athletes—builds trust and affect, creates prosocial climates, and leads to positive evaluations of sporting experiences.

Coach Confirmation

Individuals have a human need to feel endorsed, recognized, and acknowledged for who they are and who they can become (Buber, 1957, 1965). *Coach confirmation* encompasses interactions with coaches that meet athletes' needs to feel endorsed, recognized, and acknowledged. Although this state is psychological in nature, it is attributable to the reception of verbal and nonverbal messages, such as a meaningful touch, a reassuring look, or a verbal statement (Laing, 1961; Sieburg, 1985). The accumulation of these behaviors and messages creates a stimulating and encouraging relational climate, which benefits the development, experiences, and identities of recipients (Dailey, 2010; Munz & Wilson, 2014; Steinberg & Morris, 2001). Thus, confirmation is established through communicative acts associated with a particular psychological reaction within others and benefits athletes through the cultivation of relational climates (Cranmer & Brann, 2015)—similar to immediacy (see Chapter 3). The nature and quality of confirmation, however, differs based upon the situations and relationships in which it occurs, meaning that the specific acts and statements that are confirming vary across contexts (Laing, 1961).

Coaches are unique but meaningful sources of confirmation given the task-orientated nature of sport, authority of their positions, and access to millions of developing youth and adolescents (Cranmer et al., 2016). As such, understanding the manner in which coaches confirm athletes is of practical and scholarly importance. Via interviews with Division-I, women's volleyball players, Cranmer and Brann (2015) identified multiple qualitative themes of confirming communication. Their efforts suggested that coaches confirm athletes by meeting their individual needs via tailoring their communication (e.g., using preferred methods of feedback) or discussing athletes' non-sporting roles (e.g., being a student), relationships (e.g., family), and general wellbeing. Other themes addressed athlete development via calling on athletes to refine their skillsets, expressing confidence in athletes' future abilities, or recognizing their past efforts and contributions.

This seminal research was furthered by Cranmer and Spinda's (2017) observations of a Division-I football team during the 48 hours preceding a game. Their observations, which included full access to all team events and meetings, yielded novel insights regarding how confirmation manifests within large, male teams. In this study, confirmation was achieved through affectionate teasing, religious references, shared experiences and realities (e.g., "you're not in this alone" or "you need to do your job or it will be a long night for the guys behind you"), and signs or images with written mottos (e.g., "get better, show up, work hard, listen" or "best is the standard"). Of special note are the observed benefits of aggressive communication and religious appeals, which may be specific to southern football teams. The various differences between these studies indicate that confirmation is partially subject to the cultures, size, and sex composition of sport teams.

A generalizable understanding of coach confirmation, which was obtained through exploratory factor analysis, parallel analysis, and confirmatory factor analysis, has been supported across multiple populations of athletes (Cranmer, Brann, & Weber, 2017; Cranmer, Gagnon, & Mazer, 2019). These efforts indicated that coach confirmation consists of a dualistic structure of acceptance and challenge. *Acceptance* recognizes and endorses athletes' past efforts and accomplishments (i.e., confirms athletes for who they are). Receiving acceptance provides recipients with a sense of security, mitigates face threats that accompany feedback, and denotes attentiveness and positive regard.

These benefits are important for promoting healthy identities, self-esteem, and affect. Without acceptance, athletes may lack confidence or experience negative emotions stemming from a lack of reassurance or perceptions of an overly critical coach. In contrast, *challenge* validates athletes' potential to refine and improve their abilities (i.e., confirms athletes for who they can become). Challenge confronts recipients with their errors or shortcomings and demands continued efforts to improve or refine their abilities in a stimulating and prosocial manner. Without challenge, athletes may stunt their development or experience decreased engagement because of complacency or boredom. Together, acceptance and challenge function to create relational climates that are ideal for athletes' development as effective coaching often "helps achieve a balance between reinforcing appropriate responses and correcting errors" (Lockwood & Perlman, 2008, pp. 32–33).

Empirical investigations reveal mixed evidence regarding the effectiveness of coach confirmation across high school and collegiate athlete populations. Initial investigations demonstrated that only coaches' use of challenge explained increases in high school athletes' satisfaction with their sporting experiences and communication with coaches, as well as their motivation to participate in sport (Cranmer, Brann, & Weber, 2018). However, a partial replication with Division-I student-athletes revealed that coaches' use of both acceptance and challenge were associated with increases in satisfaction with sporting experiences and communication with coaches. Yet, only challenge accounted for motivation to participate in sport, competitiveness, and cognitive learning of sport (Cranmer et al., 2019). Together, these studies reveal that athletes' identities and development mostly benefit from structured and constructive feedback that acknowledges their potential and assists in refining their abilities. Such findings contradict colloquial assumptions regarding the entitlement and laziness of modern youth and adolescents. At the same time, it raises questions about the effectiveness of acceptance, which appears to become more valuable in competitive cultures of collegiate athletics or less valuable in retrospection. Confirmation literature reveals that embracing the interpersonal perspective and meeting athletes' individual needs does not mean coddling them or disregarding task accomplishment.

Developmental Messages

Since antiquity, many have argued that sport enhances the cognitive, physical, social, and moral development of athletes. Development is a broad concept that encompasses a diverse array of competencies that benefit athletes, including life skills that are applicable to non-sporting environments (Gould & Carson, 2008; Gould, Chung, Smith, & White, 2006). High school coaches recognize athletes need to learn how to listen and communicate, take responsibility for their actions, and develop a work ethic (Gould et al., 2006). Additional life skills are becoming more relevant in modern youth and adolescent sporting cultures, such as avoiding peer pressure to use drugs, alcohol, and tobacco; coping with the increased pressures on athletic performance; and managing over parenting (Gould & Carson, 2008). Coaches create the interpersonal environments that promote such development. More specifically, life skills are taught through coaches' structuring of team policies, role modeling of behaviors, providing opportunities to practice skills, and sharing of social resources (Arthur-Banning, Wells, Baker, & Hegreness, 2009; Camiré, Trudel, & Forneris, 2012; Super, Verkooijen, & Koelen, 2018). Coaches who direct their efforts toward emphasizing the process of skill development, as opposed to the outcome of games, best promote human development. Put differently, focusing on winning overshadows the potential long-term meaning and benefits of sport participation (Gould & Carson, 2008; Lockwood & Perlman, 2008). When the enjoyment of participation is valued by coaches, athletes acquire life skills and lessons more readily.

Coaches focus on the process of participating in sport by underscoring the necessity of playing in a specific manner (Kassing & Pappas, 2007). *Sportsmanship* encompasses one manner of play that emulates fairness and respect for others. Sportsmanship is crucial within athletics, as membership on sports teams requires participation throughout sets of iterative interactions (e.g., practices and live competitions). Violating the rules or sacrificing functional relationships with stakeholders for the sake of winning a single interaction comes at the cost of future participation or success across the set of interactions. Learning to abide by the agreed upon rules of a sport and/or team—even if it means losing or incurring difficulties in the short term—is an imperative life skill for athletes to learn. The most common means through which sporting stakeholders encourage sportsmanship is to role model desirable behaviors (Arthur-Banning et al., 2009) and avoid a win-at-all-cost mentality (Kassing & Barber, 2007). Sportsmanship is also encouraged through messages that advocate respecting teammates, opponents, officials, and coaches. For example, Kassing and Barber (2007) identified several such messages that encourage sportsmanship through surveying coaches and adults involved in youth soccer leagues: "winning isn't everything—it's more important how you play," "always treat opponents as you would like to be treated," "encourage your teammates, don't badmouth your teammates," and "officials do their best, respect officials."

Coaches also aid athletes' adjustment into society by imparting to them general life skills that guide their behavior, help make sense of novel situations, or frame future roles within society (Cranmer & Myers, 2017). For instance, coaches have been found to encourage work ethic (e.g., putting forth consistent effort), perseverance (e.g., not quitting or overcoming adversity), and autonomy (e.g., being independent and self-initiating performances), which are important cultural means of success within capitalistic societies (Cranmer, Anzur, et al., 2017; Cranmer & Myers, 2017; Kassing & Pappas, 2007). Likewise, coaches stress many desirable character traits within these messages—such as responsibility, cooperation, loyalty, positivity, and honesty. These interactions transcend the temporary nature of the athlete-coach relationship and benefit athletes in their personal lives and group settings, such as workplaces, families, or service groups.

Not all coaching interactions promote development, however, as coaches impede the learning of life skills by role modeling antisocial or inappropriate behaviors. Many of these behaviors fall within the scope of destructive forms of aggression, which demean or compromise the self-concepts of others. For example, athletes' enactment of sportsmanship decreases as coaches utilize character attacks, name calling, and threats, or engage in physical aggression toward them (Kassing & Infante, 1999). Such behavior creates hostile team climates and models behavior that is void of respect for others, which in turn set patterns of interaction and cultural norms that are also void of respect for rules and others. Put differently, athletes may learn to adopt and replicate coaches' destructive behaviors towards teammates, opponents, and officials. Overall, developmental literature suggests that coaches determine the values and life lessons athletes obtain from sport through their communicative patterns. With this in mind, it is important for coaches to communicate in a way that is consistent with their expectations for others.

The Future of the Interpersonal Perspective

The development of the interpersonal perspective offers insights into athletic coaching as a process reliant upon relationships. The continued advancement of the interpersonal perspective requires scholars to address a host of issues, including refining the specificity of constructs, increasing the scope of outcomes considered by researchers, and recognizing the contextual factors that shape the significance of human interaction. The interpersonal perspective illustrates a lack of specificity and distinction between commonly studied behaviors—a concern of all social science researchers and the point of establishing discriminant validity. Establishing such distinctions provides nuanced understandings of coach behaviors, facilitates the connection between empirical studies, and prevents parallel lines of research that are overly redundant. The lack of distinctions between dimensions of interpersonal coaching behaviors is evident in research on social support, which often utilizes a unidimensional understanding of support (i.e., as within the MDLM) or focuses exclusively on emotional support (e.g., Westre & Weiss, 1991). Such approaches overlook the various types of support that coaches provide to athletes.

Moreover, there is potential for conceptual overlap between coaches' use of social support and confirmation. For instance, identifying mistakes and providing correction is consistent with informational support and challenge, and recognizing athletes' abilities is consistent with esteem support and acceptance. In an effort to articulate the theoretical distinctions between these concepts, Cranmer et al. (2018) argued that social support is characterized by efforts to help recipients overcome adversity, whereas confirmation is characterized by a meaningful psychological response within recipients. Additional distinctions are evident in acceptance being a response to successful performances and efforts (as opposed to adversity) and reinforcing the status quo. While theorizing may parse out how variables are related, it is imperative for such distinctions to be supported by empirical evidence—not just reasoning.

It is also important to address the overwhelmingly prosocial nature of the interpersonal perspective. The emphasis on the benefits of meeting athletes' needs is unsurprising, as it is germane to the purpose of effective coaching research. However, the sole focus on the benefits of specific coaching behaviors overlooks that all relationships feature some degree of conflict and tension. For example, close interpersonal relationships within task-focused groups are accompanied by dialectical tensions between task and social objectives (Bridge & Baxter, 1992), informational clutter (Kramer, 2004), emotional distress (Waldron, 2012), and negative affect (Berman, West, & Richter, 2002). For coaches, their efforts to facilitate and maintain close relationships with athletes may impede or make it more difficult to provide critical feedback or distribute resources (e.g., playing time or attention) efficiently. As such, it is important for communication researchers to consider how coaches manage the boundaries of their relationships (Rhind & Jowett, 2010, 2012) and resolve conflicts with athletes (Wachsmuth, Jowett, & Harwood, 2018). The ability to reap the benefits of close relationships, without impeding efforts to be effective, rests within the negotiation of these interpersonal dynamics (Becker, 2009; Nash, Sproule, & Horton, 2011). Further, it is just as relevant for coaches to understand when prosocial behaviors are ineffective or inspire negative outcomes for athletes. For instance, the reception of social support is a complex process and not all attempts to enact support are successful (Bodie & Burleson, 2008). Athletes must be motivated and able to process coaches' prosocial messages, and coaches' messages must be useful to some extent. In the absence of these criteria, attempts to be supportive may go unrecognized (i.e., *invisible support*) (Bolger, Zuckerman, & Kessler, 2000).

The interpersonal perspective also needs to integrate the contextual and personal elements that influence the formation and maintenance of interpersonal relationships. The incorporation of social structures (e.g., sex, race, socio-economic status) acknowledged within sport sociology may aid communication researchers who operate from an interpersonal perspective. For example, sex and ethnicity are important factors in the evaluation of social support (Bodie & Burleson, 2008). In general, women value and are more critical of support—arguably, because they possess greater abilities and motivation to examine their interpersonal relationships. Additionally, ethnicity is relevant for interpreting support, as individuals from high-context cultures (i.e., cultures that rely more heavily on inferring meaning from contexts surrounding interaction as opposed to the content exchanged during an interaction) are able to draw more meaning from simplified and generalized messages. Additionally, numerous personality and communication dispositions—such as attachment styles, needs for affection and affiliation, and communicator styles—may determine athletes' interpersonal needs and preferred modes of interaction (McCroskey, Daly, Martin, & Beatty, 1998). The utility of the interpersonal perspective will increase with the incorporation of new frameworks that account for the role of individual differences.

Conclusion

The interpersonal perspective offers numerous opportunities for the investigation of the relational dynamics that undergird athletic coaching. More specifically, this perspective emphasizes that effective coaching is a social process that requires establishing and maintaining personalized relationships with athletes. By fostering close relationships defined by trust, respect, and affection, coaches are able to better impart knowledge and develop athletes within sport and as people (Jowett, 2017; Turman, 2017). The continued development of this perspective requires a more complex understanding of the dynamics of interpersonal relationships and the contexts in which they occur. This progress may be accomplished through considering detrimental and ineffective athlete-coach interactions, the maintenance of these relationships, and the distinctness of particular behaviors. The development of the interpersonal perspective has the potential to address recent and destructive trends within youth and adolescent sporting cultures.

Note

1. Kline, M. (2011, March 1). Mike Krzyzewski's 20 best quotes from his time as Duke's coach. *BleacherReport.com*. Retrieved from https://bleacherreport.com/articles/623308-mike-krzyzewskis-20-best-quotes-from-his-time-as-dukes-coach

References

Albrecht, T. L., & Adelman, M. B. (1987). *Communicating social support*. Newbury Park, CA: Sage.

Arthur-Banning, S., Wells, M., Baker, B., & Hegreness, R. (2009). Parents behaving badly? The relationship between the sportsmanship behaviors of adults and athletes in youth basketball games. *Journal of Sport Behavior, 32*, 3–18.

Atkinson, J. L. (2009). Age matters in sport communication. *The Electronic Journal of Communication, 19*. Online Journal. Retrieved from http://www.cios.org/EJCPUBLIC/019/2/019341.html

Becker, A. J. (2009). It's not what they do, it's how they do it: Athlete experiences of great coaching. *International Journal of Sports Science & Coaching, 4*, 93–119.

Berman, E. M., West, J. P., & Richter, M. N. Jr. (2002). Workplace relations: Friendship patterns and consequences (according to managers). *Public Administration Review, 62*, 217–230.

Bodie, G. D., & Burleson, B. R. (2008). Explaining variations in the effects of supportive messages: A dual-process framework. *Annals of the International Communication Association, 32*, 355–398.

Bolger, N., Zuckerman, A., & Kessler, R. C. (2000). Invisible support and adjustment to stress. *Journal of Personality and Social Psychology, 79*, 953–961.

Bridge, K., & Baxter, L. A. (1992). Blended relationships: Friends as work associates. *Western Journal of Communication, 56*, 200–225.

Buber, M. (1957). Distance and relation. *Psychiatry, 20*, 97–104.

Buber, M. (1965). *The knowledge of man.* New York, NY: Harper & Row.

Camiré, M., Trudel, P., & Forneris, T. (2012). Coaching and transferring life skills: Philosophies and strategies used by model high school coaches. *The Sport Psychologist, 26,* 243–260.

Clement, D., & Shannon, V. R. (2011). Injured athletes' perceptions about social support. *Journal of Sport Rehabilitation, 20,* 457–470.

Cohen, S. (1988). Psychosocial models of the role of social support in the etiology of physical disease. *Health Psychology, 7,* 269–297.

Cohen, S., & Wills, T. A. (1985). Stress, social support, and the buffering hypothesis. *Psychological Bulletin, 98,* 310–357.

Cranmer, G. A. (2016). A continuation of sport teams from an organizational perspective: Predictors of athlete-coach leader-member exchange. *Communication & Sport, 4,* 43–61.

Cranmer, G. A., Anzur, C. K., & Sollitto, M. (2017). Memorable messages of social support that former high school athletes received from their head coaches. *Communication & Sport, 5,* 604–621.

Cranmer, G. A., & Brann, M. (2015). "It makes me feel like I am an important part of this team": An exploratory study of coach confirmation. *International Journal of Sport Communication, 8,* 193–211.

Cranmer, G. A., Brann, M., & Anzur, C. K. (2016). Putting coach confirmation theory into practice: How to confirm youth and high school athletes and coach more effectively. *Strategies: A Journal for Physical and Sport Educators, 29*(6), 25–29.

Cranmer, G. A., Brann, M., & Weber, K. D. (2017). Quantifying coach confirmation: The development and preliminary validation of the coach confirmation instrument. *Communication & Sport, 5,* 751–769.

Cranmer, G. A., Brann, M., & Weber, K. D. (2018). "Challenge me!": Using confirmation theory to understand coach confirmation as an effective coaching behavior. *Communication & Sport, 6,* 239–259.

Cranmer, G. A., Gagnon, R. J., & Mazer, J. P. (2019). A continued application of confirmation theory: Division-I student-athletes' responses to coach confirmation. *Communication & Sport.* Advanced online publication. Retrieved from https://journals.sagepub.com/doi/pdf/10.1177/2167479518824868

Cranmer, G. A., & Myers, S. A. (2015). Sports teams as organizations: A leader-member exchange perspective of player communication with coaches and teammates. *Communication & Sport, 3,* 100–118.

Cranmer, G. A., & Myers, S. A. (2017). Exploring Division-I student-athletes' memorable messages from their anticipatory socialization. *Communication Quarterly, 65,* 125–143.

Cranmer, G. A., & Sollitto, M. (2015). Sport support: Received social support as a predictor of athlete satisfaction. *Communication Research Reports, 32,* 253–264.

Cranmer, G. A., & Spinda, J. (2017). *Coaches' use of confirmation during the preparation for a Division-I football game.* Paper submitted to the annual meeting of the National Communication Association, Dallas, TX.

Dailey, R. M. (2010). Testing components of confirmation: How acceptance and challenge from mothers, fathers, and siblings are related to adolescent self-concept. *Communication Monographs, 77,* 592–617.

Defreese, J. D., & Smith, A. L. (2013). Teammate social support, burnout, and self-determined motivation in collegiate athletes. *Psychology of Sport and Exercise, 14,* 258–265.

European Coaching Council (2007, September). Review of the EU 5-level structure for the recognition of coaching qualifications. *European Network of Sports Science, Education and Employment.* Retrieved from https://www.icce.ws/_assets/files/documents/ECC_5_level_review.pdf

Goldsmith, D. J. (2004). *Communicating social support.* Cambridge, MA: Cambridge University.

Gould, D., & Carson, S. (2008). Life skills development through sport: Current status and future directions. *International Review of Sport and Exercise Psychology, 1,* 58–78.

Gould, D., Chung, Y., Smith, P., & White, J. (2006). Future directions in coaching life skills: Understanding high school coaches' views and needs. *The Online Journal of Sport Psychology, 8.* Retrieved from http://citeseerx.ist.psu.edu/viewdoc/download?doi=10.1.1.498.6098&rep=rep1&type=pdf

Ishak, A. W. (2017). Communication in sports teams: A review. *Communication Research Trends, 36,* 4–38.

Jowett, S. (2008). Outgrowing the familial coach-athlete relationship. *International Journal of Sport Psychology, 39,* 20–40.

Jowett, S. (2017). Coaching effectiveness: The coach–athlete relationship at its heart. *Current Opinion in Psychology, 16,* 154–158.

Jowett, S., & Meek, G. A. (2000). The coach-athlete relationship in married couples: An exploratory content analysis. *The Sport Psychologist, 14,* 157–175.

Jowett, S., Paull, G., & Pensgaard, A. M. (2005). Coach-athlete relationship. In J. Taylor & G. S. Wilson (Eds.), *Applying sport psychology: Four perspectives* (pp. 153–170). Champaign, IL: Human Kinetics.

Jowett, S., Timson-Katchis, M., & Adams, R. (2007). Too close for comfort? Dependence in the dual role parent/coach-child/athlete relationship. *International Journal of Coaching Science, 1,* 59–78.

Kassing, J. W., & Barber, A. M. (2007). "Being a good sport": An investigation of sportsmanship messages provided by youth soccer parents, officials, and coaches. *Human Communication, 10,* 61–68.

Kassing, J. W., & Infante, D. A. (1999). Aggressive communication in the coach-athlete relationship. *Communication Research Reports, 16,* 110–120.

Kassing, J. W., & Pappas, M. E. (2007). "Champions are built in the off season": An exploration of high school coaches' memorable messages. *Human Communication, 10,* 537–546.

Kramer, M. W. (2004). *Managing uncertainty in organizational communication.* Mahwah, NJ: Lawrence Erlbaum Associates.

Laing, R. D. (1961). *Self and others.* London: Tavistock Publications.

Lockwood, P., & Perlman, D. (2008). Enhancing the youth sport experience: A re-examination of methods, coaching style, and motivational climate. *The Journal of Youth Sports, 4,* 30–34.

Lu, F. J., & Hsu, Y. (2013). Injured athletes' rehabilitation beliefs and subjective well-being: The contribution of hope and social support. *Journal of athletic training, 48,* 92–98.

Mazer, J. P., Barnes, K., Grevious, A., & Boger, C. (2013). Coach verbal aggression: A case study examining effects on athlete motivation and perceptions of coach credibility. *International Journal of Sport Communication, 6*, 203–213.

McCroskey, J. C., Daly, J. A., Martin, M. M., & Beatty, M. J. (1998). *Communication and personality: Trait perspectives.* Cresskill, NJ: Hampton Press.

Munz, E. A., & Wilson, S. R. (2014). Caregiver confirmation and children's attachment security during the transition to kindergarten. *Communication Research, 44*, 668–690.

Nash, C., Sproule, J., & Horton, P. (2011). Excellence in coaching. *Research Quarterly for Exercise and Sport, 82*, 229–238.

Project Play. (2018). What we do. AspenProjectPlay.org. Retrieved from https://www.aspen projectplay.org/whatwedo/

Rees, T., & Freeman, P. (2007). The effects of perceived and received support on self-confidence. *Journal of Sports Sciences, 25*, 1057–1065.

Rees, T., & Hardy, L. (2000). An investigation of the social support experiences of high-level sports performers. *The Sport Psychologist, 14*, 327–347.

Rees, T., Hardy, L., & Freeman, P. (2007). Stressors, social support, and effects upon performance in golf. *Journal of Sports Sciences, 25*, 33–42.

Rees, T., Ingledew, D. K., & Hardy, L. (1999). Social support dimensions and components of performance in tennis. *Journal of Sports Sciences, 17*, 421–429.

Rhind, D. J. A., & Jowett, S. (2010). Relationship maintenance strategies in the coach-athlete relationship: The development of the COMPASS model. *Journal of Applied Sport Psychology, 22*, 106–121.

Rhind, D. J. A., & Jowett, S. (2012). Working with coach-athlete relationships: Their quality and maintenance. In S. Hanton & S. D. Mellalieu (Eds.), *Professional practice in sport psychology: A review* (pp. 219–248). New York, NY: Routledge.

Sagar, S. S., & Jowett, S. (2012). Communicative acts in coach-athlete interactions: When losing competitions when making mistakes in training. *Western Journal of Communication, 76*, 148–174.

Sieburg, E. (1985). *Family communication: An integrated systems approach.* Boston, MA: Allyn & Bacon.

Steinberg, L., & Morris, A. S. (2001). Adolescent development. *Annual Review of Psychology, 52*, 83–110.

Super, S., Verkooijen, K., & Koelen, M. (2018). The role of community sports coaches in creating optimal social conditions for life skill development and transferability—A salutogenic perspective. *Sport, Education and Society, 23*, 173–185.

Turman, P. D. (2017). Sports as interpersonal communication. In A. C. Billings (Ed.), *Defining sport communication* (pp. 165–177). New York, NY: Routledge.

Vella, S., Oades, L. G., & Crowe, T. P. (2011). The role of coach in facilitating positive youth development: Moving from theory to practice. *Journal of Applied Sport Psychology, 23*, 33–48.

Wachsmuth, S., Jowett, S., & Harwood, C. G. (2018). On understanding the nature of interpersonal conflict between coaches and athletes. *Journal of Sports Sciences, 36*, 1955–1962.

Waldron, V. R. (2012). *Communicating emotion at work.* Malden, MA: Polity.

Weiss, M. R., & Fretwell, S. D. (2005). The parent-coach/childe-athlete relationship in youth sport: Cordial, contentious, or conundrum? *Research Quarterly for Exercise and Sport, 76,* 286–305.

Westre, K. R., & Weiss, M. R. (1991). The relationship between perceived coaching behaviors and group cohesion in high school football teams. *The Sport Psychologist, 5,* 41–54.

· 7 ·

SETTING A SCHOLARLY AGENDA: BUILDING TOWARD A HOLISTIC FRAMEWORK

All coaching is, is taking a player where he [sic] can't take himself.—Bill McCartney[1]

Historically, knowledge within coaching science (Gilbert, 2002; Gilbert & Trudel, 2004; Potrac, Denison, & Gilbert, 2013) and sport communication (Abeza, O'Reilly, & Nadeau, 2014; Kassing et al., 2004; Wenner, 2015) has been generated through assessments and constructive critiques of empirical research. It is through such reflection, synthesis, and criticism that pathways for advancement become apparent and the tools that produce knowledge are refined. The initial two chapters of this text created a foundation for a communicative approach to coaching. These chapters established coaching as a social process within which effectiveness is dependent on the strategic exchange of verbal and nonverbal messages. The next four chapters built upon this foundation and detailed distinct perspectives utilized by coach communication scholars (i.e., instructional, organizational, group, and interpersonal perspectives). The chapters on these perspectives established and organized the conceptualization, history, and state of coach communication research for readers. Together, these six chapters offer a fundamental understanding from which to outline a scholarly agenda.

A continual theme across each of these chapters was the tremendous potential of coach communication research to inform a range of applied and scholarly communities. Despite nearly two decades of research, Kassing et al.'s (2004) assessment of the unmet and seemingly unlimited potential of communicative approaches to coaching is still quite suitable. In order for researchers to fulfill this potential, there is a great need to advance existing approaches, as well as cultivate new ones. This chapter seeks to contribute to this advancement in two ways. First, it identifies a host of issues that provide opportunities to develop research practices and garner scientific knowledge of coaching. In other words, through the identification of problematic aspects of past research and the provision of potential solutions to those problems, this chapter intends to stimulate the refinement and growth of coach communication scholarship. Second, this chapter considers the benefits and challenges of creating a holistic framework of coaching. A holistic approach involves connecting the previously outlined perspectives (featured in Chapters 3-6) and offering an encompassing framework for scholars and practitioners—an ambitious pursuit. Together, with the future research recommendations made within the previous chapters, this chapter guides the construction of a scholarly agenda for coach communication researchers.

The foci of this chapter are timely as coaching is a budding topic of inquiry. Multiple assessments of sport communication research have called for a renewed focus on interpersonal interactions within sport, including those between coaches and athletes (Abeza et al., 2014; Kassing et al., 2004; Pedersen, 2013; Wenner, 2015). These efforts are imperative to the future of sport communication because coaching is one of the central processes that defines sport participation. Moreover, this knowledge may assist coaches in developing athletes, improving their performances, and managing sporting environments through strategic communication. Providing such prescriptive information fills several voids within coaching science literature and increases its practical implications (Duffy et al., 2011). For instance, Potrac, Brewer, Jones, Armour, and Hoff (2000) suggested: "… it can be argued that coaches, far from being merely technicians, need to be educated as intellectuals with social and cognitive skills and values … [and that] coach education should focus on the problems and realities of human interaction …" (p. 188). Thus, communication scholars are ideally positioned to produce knowledge with practical and heuristic value to multiple fields of inquiry.

Opportunities for Advancement

A means of promoting the advancement of a field of inquiry is to identify its shortcomings or topics for further consideration. It is through the identification of problematic practices and the forwarding of potential solutions that coach communication scholarship may continue to develop into a rigorous scientific pursuit that benefits coaches and researchers. The current efforts to identify weaknesses in research practices and designs are a constructive means to contribute to scholarly discourse. Indeed, myself and other established scholars have perpetuated many of the practices featured in this chapter. As such, these issues are framed as opportunities for the progression of coach communication research and not condemnations of individuals. Five specific opportunities that address foundational elements of research are a good starting point for forwarding coach communication scholarship: sampling, measurement, research designs, application, and epistemological diversity.

Sampling

Social scientists procure knowledge through the collection and analysis of data from samples of athletes and coaches. Access to appropriate samples is incredibly important for obtaining replicable and valid findings (Carpenter, 2017; Tye-Williams, 2017). There are several issues that coaching scholars might consider when determining the best sample for their research. A common practice within coaching scholarship is the use of retrospective samples of former athletes who are no longer members of the teams on which they are reporting. It is understandable why retrospective data is commonplace in coaching literature. The majority of athlete populations within the United States consist of minors (i.e., between the ages of 4 and 17) (Kelley & Carchia, 2013; National Federation of State High School Associations, 2017). These populations are insulated and more difficult to access without developed social networks. Additionally, working with minors requires rigorous oversight and lengthy institutional review board (IRB) applications, as well as parental consent. In contrast, samples of young adults (i.e., often college students) who played organized sports earlier in their lives are abundant, easily accessible, and require fewer restrictions and oversight—a sample of pure convenience. However, the traditional limitations of self-report data compound with retrospection, which is subject to greater degrees of omission, rumination, and other sources of inaccuracies (Bernard, Kilworth, Kronenfeld, & Sailer, 1984).

As such, retrospective data should be avoided, at least without significant rationale, and data from current athletes sought. Researchers have moved in this direction, with the parameters on retrospective data becoming increasingly restrictive; progressing from unspecified criteria (Kassing & Infante, 1999; Martin, Rocca, Cayanus, & Weber, 2009; Rocca, Martin, & Toale, 1998), to within 10 years (Kassing & Anderson, 2014), five years (Cranmer, 2016), two years (Cranmer & Buckner, 2017), and a year of athletes' last sports participation (Cranmer, Brann, & Weber, 2018). A notable exception to the prioritization of current athlete populations is when researchers explore concepts that require retrospection, such as memorable messages or sense making (Cranmer, Anzur, & Sollitto, 2017; Kassing & Pappas, 2007); Retrospective samples are entirely appropriate in these contexts.

Another potential issue is the sampling of athletes across sports. Particular sports arguably have unique histories, norms, and general team cultures. As such, researchers may consider the sports in which their samples participate when seeking to generalize about athlete-coach interactions. Because of this concern, some researchers restrict the range of sports they consider, as Cranmer and Brann (2015) did with volleyball or Turman (2001, 2003a; Turman & Schrodt, 2004) did with wrestling. Qualitative evidence indicates that such an approach can reveal nuanced differences within coach communication. For instance, within the hegemonic sport of football, some forms of aggressive communication (e.g., teasing) appear to promote positive psychological states and relationships (Cranmer & Spinda, 2017; Turman, 2003b)—a finding not replicated among female teams. Another strategy to account for sporting cultures is to categorize sports based upon the interdependence required between athletes (i.e., individual, independent, and interdependent sports). The interdependence between athletes is theorized to shape interactions and social dynamics among teams. Despite these assertions, quantitative differences in athlete-coach communication across independent and interdependent sports have remained elusive. For instance, no differences have been observed in relation to orientations toward coach feedback (Cranmer & Goodboy, 2015), the provision of organizational resources (Cranmer, 2016), expressions of athlete dissent (Cranmer & Buckner, 2017), or socialization into teams (Cranmer, 2018). A notable exception to this trend is that athletes who play independent sports report feeling closer to their coaches (Cranmer & Goodboy, 2015; Rhind, Jowett, & Yang, 2012). This general lack of evidence suggests that potential differences between sporting cultures might not be readily generalizable based upon interdependence. Researchers should carefully consider the sporting contexts from which they derive their samples as a potential explanation for observed phenomenon and collect data with consideration of such realities.

There also remains opportunities to consider multiple perspectives within samples. To date, researchers have largely relied on athletes' reports of coach behaviors, their own affective and cognitive states, or perceptions of relationships with others—a singular perspective of athlete-coach interactions. Coaching science scholars have encouraged the collection of data that considers both athlete and coach perspectives of interaction (Jowett & Wylleman, 2006; Potrac et al., 2000; Rhind & Jowett, 2012). Dyadic data has not been a common feature within coach communication research, with few notable exceptions (Turman, 2001, 2003a). Dyadic data offers coaching scholars the opportunity to determine if others (e.g., coaches or teammates) more broadly share the social realities identified within data obtained from athletes. This type of sampling makes an important contribution to the empirical record, as social interaction is comprised of multiple individuals, who have valid understandings of relationships and sporting experiences.

The addition of multiple perspectives may reveal and provide means to adjust for the influence of social desirability and issues that threaten the validity of self-report data. For instance, coaches may underreport their use of antisocial behaviors or athletes may overreport their socialization into a team, self-confidence, or abilities. Incorporating the perspectives of additional stakeholders may reveal and account for such patterns. With that said, the use of dyadic data accompanies increasing methodological complexities and statistical issues that are too lengthy for this text; see Kenny, Kashy, and Cook (2006) for information regarding the examination of such data. Researchers should make efforts to collect dyadic data but should not lose focus on the reality that many outcomes of effective coaching are only knowable through athletes' self-reports, such as affective and cognitive learning, motivation, satisfaction, or knowledge relevant to socialization. Overall, it is important that coach communication researchers commit to obtaining quality and rigorous samples, rather than seeking convenience when obtaining participants for research.

Measurement

The development of valid and reliable psychometric measurement is essential to the creation of meaningful knowledge about human behavior (DeVellis, 2012). Measurement comprises the tools through which we obtain generalizable information about athlete and coach experiences. Unfortunately, serious measurement issues underlie sport communication research (Denham, in press). Cranmer, Brann, and Weber (2017) summarized these issues as follows:

> The lack of appropriate measurement raises some concern regarding whether the foundation of research [about coach communication] is built on sturdy terrain. Further, the lack of such measurement may impede the development of future athlete-coach communication research, which will be restricted without the availability of true sport communication measures. (p. 764)

Given these concerns, Cranmer and colleagues called for the continued development and refinement of coaching measures. Three measurement issues merit specific attention: the reliance on non-sporting measures, the lack of measurement creation, and the absence of measurement validation.

Coach communication researchers frequently rely upon measures from alternative contexts of interaction, including instructional, organizational, and interpersonal communication. Although this reliance is unsurprising given the novelty of coach communication as a topic of inquiry and the use of alternative contexts for conceptual frameworks, the incorporation of such instrumentation can be troublesome. Sport is a distinct context of human interaction; behavior can manifest in novel ways within the athlete-coach relationship. For instance, coaches' use of confirmation (Cranmer & Brann, 2015) varies greatly from that of instructors or parents, especially regarding challenging athletes to refine performances. Scholars who borrow measurement from non-sporting contexts, therefore, may not accurately assess coaches' behaviors or athletes' reactions. With this in mind, researchers should avoid importing measures from non-sporting contexts whenever possible. Measures from sport psychology and management may help fill these voids until new communicative measures are developed and validated. For example, the Coach-Athlete Relationship Maintenance Questionnaire (Rhind & Jowett, 2012), the Coach-Athlete Relationship Questionnaire (Jowett & Ntoumanis, 2004), or the Leadership Scale for Sports (Zhang, Jensen, & Mann, 1997) may serve such purposes. In the event importing measures from non-sporting contexts is unavoidable, empirical demonstrations of scale performance should be required (at a minimum) as evidence of validity, given the functionality of measures is subject to change across distinct populations (Levine, 2005; Levine, Hullett, Mitchell-Turner, & Lapinski, 2006).

The historical reliance on non-sporting measurement may be attributable to a lack of novel measures created by communication scholars. To date, only two measures encompassing coaching behaviors have been forwarded, including those that assess coaches' verbal aggression (Kassing & Infante, 1999) and confirmation (Cranmer, Brann, et al., 2017). Additionally, communication researchers have produced a limited number of measures that assess outcomes of effective coaching, like athlete-coach relational satisfaction (Kassing & Infante, 1999), holistic sport satisfaction (Turman, 2006), and sportsmanship behaviors (Kassing & Infante, 1999). There are countless additional behaviors and outcomes of effective coaching that provide researchers with opportunities to develop and validate new measures; these tools of inquiry are necessary for coach communication research to meet its potential.

While the creation of such measurement is needed for the continued advancement of coach communication research, most of the previously mentioned measures lack validation (Denham, in press). Denham (in press), however, highlighted the Coach Confirmation Instrument (CCI) (Cranmer, Brann, et al., 2017) as an exemplar of scale development. The development and validation of the CCI is especially noteworthy for four reasons. First, these efforts have occurred over multiple studies that consider different populations of athletes (Cranmer, Arnson, et al., 2019; Cranmer, Brann, et al., 2017, 2018; Cranmer, Gagnon, & Mazer, 2019). Second, multiple demonstrations of the measure's reliability have been made—both with Cronbach's alpha and Tarkkonen's rho. These efforts demonstrate that there is little random error in participants' responses to the CCI and its items are not overly redundant. Third, the structure of the CCI was established and confirmed via exploratory and confirmatory factor analyses, parallel analysis, and the average variance extracted between dimensions. Fourth, the CCI has demonstrated degrees of multiple types of validity. It demonstrated *face validity* through its inductively derived items and expert appraisal. It displayed *content validity* through the full representation of qualitative themes from previous research and Confirmation theory (Cranmer & Brann, 2015). It exhibited *concurrent validity* via its relationship to reports of psychological feelings of confirmation. It revealed *construct validity* via its relationships with verbal aggression, satisfaction, motivation, and cognitive learning (Cranmer, Brann, et al., 2017, 2018; Cranmer, Gagnon, et al., 2019). The CCI is of value as an example of scale construction because it illustrates that the validation of measurement is a continual process and an integral part of research. There needs to be a concerted and collective effort among coaching scholars to focus on the creation, validation, and continual assessment of the performance of measures as a standard component of all quantitative research studies.

Research Designs

There remain opportunities to integrate more complex and diverse methodological approaches into investigations of coach communication. The selection of a methodology is one of the most basic decisions that scholars make, and it defines the type of insights provided by research (Wilson, 2017). To date, coach communication research is mostly comprised of self-report, surveys and few examples of quasi-experiments (Mazer, Barnes, Grevious, & Boger, 2013), observational studies (Turman, 2005, 2007; Webster, 2009), and interviews (Cranmer & Brann, 2015; Turman, 2003b). As such, the knowledge that scholars have created is reliant upon athletes' perceptions—and to a lesser extent those of coaches. The reliance on a single methodology across a body of research is concerning, as methodologies offer unique advantages and disadvantages. For example, surveys best reveal perceptions and internal states, observations offer insight into the aspects of team cultures and coaching that are taken for granted by participants, experiments reveal the effects of coaching behaviors within controlled environments, and interviews yield the nuances within athlete and coach experiences and sense-making. Ideally, scholars will use multiple methods across literature or even within studies to gain comparative insights. The incorporation of a diverse array of methodologies is crucial for gaining a holistic understanding of coaching (Potrac et al., 2000). Coach communication scholars should consider their research aims and select a methodology or multiple methodologies based upon what best assists in accomplishing their aims.

There are also numerous considerations that can strengthen the rigor and validity of current survey research (e.g., reduce method or measurement error). One such concern is the recognition of *halo effects*. Halo effects are the consequence of the tendency to form generalized impressions of individuals, which subsequently cloud the ability of survey participants to distinguish between aspects of others' behavior. For example, athletes' reports of coach behavior may stem from their affect or liking for a coach, with well-liked coaches being perceived as funnier, nicer, smarter, etc. than objectively supported. Similar patterns occur within other contexts of communication but can be minimized by placing measures assessing irrelevant variables at the beginning of a survey (Feeley, 2002).

A second concern within survey research is that of *order effects*. This effect acknowledges that the order of measures within a survey influences data obtained from participants. For example, order effects could result from a survey that features measures assessing coaches' use of specific behaviors—especially those that are highly valenced (e.g., verbal aggression or social support)—followed by subsequent assessments that are broad and holistic in nature (e.g., sport satisfaction or relational quality). In such a scenario, reading and completing the behavioral measure would alter participants' assessments of sporting experiences (e.g., reflecting on coaches' use of prosocial behaviors would inflate holistic assessments). Order effects may be addressed through the randomization of measures within a survey, which is easily facilitated with online data collection websites (e.g., qualtrics.com), or the ordering of measures from broad to specific in focus (McFarland, 1981).

A third concern is that of *common method variance*, which references the potential for an altered relationship between constructs when data is obtained through a shared method. For example, collecting athletes' reports of a coaching behavior and sporting outcomes within a single survey and via similar measurements (i.e., design, format, etc.) may alter the relationship between those constructs. Most commonly, such alterations manifest in inflated amounts of shared variance between constructs. Common method variance has been identified across numerous fields that examine human behavior, including psychology, sociology, marketing, business, and education (Côté & Buckley, 1987; Podsakoff, MacKenzie, Lee, & Podsakoff, 2003). Ideally, scholars will preemptively address common method variance through their research designs, including collecting data from multiple individuals or longitudinally. However, researchers may also relieve these concerns through post-hoc alternatives, such as demonstrations that participations were able to distinguish between measures or that observed relationships were comparable to those from studies that controlled for common method variance. Together, concerns about research design demonstrate that coach communication scholars need to continue to incorporate novel methods into their research and refine the rigor of established methods.

Application

Another opportunity for coach communication scholars is a renewed and focused effort to promote the practical implications of their research. The purpose of coaching science scholarship is to assist in and promote effective coaching. In other words, those who conduct coaching research have an obligation to facilitate the translation of their scholarship into practice. The efforts of scholars, practitioners, and administrators must be amalgamated for coach communication literature to meet its aim. There are several potential remedies for the current lack of application of coach communication research. First, scholars need to make an exerted effort to emphasize the practical implications of each study. These efforts naturally fit within the scope and purpose of a thoughtful and well-reasoned discussion section (Omori, 2017). The lack of articulation regarding how sporting stakeholders may benefit from research is a worthy justification for disqualifying a manuscript from publication regardless of its theory, arguments, sample, or method. Moreover, these discussion sections need specificity and must illustrate how coaches or others are to implement findings. It is not sufficient to encourage the replication of a particular behavior in a general sense; details regarding how to implement a behavior and under what conditions are relevant information. If scholarly culture, editors, and peer reviewers develop a more rigorous emphasis on application, research design and writing will eventually reflect this emphasis and in turn may increase the practical value of our scholarship.

Second, coach communication scholars should seek opportunities to share research with practitioners whenever possible. This may come in the form of attending and presenting at coaching, rather than communication, conferences (e.g., The United States Center for Coaching Excellence annual summit) or publishing in popular press formats (e.g., newspapers or online sport websites). Additionally, scholars should make use of applied journals that target coaches and sport practitioners. One good example of such an outlet is *Strategies: A Journal for Physical and Sport Educators*, which seeks to publish practical, how-to articles for coaches and physical educators. This journal readily features "theory into practice" articles that distill research into accessible and practical essays that have prescriptive value. These articles allow scholars to remove the jargon and statistics that may hinder the layperson from understanding and applying academic research. Moreover, SHAPE America distributes the journal to thousands of coaches and teachers. If coach communication research is to reach its potential as a field of inquiry, application needs to become a stronger focal point of scholars from research design to the sharing of findings.

Epistemological Diversity

To date, coach communication research has been the product of post-positivists (e.g., Turman, Kassing, Cranmer, Martin, or Myers), who take a behaviorist approach to coaching. The prevalence of these scholars within the empirical record should not be surprising given the emphasis on producing generalizable results and identifying effective messages and behaviors within coaching science. Yet, there is room for additional epistemological perspectives. In particular, interpretivist or humanist approaches that recognize the importance of individual differences may be of benefit to the empirical record (Nelson & Colquhoun, 2013). Sport sociologists have identified numerous demographic characteristics that shape patterns of participation within sport. For example, regional differences (e.g., sporting popularity and geographic resources), socio-economic status, birth order, sex and race determine athletes' opportunities and social expectations for sport participation (Coakley, 1993; McPherson, 1981). The addition of such perspectives, however, are only productive to the extent that novel arguments are based in empirical evidence and build upon the established scientific approach.

The consideration of gender and sex—or at least patterns of socialization, personality, and interaction associated with these demographics—might be especially fruitful. Sport sociologist widely argue that sport is a gendered environment that produces masculine norms and expectations for human behavior (Messner, 1992). Yet coaching scholars and practitioners have been hesitant to integrate such notions into their practice. For example, Patt Summitt famously reflected on a question regarding the intersections of coaching and gender during a coaching clinic:

> I remember teaching a clinic to other coaches, and a guy raised his hand and asked if I had any advice when it came to coaching women. I leveled him with a death-ray stare, and said, "go home and coach basketball."

Likewise, within coaching science literature, there is little emphasis on gender or sex, with the *Routledge Handbook of Sport Coaching* and Lyle and Cushion's (2010) *Sports Coaching: Professionalization and Practice* dedicating zero chapters to the subject. Sex is commonly excluded as a determinant of athlete-coach interactions within communication research. Yet, there are some assertions that athlete-coach interactions differ, especially regarding the prevalence and effectiveness of aggressive communication with male coaches and participants (Cranmer & Spinda, 2017; Martin et al., 2009; Turman, 2003b). Many of these studies, however, do not directly compare or test such notions (e.g., Ruggiero & Lattin, 2008). Communication scholars could rely upon and extend physical education literature, which offers evidence of gendered patterns of teacher-student interactions during physical education classes (e.g., weight lifting and badminton). These patterns include the intersections of athlete sex and sport type in determining the amount and nature of sport-related feedback (Nicaise, Cogerino, Fariclough, Bois, & Davis, 2007). A more diverse array of scholarly perspectives (e.g., interpretive) may assist in raising attention toward potential issues that are currently being overlooked by postpositivists.

Building Holistic Frameworks of Coaching

A central focal point of coaching science researchers over the past decade has been to build a holistic framework that accounts for the dynamic and complex realities that coaches endure (Duffy et al., 2011; Potrac et al., 2000). Although many scholars have called for holistic approaches toward coaching, what is meant by the term *holistic* is seldom explained and appears to vary across literature (Cassidy, 2013). Within this text, holism refers to the notion of the whole being greater than the sum of the parts. Put differently, holism recognizes that communicative, dispositional, and situational variables interact in a manner that produces unique circumstances that determine coach effectiveness (Jones & Turner, 2006). Such a framework transcends a process-product orientation, which asserts behaviors are inherently effective, and allows for the investigation of how individual, relational, and contextual features shape interaction. The development of such a framework allows for the codification of professional standards and facilitates the evaluation of coaches (European Coaching Council, 2007). For communication scholars, building toward a holistic framework requires the integration of the existing perspectives of coaching and the inclusion of the contexts that surround athlete-coach relationships.

Integrating Existing Perspectives

It is beneficial to unify and transcend the multiple communicative perspectives used to examine coaching, as "… a fragmented or episodic approach to coaching knowledge tends to underestimate the complexity of the coaching process" (Cushion & Lyle, 2010, p. 3). The previous four chapters articulated the instructional, organizational, group, and interpersonal perspectives of coaching; (see Table 7.1 for a brief summary). These perspectives posit that coaches teach sporting knowledge and skills; manage, structure, and lead teams in a way that facilitates the accomplishment of shared tasks; create climates and cultures that benefit teams as collectives; or form quality relationships that meet athletes' needs. Yet, coaches must fulfill *all* of these roles, as coaching requires "…not only expansive technical knowledge of their sport but also the pedagogical skills of a teacher, the counseling wisdom of a psychologist, the training expertise of a physiologist, and the administrative leadership of a business executive" (Potrac et al., 2000, p. 187). In other words, coaches must learn to be a teacher, manager, group member, and a relational partner to inspire athlete development and performance, as well as manage sporting environments effectively.

A holistic approach requires scholars to articulate the interdependence between these perspectives, which are arguably artifacts of the structure of communication studies and expertise of seminal scholars. Coach communication research may be forwarded through determining the mutual influence that coaches' roles exert on each other. Some potential intersections may include: (a) the effect of managerial styles, team climates, and interpersonal relationships on coaches' instructional approaches and athlete learning; (b) the consequences of coaches' distributions of organizational resources for shaping athlete learning, team dynamics, and athlete-coach relationships; (c) the influence of team social dynamics for the processing of instruction, managerial choices, or attempts to meet athletes' interpersonal needs; or (d) the benefits of interpersonal closeness in improving corrective instruction, management, or team climates.

Table 7.1. *Summary of Four Coaching Perspectives*

Perspective	Role of Coach	Role of Athlete	Outcomes
Instructional	Coaches are instructors, who gather information and insight regarding sport and share it with athletes through verbal and nonverbal communication in an effort to promote athlete learning and develop stimulating sporting environments.	Athletes are learners, who receive and process coaches' verbal and nonverbal communication in an attempt to understand instruction and bring it to fruition via their physical performance.	Affective, Cognitive, & Behavioral Learning Motivation Evaluations of Coaches
Organizational	Coaches are managers, who are responsible for their teams' performances and use verbal and nonverbal communication to direct athletes' task performances and optimize team functioning.	Athletes are subordinates, who receive direction and are influenced by coaches' verbal and nonverbal communication toward the accomplishment of assigned tasks and roles.	Distribution of Organizational Resources Orientations and Knowledge toward Tasks & Roles Winning

Table 7.1. *Continued*

Group	Coaches are members of social collectives, who use verbal and nonverbal communication to oversee team social dynamics, collective processes (e.g., conflict resolution), and the setting and accomplishment of group and individual goals.	Athletes are members of social collectives, who comprise the bulk of teams and forge relationships with each other and their coaches as they seek to accomplish group and individual goals.	Cohesion Team Cultures Perceptions of Team Environments/Atmospheres Shared Motivational States
Interpersonal	Coaches are relational partners, who utilize their verbal and nonverbal communication to form relationships with athletes and provide them with social and emotional resources, either directly or indirectly through the structuring of sporting environments.	Athletes are developing individuals, who have unique psychological, social, and communicative needs, which when met better facilitate their performance and development.	Communication Satisfaction Coach Satisfaction Socialization via Sport Sportsmanship Life Skills

Some examples of such efforts include articles that consider improving learning through meeting athletes' interpersonal needs (Cranmer et al., 2019) or enacting particular group leadership styles (Turman, 2003a). Others have considered the influence of coaches' instructional behaviors in determining team cohesion (Turman, 2008), or how the distributions of interpersonal resources function as a consequence of organizational strategies (Cranmer, Arnson, Moore, Scott, & Peed, 2019). These studies bring coach communication scholars closer to a holistic framework that transcends the limited perspectives of coaches as teachers, managers, group members, and relational partners.

The existence of multiple perspectives, while useful for understanding aspects of coaching, are individually inadequate. Unifying these various perspectives better encompasses the complexities of coaching as a social process that spans teaching, managing, and relating to athletes as groups and individuals. A holistic framework, however, requires recognizing the roles that come to define these perspectives intersect and influence one another. Further complexity is achieved when scholars recognize that athlete-coach interactions are also shaped by the contexts in which coaching occurs, including by the characteristics of teams and athletes.

Contextual Features

Coaching is a process that takes place within a larger social context (Horn, 2002; Potrac et al., 2000). The definition of coaching forwarded by this text (see Chapter 1) acknowledges that coaching occurs within sporting environments and effective coaching requires the management of those environments toward athlete development and performance (see Chapter 2). To date, communication researchers have largely overlooked the context in which coaches implement behaviors and messages. A holistic approach recognizes both situational features and the dispositional characteristics of athletes and coaches, which come to define sporting contexts. Situational features encompass the external sporting environment, including specific game situations, the time within a sporting season, the sport being played, and the levels of intensity and competition attributable to specific sports leagues (Strean, 1995). For instance, pointing out mistakes and assisting athletes in refining their efforts are most effective during developmental periods (e.g., practice or off-season workouts) (Cranmer & Brann, 2015) or immediately before competitions (Cranmer & Spinda, 2017).

Dispositional characteristics of athletes and coaches include their personalities, knowledge, biological traits, and various predispositions (e.g., anxiety, competitiveness, or personality). These types of characteristics influence how coaches communicate with athletes. For instance, coaches rely on their intrapersonal knowledge to guide self-reflection and control themselves, interpersonal knowledge to inform how they relate to athletes, and professional knowledge to determine what and how they instruct athletes (Côté, Young, North, & Duffy, 2007). Similarly, athletes' characteristics determine how they respond to coach communication. For example, athletes with low self-esteem respond most favorably to coaches' reinforcement and encouragement but most negatively to an absence of support (Smoll & Smith, 1989). Together, dispositional characteristics are logical moderators that determine the effectiveness of coach behaviors. Scholars would be wise to include such factors in future frameworks, as accounting for these characteristics would determine when and with whom coaches should use behaviors.

A holistic approach to coaching must recognize the interplay between coach communication and roles, situational features, and dispositional characteristics when determining the nature and consequences of athlete-coach interaction. The unique combination of these variables yields insight into how, when, and why coach communication is effective, rather than merely what is effective. With this in mind, coach communication scholars "… should shift away from the plotting of one-dimensional models, and towards the interactive process of coaching in order to sensitize coaches to understand the unique dynamics of the particular situation and how to act accordingly" (Jones & Turner, 2006, p. 185). These efforts would address critiques of overly reductionist approaches to coaching and more accurately provide prescriptive advice to practitioners.

Conclusion

A holistic approach to coaching is of tremendous value and offers communication scholars opportunities to create more elaborate and accurate research models. As coach communication scholars develop holistic frameworks, transferability and accessibility of these models needs to be a continual focal point. The value of coaching research is in its application, and coaches often rely upon simplified frameworks, such as heuristic cues and experience (Cushion & Lyle, 2010). Overly complex and large frameworks are difficult to implement in contexts that are incredibly dynamic and require quick decision-making. As such, holistic models will continually need to be refined, and scholars must balance the functionality and scope of such models. It may help scholars to keep in mind that scientific knowledge rests within a collection of empirical knowledge obtained across samples and researchers, whereby no single study, theory, or perspective provides a complete understanding of any process or context of interaction.

Note

1. Brainy Quote. (2019). Bill McCartney quotes. *BrainyQuote.com*. Retrieved from https://www.brainyquote.com/quotes/bill_mccartney_381122

References

Abeza, G., O'Reilly, N., & Nadeau, J. (2014). Sport communication: A multidimensional assessment of the field's development. *International Journal of Sport Communication, 7,* 289–316.

Bernard, H. R., Kilworth, P., Kronenfeld, D., & Sailer, L. (1984). The problem of informant accuracy: The validity of retrospective data. *Annual Review of Anthropology, 13,* 495–517.

Carpenter, G. W. (2017). Sampling, methodological issues in. In M. Allen (Ed.), *Sage encyclopedia of communication research methods* (pp. 1531–1533). Thousand Oaks, CA: Sage.

Cassidy, T. (2013). Holistic sports coaching: A critical essay. In P. Protrac, W. Gilbert, & J. Denison (Eds.), *The Routledge handbook of sports coaching* (pp. 172–183). New York, NY: Routledge.

Coakley, J. (1993). Sport and socialization. *Exercise and Sport Sciences Reviews, 21*, 169–200.

Côté, J. A., & Buckley, R. (1987). Estimating trait, method, and error variance: Generalizing across 70 construct validation studies. *Journal of Marketing Research, 24*, 315–318.

Côté, J. A., Young, B., North, J., & Duffy, P. (2007). Towards a definition of excellence in sport coaching. *International Journal of Coaching Science, 1*, 3–16.

Cranmer, G. A. (2016). A continuation of sport teams from an organizational perspective: Predictors of athlete-coach leader-member exchange. *Communication & Sport, 4*, 43–61.

Cranmer, G. A. (2018). An application of socialization resources theory: Collegiate student-athletes' team socialization as a function of their social exchanges with coaches and teammates. *Communication & Sport, 6*, 349–367.

Cranmer, G. A., Anzur, C. K., & Sollitto, M. (2017). Memorable messages of social support that former high school athletes received from their head coaches. *Communication & Sport, 5*, 604–621.

Cranmer, G. A., Arnson, E., Moore, A., Scott, A., & Peed, J. (2019). High school athletes' reports of confirmation as a function of starting status and leader-member exchange. *Communication & Sport, 7*, 510–528. doi:10.1177/2167479518783838

Cranmer, G. A., & Brann, M. (2015). "It makes me feel like I am an important part of this team": An exploratory study of coach confirmation. *International Journal of Sport Communication, 8*, 193–211.

Cranmer, G. A., Brann, M., & Weber, K. D. (2017). Quantifying coach confirmation: The development and preliminary validation of the coach confirmation instrument. *Communication & Sport, 5*, 751–769.

Cranmer, G. A., Brann, M., & Weber, K. D. (2018). "Challenge me!": Using confirmation theory to understand coach confirmation as an effective coaching behavior. *Communication & Sport, 6*, 239–259.

Cranmer, G. A., & Buckner, M. (2017). High school athletes' relationships with head coaches and teammates as predictors of their expressions of upward and lateral dissent. *Communication Studies, 68*, 37–55.

Cranmer, G. A., Gagnon, R. J., & Mazer, J. P. (2019). A continued application of confirmation theory: Division-I student-athletes' responses to coach confirmation. *Communication & Sport*. Advanced online publication. Retrieved from https://journals.sagepub.com/doi/pdf/10.1177/2167479518824868

Cranmer, G. A., & Goodboy, A. K. (2015). Power play: Coach power use and athletes' communicative evaluations and responses. *Western Journal of Communication, 79*, 614–633.

Cranmer, G. A., & Spinda, J. (2017). *Coaches' use of confirmation during the preparation for a Division-I football game.* Paper submitted to the annual meeting of the National Communication Association, Dallas, TX.

Cushion, C., & Lyle, J. (2010). Conceptual development in sports coaching. In J. Lyle & C. Cushion (Eds.), *Sports coaching: Professionalisation and practice* (pp. 1–13). Edinburgh: Churchill Livingstone.

Denham, B. (in press). Measurement issues and trends in sport communication research. In E. E. Graham & J. P. Mazer (Eds.), *Communication research measures III: A sourcebook*. New York, NY: Routledge.

DeVellis, R. F. (2012). *Scale development: Theory and applications*. Los Angeles, CA: Sage.

Duffy, P., Hartley, H., Bales, J., Crespo, M., Dick, F., Vardhan, D., … Curado, J. (2011). Sport coaching as a "profession": Challenges and future directions. *International Journal of Coaching Science, 5*, 93–123.

European Coaching Council (2007, September). Review of the EU 5-level structure for the recognition of coaching qualifications. *European Network of Sports Science, Education and Employment*. Retrieved from https://www.icce.ws/_assets/files/documents/ECC_5_level_review.pdf

Feeley, T. H. (2002). Evidence of halo effects in student evaluations of communication instruction. *Communication Education, 51*, 225–236.

Gilbert, W. D. (2002, June). *An annotated bibliography and analysis of coaching science: 1970-2001*. Washington, DC: American Alliance for Health, Physical Education, Recreation. Retrieved from www.aahperd.org/rc/programs/upload/grantees_coaching_science.pdf.

Gilbert, W. D., & Trudel, P. (2004) Analysis of coaching science research published from 1970-2001. *Research Quarterly for Exercise and Sport, 75*, 388–399.

Horn, T. S. (2002). Coaching effectiveness in the sport domain. In T. S. Horn (Ed.), *Advances in sport psychology* (2nd ed., pp. 309–354). Champaign, IL: Human Kinetics.

Jones, R. L., & Turner, R. (2006). Teaching coaches to coach holistically: Can problem-based learning (PBL) help? *Physical Education and Sport Pedagogy, 11*, 181–202.

Jowett, S., & Ntoumanis, N. (2004). The coach–athlete relationship questionnaire (CART Q): Development and initial validation. *Scandinavian Journal of Medicine & Science in Sports, 14*, 245–257.

Jowett, S., & Wylleman, P. (2006). Interpersonal relationships in sport and exercise: Crossing the chasm. *Psychology of Sport and Exercise, 7*, 119–123.

Kassing, J. W., & Anderson, R. L. (2014). Contradicting coach or grumbling to teammates: Exploring dissent expression in the coach–athlete relationship. *Communication & Sport, 2*, 172–185.

Kassing, J. W., Billings, A. C., Brown, R. S., Halone, K. K., Harrison, K., Krizek, B., … Turman, P. D. (2004). Communication in the community of sport: The process of enacting, (re) producing, consuming, and organizing sport. In P. J. Kalbfleisch (Ed.), *Communication yearbook* (Vol. 28, pp. 373–409). Mahwah, NJ: Erlbaum.

Kassing, J. W., & Infante, D. A. (1999). Aggressive communication in the coach-athlete relationship. *Communication Research Reports, 16*, 110–120.

Kassing, J. W., & Pappas, M. E. (2007). "Champions are built in the off season": An exploration of high school coaches' memorable messages. *Human Communication, 10*, 537–546.

Kelley, B., & Carchia, C. (2013, July 11). Hey, data data—Swing! The hidden demographics of youth sports. *ESPN.com*. Retrieved from http://espn.go.com/espn/story/_/id/9469252/hidden-demographics-youth-sports-espn-magazine.

Kenny, D. A., Kashy, D. A., & Cook, W. L. (2006). *Dyadic data analysis*. New York, NY: Guilford Press.

Levine, T. R. (2005). Confirmatory factor analysis and scale validation in communication research. *Communication Research Reports, 22,* 335–338.

Levine, T. R., Hullett, C. R., Mitchell-Turner, M., & Lapinski, M. K. (2006). The desirability of using confirmatory factor analysis on published scales. *Communication Research Reports, 23,* 309–314.

Lyle, J., & Cushion, C. (2010). *Sports coaching: Professionalisation and practice*. Edinburgh: Churchill Livingstone.

Martin, M. M., Rocca, K. A., Cayanus, J. L., & Weber, K. (2009). Relationship between coaches' use of behavior alteration techniques and verbal aggression on athletes' motivation and affect. *Journal of Sport Behavior, 32,* 227–241.

Mazer, J. P., Barnes, K., Grevious, A., & Boger, C. (2013). Coach verbal aggression: A case study examining effects on athlete motivation and perceptions of coach credibility. *International Journal of Sport Communication, 6,* 203–213.

McFarland, S. G. (1981). Effects of question order on survey responses. *Public Opinion Quarterly, 45,* 208–215.

McPherson, B. D. (1981). Socialization into and through sport involvement. In G. R. F. Luschen & G. H. Sage (Eds.), *Handbook of social science of sport* (pp. 246–273). Champaign, IL: Stipes.

Messner, M. A. (1992). *Power at play: Sports and the problem of masculinity*. Boston, MA: Beacon Press.

National Federation of State High School Associations. (2017). High school participation increases for 25th consecutive year. *NFHS.org*. Retrieved from http://www.nfhs.org/ParticipationStatistics/PDF/2016-17_Participation_Survey_Results.pdf

Nelson, L., & Colquhoun, D. (2013). Athlete (non)learning: Is it time for an interdisciplinary understanding? In P. Potrac, W. Gilbert, & J. Denison (Eds.), *Routledge handbook of sports coaching* (pp. 284–295). London: Routledge.

Nicaise, V., Cogerino, G., Fariclough, S., Bois, J., & Davis, K. (2007). Teacher feedback and interactions in physical education: Effects of student gender and physical activities. *European Physical Education Review, 13,* 319–337.

Omori, K. (2017). Writing a discussion section. In M. Allen (Ed.), *Sage encyclopedia of communication research methods* (pp. 1883–1885). Thousand Oaks, CA: Sage.

Pedersen, P. M. (2013). Reflections on communication and sport: On strategic communication and management. *Communication & Sport, 1,* 55–67.

Podsakoff, P. M., MacKenzie, S. B., Lee, J., & Podsakoff, N. P. (2003). Common method biases in behavioral research: A critical review of the literature and recommended remedies. *Journal of Applied Psychology, 88,* 879–903.

Potrac, P., Brewer, C., Jones, R., Armour, K., & Hoff, J. (2000). Toward an holistic understanding of the coaching process. *Quest, 52,* 186–199.

Potrac, P., Denison, J., & Gilbert, W. (2013). Introduction. In P. Potrac, W. Gilbert, & J. Denison (Eds.), *Routledge handbook of sports coaching* (pp. 1–2). New York, NY: Routledge.

Rhind, D. J., & Jowett, S. (2012). Development of the coach-athlete relationship maintenance questionnaire (CARM-Q). *International Journal of Sports Science & Coaching, 7*, 121–137.

Rhind, D. J. A., Jowett, S., & Yang, S. X. (2012). A comparison of athletes' perceptions of the coach-athlete relationship in team and individual sports. *Journal of Sport Behavior, 35*, 433-452.

Rocca, K. A., Martin, M. M., & Toale, M. C. (1998). Players' perceptions of their coaches' immediacy, assertiveness, and responsiveness. *Communication Research Reports, 15*, 445–450.

Ruggiero, T. E., & Lattin, K. S. (2008). Intercollegiate female coaches' use of verbally aggressive communication toward African American female athletes. *The Howard Journal of Communications, 19*, 105–124.

Smoll, F. L., & Smith, R. E. (1989). Leadership behaviors in sport: A theoretical model and research paradigm. *Journal of Applied Social Psychology, 19*, 1522–1551.

Strean, W. (1995). Youth sport contexts: Coaches' perceptions and implications for intervention. *Journal of Applied Sport Psychology, 7*, 23–37.

Turman, P. D. (2001). Situational coaching styles: The impact of success and athlete maturity level on coaches' leadership styles over time. *Small Group Research, 32*, 576–594.

Turman, P. D. (2003a). Athletic coaching from an instructional communication perspective: The influence of coach experience on high school wrestlers' preferences and perceptions of coaching behaviors across a season. *Communication Education, 52*, 73–86.

Turman, P. D. (2003b). Coaches and cohesion: The impact of coaching techniques on team cohesion in the small group sport setting. *Journal of Sport Behavior, 26*, 86–104.

Turman, P. D. (2005). Coaches' use of anticipatory and counterfactual regret messages during competition. *Journal of Applied Communication Research, 33*, 116–138.

Turman, P. D. (2006). Athletes' perception of coach power use and the association between playing status and sport satisfaction. *Communication Research Reports, 23*, 273–282.

Turman, P. D. (2007). The influence of athlete sex, context, and performance on high school basketball coaches' use of regret messages during competition. *Communication Education, 56*, 333–353.

Turman, P. D. (2008). Coaches' immediacy behaviors as predictors of athletes' perceptions of satisfaction and team cohesion. *Western Journal of Communication, 72*, 162–179.

Turman, P. D., & Schrodt, P. (2004). New avenues for instructional communication research: Relationships among coaches' leadership behaviors and athletes' affective learning. *Communication Research Reports, 21*, 130–143.

Tye-Williams, S. (2017). Sample versus population. In M. Allen (Ed.), *Sage encyclopedia of communication research methods* (pp. 1523–1526). Thousand Oaks, CA: Sage.

Webster, C. A. (2009). Expert teachers' instructional communication in golf. *International Journal of Sport Communication, 2*, 205–222.

Wenner, L. A. (2015). Communication and sport, where art thou? Epistemological reflections on the moment and field(s) of play. *Communication & Sport, 3*, 247–260.

Wilson, S. R. (2017). Selection of methodology. In M. Allen (Ed.), *Sage encyclopedia of communication research methods* (pp. 1019–1023). Thousand Oaks, CA: Sage.

Zhang, J., Jensen, B. E., & Mann, B. L. (1997). Modification and revision of the leadership scale for sport. *Journal of Sport Behavior, 20*, 105–122.

· 8 ·

BUILDING ATHLETIC COACHING THEORY: EXTENDING CONFIRMATION THEORY TO ATHLETIC COACHING

There's always ways of motivating yourself to higher levels. Write about it, dream about it.
But after that, turn it into action. Don't just dream.—Dan Gable[1]

The purpose of this text is to synthesize and advance the scientific exploration of coach communication through outlining, connecting, and promoting applied and generalizable means of inquiry regarding how coaches can effectively guide athlete performance and development, as well as manage their sporting environments. Andersen (1989) argued that "science is a process of discovering order amid chaos and regularity in randomness" (p. 4). A central means of finding such order and regularity is through the creation and refinement of social scientific theory (Berger, Roloff, & Roskos-Ewoldsen, 2010). Communicative theories are comprised of a set of statements that address the realities of human interaction with "a set of interrelated propositions that stipulate relationships among theoretical constructs and account of a mechanism or mechanisms that explain the relationships stipulated in the propositions" (Berger, 1995, p. 417). Simply, communication theories identify and explain relationships between communicative concepts, including why those relationships exist. Theory is useful because it provides scholars with frameworks to simplify and generalize about human interaction (Littlejohn, 2009), as well as investigate and test new ideas (Berger, 1991, 1995). Empirical investigations subsequently build and refine theory, which continues the generation of knowledge. Unsurprisingly, a goal of communication research is the creation and testing of theory (Andersen, 1989).

To date, sport communication researchers have placed limited emphasis on creating and building theory. The use of theory within sport communication is problematic on three fronts: its origins, features, and topics. Much of the utilized theory within sport communication originated in other disciplines. For instance, commonly utilized theories within sport communication were developed within journalism, media studies, or psychology (e.g., Framing theory, Agenda Setting theory, Uses and Gratifications theory) (Yoo, Smith, & Kim, 2013). Coach communication research relies upon theories from organizational studies (e.g., LMX or Socialization Resources theory) or sociology (e.g., Sport Socialization). Berger (1991) reflected on such circumstances and argued that the justification for the existence of the field of communication is dependent upon the necessity to explain human interaction with theories that emphasize the role of messages and behaviors and the context in which it occurs. Although the existence of sport communication is justifiable, its scholars are hesitant to develop theories.

More concerning, many theories, including those frequently used within sport communication research (e.g., Framing theory), lack mechanisms that explain the theoretical relationships between constructs (Berger et al., 2010). Without such explanatory mechanisms, these frameworks fall short of true theories. It is not enough to merely describe *what* occurs during interactions; understanding *why* a phenomenon or process occurs is crucial for explaining and predicting human behavior. The most common interdisciplinary theoretical approach used in coach communication research (i.e., Multidimensional Leadership Model; MDLM) also lacks such explanatory mechanisms. MDLM merely asserts coaching behaviors manifest in five generalizable forms and determine athletes' experiences. Yet, why coaches select to use specific behaviors, or why some behaviors are effective and others are not, remains unclear. If coach communication scholars are to offer prescriptive advice to coaches, an understanding of why behaviors and messages are effective is mandatory.

An additional concern among coach communication scholars is much of the theoretically driven research within sport communication is specific to mediated communication (e.g., patterns of media coverage, consumption of sports media, or effects of consumption) (Yoo et al., 2013). Although this work is important and must continue, the most common form of daily communication within sport is interpersonal in nature (Pedersen, Laucella, Kian, & Geurin, 2017). Large swaths of Americans participate in organized sport during childhood and into adolescence, and even more parents, family members, and coaches support these individuals. Interactions with coaches, who structure sporting environments, determine the experiences of these individuals (see Chapters 3–6). A lack of theorizing about coaching is consequential given their significance. Yoo et al. (2013) recognized that the contribution of sport communication as an academic discipline will be determined, in part, by its ability to develop theories.

The Need for Quality Theory

Theory is the cornerstone upon which knowledge and application rest. Multiple scholars have called on sport scholars to embrace a mindset in which theory and practice are mutually enforcing objectives (Cassidy, 2010; Haag, 1994). Such a mindset recognizes that theorizing allows for innovative practices, whereas application provides data that may create and advance theory. It is for these reasons Kurt Lewin's (1951) assertion that "there is nothing so practical as a good theory" remains engrained in scholarly discourse to this day (p. 169). A good theory demonstrates degrees of several core features. A quality theory is *accurate*, which means that it is supported by empirical evidence. The empirical support for theoretical assertions may come before or after a theory is initially forwarded but should be continually sought and tested. A theory that is not testable and does not hold true under scrutiny is of little use to anyone.

A quality theory also demonstrates *consistency*—both internally and externally. Internal consistency requires the assumptions, mechanisms, constructs, and relationships within a theory to align and be void of contradictions. A good theory is logically constructed, and its propositions build upon each other toward a logical conclusion. External consistency refers to the extent to which a theory is consistent with the notions of established and supported theories. Demonstrating external consistency does not mean that good theories always agree with past assertions about the realities or underlying mechanisms of human interaction. In fact, the existence of competing theoretical explanations for a given phenomenon is an indicator of a robust field of inquiry and offers opportunities for scientific advancement (Berger et al., 2010). Instead, external consistency recognizes that knowledge builds upon itself and that new knowledge should be consistent with widely accepted and established findings.

Another central feature of a quality theory is *parsimony*, which refers to the simplicity of a theory. A parsimonious theory is succinct, and encompasses a given communicative process or interaction with the fewest possible concepts. The inclusion of unnecessary and superfluous constructs creates overly complex and cumbersome frameworks that are more difficult for researchers to manage and validate, and nearly impossible for practitioners to integrate. The goal of a good theory is to demonstrate acuity by accounting for complex interactions in a manner that makes them readily accessible to those who wish to test and apply the theory.

Finally, a good theory is *practical*, which means that it offers applied value to real world settings and practitioners. A theory is not of much use if practitioners cannot apply it to better their lives. A purpose of science, at least partially, is to assist those who are the subjects of research, which is why generalizability is crucial to the creation of knowledge. This is especially true for research on coaching, which aims to assist coaches in their efforts to promote athlete performance and development (Duffy et al., 2011). The applicability of coaching research, however, has been limited. The development of quality coaching theory can address this limitation by encouraging additional explanations and knowledge regarding effective coaching (Haag, 1994). Fortunately, as articulated in Chapter 1, the scientific exploration of coaching offers numerous opportunities for practical implications with vast populations of athletes who stand to benefit from research and numerous organizations that seek to implement research findings. All that remains for scholars to do is engage in the creation and refinement of coaching theories that might benefit these stakeholders.

The creation and refinement of theory is a central goal of the scientific process because of its value to researchers and practitioners. Theory offers description, explanation, prediction, and control of human interaction (Andersen, 1989; Dainton & Zelley, 2011; Miller, 2005; West & Turner, 2018). Description and explanation are criterion of theory and establish which communicative constructs are related and why (Berger et al., 2010; Monge, 1973). In this regard, a rigorous theory extends beyond description. It is not enough to merely describe what is being observed; a theory must explain why such observations are possible. These explanations provide an abstract understanding of human communication (Miller, 2005) and a way of viewing the world

(Dainton & Zelley, 2011). Addressing why communication events are related requires the identification of causes or mechanisms of human behavior and subsequent responses. The identification of such mechanisms contributes to a theory's falsifiability and provides explanations that may facilitate subsequent predictions.

Prediction encompasses determining future behaviors or responses to communicative events or stimuli. This function extends beyond explaining what has already occurred to *what will occur*. Charles Redding (1970) reflected: "many writers have maintained that the most important—or perhaps even the sole—ultimate goal of all science is discovering and testing theories which yield hypotheses subject to tests for predictability" (p. 117). The ability to predict responses to behaviors or messages requires a theory to identify causes and effects of interaction in a generalizable manner. With the ability to successfully predict aspects or outcomes of social interaction, theory offers scholars and practitioners control. Control refers to the ability to intentionally cultivate a desired goal or state through strategic efforts. This function enables those who use theory to be proactive in shaping their environments or the experiences of themselves and others. Together, these functions underscore that theory development is crucial for the advancement of scholarship as it offers insight into the causes, outcomes, and modes of coaching effectiveness.

Despite extensive rationale to develop theory, theorizing within coach communication has remained elusive, with scholars primarily using atheoretical and variable analytic approaches (Cranmer & Sollitto, 2015; Turman, 2008) or relying upon non-communicative theories such as Leader-Member Exchange (LMX) (Cranmer, Arnson, Moore, Scott, & Peed, 2019; Cranmer & Myers, 2015), Socialization Resources theory (Cranmer, 2018), or the Multidimensional Leadership Model (Turman, 2003). The lack of theoretical development is not unique to coach communication scholarship. Communication as a field has produced few theoretical advancements, with some notable exceptions (see Berger, 1991; Waldeck, Kearney, & Plax, 2001). The lack of theoretical advancement has multiple explanations. Theory development is a creative process that requires innovative thought (Berger, 1991; Berger et al., 2010), which may not align perfectly with the pragmatic and regimented nature of a scientific approach to human interaction. Further, testing developed theories requires less ingenuity than creating a new one. Another potential explanation is that the field of communication has fragmented over time; making it harder to build upon each other's work (Berger, 1991). This assertion is even truer today, as evidenced by the increasing number and diversity of divisions and interest groups across communication associations.

Another compelling explanation for the lack of theoretical development may be that creating communication theory is a risky endeavor, at least for the creator(s) of said theory. Berger et al. (2010) noted that ego and reputation of scholars are often at risk when their theories are tested. A theory gains credibility through its application and the finding of evidence that its assumptions are plausible. Empirical support is especially salient when it is found by scholars who are not closely affiliated with a theory's creator(s). Berger (1991) noted that in such a scenario those who subsequently test the theory are able to take some of the credit and scholarly capital from the creator(s). However, if empirical evidence indicates that the assumptions of a theory seem less plausible, the consequences of the rejected propositions fall at the feet of its creator(s). With this in mind, Berger and colleagues suggested "… it is much less risky and ego threatening to test someone else's theory or theories than to make public one's own, clearly articulated theory and risk the possibility of its disconfirmation" (p. 14). Under these conditions, it might seem odd that anyone would want to create a theory and endure such risks. Yet, such a view is counterproductive and operates from unrealistic assumptions about the creation and refinement of theory.

The development of theory is a complex and messy process. It is unrealistic to expect that the initial proposal of a theory will be without flaw. Theories often contain propositions or elements that, upon further testing, appear to be less plausible than initially believed. Berger et al. (2010) estimated that in their experience only 60% of theoretical propositions are supported. For this reason, theories develop over time and should not be viewed as stagnate and unchanging frameworks. Simply, the proposal of a theory is not a conclusion but a starting point for additional research. Researchers refine their understandings of a process, phenomenon, or situation through testing and revising theories (Dainton & Zelley, 2011). Even when evidence indicates that a theory appears implausible, its existence has served as the catalyst for additional research and, hopefully, novel theorizing (Andersen, 1989). Thus, the debunking of theories still yields functional knowledge. In this manner, the subsumption of one theory by another is an indicator of scientific progress rather than the failure of its creator(s) (Berger, 1991). These realities reveal that theorizing is an ongoing process and that for the sake of scientific advancement creators must strive to be correct but be willing to be at least partially wrong. It is under these conditions that a working theory of coaches' use of confirmation is forwarded below.

Extending Confirmation Theory to the Coaching Context

As aforementioned, coach communication scholars have yet to build theory, opting to utilize atheoretical approaches or rely upon theories that are either not specific to coaching or are not communicative in nature. Recently, Cranmer, Gagnon, and Mazer (2019) recognized a potential opportunity to extend theorizing about confirmation to task-oriented collectives. A small collection of studies have utilized Dailey's (2006) Confirmation theory, which has shown promise as a framework that explains athlete-coach interaction (Cranmer, Arnson, et al., 2019; Cranmer & Brann, 2015; Cranmer, Brann, & Anzur, 2016; Cranmer, Brann, & Weber, 2017, 2018; Cranmer et al., 2019). As is, Confirmation theory considers how communication (dichotomized as acceptance and challenge) between two individuals engaged in an interpersonal relationship makes those individuals feel regarded. Extant coaching literature has independently replicated the structure of confirmation using inductive data derived from athlete-coach interactions (Cranmer et al., 2017) and demonstrated that confirmation aids athletes' development and sporting experiences (Cranmer, Brann, et al., 2018; Cranmer et al., 2019). These efforts suggest Confirmation theory has utility within the coaching context.

Yet, there are some important distinctions observed within data obtained on coaches' use of confirmation and voids in Confirmation theory that may warrant additional consideration or extension. First, the team dynamics and emphasis on task accomplishment within sport distinguish coaching from traditional interpersonal contexts, which focus on the initiation, definition, or maintenance of personal relationships (Berger, 1995; Dainton & Zelley, 2011). Confirmation theory was developed within dyadic and interpersonal relationships (e.g., familial and romantic relationships) that are rooted in kinship or affect for one another (Dailey, Crook, Glowacki, Prenger, & Winslow, 2016). In contrast, the athlete-coach relationship occurs within larger team and sporting league structures, and exists to facilitate task accomplishment. The focus on tasks is evident at nearly every level of sport. Even for coaches who do not overly prioritize winning, the focus on developing athletes' abilities to perform sporting skills is still present (Lockwood & Perlman, 2008).

Sporting environments are structured accordingly; whether it be emphasizing the importance of sport outcomes (Turman, 2005, 2007), distributing coaching resources (at least partially) based upon athletes' abilities (Case, 1998; Cranmer & Myers, 2015), or organizing practices to facilitate success during competitions (Becker, 2009; Lockwood & Perlman, 2008). These realities are evident in novel findings that diminish the importance of some aspects of confirmation (Cranmer, Brann, et al., 2018; Cranmer et al., 2019) and highlight the role of athlete ability as a determinant of such interpersonal interactions (Cranmer, Arnson, et al., 2019).

Second, if Confirmation theory is to remain useful for coach communication scholars, moderators that determine the effectiveness of confirmation should be forwarded. As part of the call to build holistic understandings of coaching, scholars are encouraged to recognize the importance of interaction (e.g., communicative behaviors), the characteristics of those involved in interaction (i.e., athletes and coaches), and the situational elements of sport in determining coaching effectiveness. Current understandings of Confirmation theory may be refined toward these efforts by (a) providing specificity to the outcomes of confirmation (i.e., currently including general notions of identity, attitudes, emotions, or behaviors), (b) recognizing contextual mechanisms that explain why confirmation is communicated, and (c) adding situational and interpersonal variables that may alter how confirmation is processed. Within this chapter, these efforts are contextualized within athletic coaching but could be extended to other task-oriented collectives (e.g., volunteer groups, small companies, or political campaigns). The remaining portion of this chapter seeks to extend theorizing regarding confirmation into a working theory that explains the effectiveness of coaches' use of confirmation within sports teams.

What Is Coach Confirmation?

Confirmation originated as a theological and philosophical concept and references interactions that recognize, acknowledge, and endorse others (Buber, 1957, 1965). Although feeling confirmed is a psychological state (Sieburg, 1975), it is attributable to the reception and interpretation of specific verbal (e.g., personal language or indications of worth) and nonverbal messages (e.g., a look, touch, or smile) (Laing, 1961; Sieburg, 1985). With this in mind, *coach confirmation* may be understood as the interactions by which coaches communicate to players that they are recognized, acknowledged, and endorsed as valuable, significant individuals (Cranmer & Brann, 2015). A testable assumption that underlies Confirmation theory, therefore, is that confirmation behaviors are validly and reliably identifiable.

Specifically, Confirmation theory forwards that *confirmation manifests in communication that conveys either acceptance or challenge* (Proposition 1). As previously discussed within Chapter 6, coaches' use of *acceptance* demonstrates attentiveness and warmth through recognizing and endorsing athletes' past efforts and accomplishments, whereas their use of *challenge* refers to the validation of athletes' potential through pointing out mistakes, teaching new techniques, calling for improvement, and holding athletes to high standards. The understanding of confirmation as acceptance and challenge is *externally consistent* with the assertions of seminal confirmation theorists, who argued that confirmation recognizes, acknowledges, and endorses individuals for *who they are* and *who they can become* (Buber, 1957, 1965; Laing, 1961). Such assertions also appear *accurate* based on empirical evidence from coach communication scholarship, which independently replicated the dual structure of acceptance and challenge across multiple populations of athletes (i.e., high school and collegiate) and analyses (e.g., scree test [Cattell, 1966], parallel analysis [Horn, 1965], and exploratory and confirmatory factor analyses) (Cranmer et al., 2017, 2019). Moreover, the dualistic approach to confirmation offers a *parsimonious* understanding of coaching that is accessible to practitioners. This understanding is *practical* enough to address coaches' efforts to reinforce what athletes do well and correct their mistakes (Lockwood & Perlman, 2008).

Coach Confirmation as Effective Coaching

The most rudimentary element of a theory is the *description of relationships* between concepts, which may lead to propositions that offer *prediction* about human interaction (Berger et al., 2010; West & Turner, 2018). Confirmation theory broadly asserts that confirmation produces desirable identities, attitudes, emotions, and behaviors for those who receive it (Dailey, 2006, 2010). These assertions are quite broad—arguably to facilitate the extension of the theory to a multitude of relationships and contexts. To address the needs of coaches, this assertion needs to be refined to suggest that *confirmation fosters outcomes of effective coaching* (Proposition 2). As outlined within Chapter 2, effective coaching occurs via athlete development or performance, as well as the management of sporting environments toward these aims. More specifically, effectiveness is evident in the domains of athlete learning, athlete-coach and teammate relationships, athletes' psychological orientations toward sport, athlete socialization into teams and society, team environments, and winning. At a bivariate level (i.e., that which is focused on the relationships between a singular dimension of confirmation and a select outcome of effectiveness), this proposition appears *accurate* based on studies that have considered athletes' cognitive learning, athlete-coach relationships, satisfaction, and motivation (Cranmer et al., 2017, 2019; Cranmer, Brann, et al., 2018). Scholars may continue to test this proposition by determining the relationships between acceptance or challenge and additional effective coaching outcomes. Efforts that expand effectiveness to include issues of behavioral learning, teammate relationships, athlete socialization, team environments, or winning remain unaddressed within literature and are particularly of merit.

Multivariate explorations of acceptance and challenge (i.e., that which considers both dimensions of confirmation simultaneously in explorations of coaching effectiveness) provide further nuance regarding the comparative effectiveness of aspects of confirmation. Originally, Dailey (2006, 2010) theorized that *acceptance and challenge interact to produce the best outcomes for recipients of confirmation* (Proposition 3). The empirical record has provided limited support for this proposition but it remains a core component of the theory (Dailey et al., 2016). In contrast, data obtained from coaching research indicate that aspects of confirmation appear to function independently and differently within sporting environments; offering evidence that the theorized interaction is implausible. Specifically, challenge accounts for unique variance across the full spectrum of explored outcomes (Cranmer et al., 2017, 2019; Cranmer, Brann, et al., 2018). Yet, acceptance contributes only to affective evaluations of interactions with coaches and broad sporting experiences (Cranmer et al., 2019). The supremacy of challenge within these studies may be attributable to sport being a task-oriented environment, as many athletes prioritize their performances and skill development (Cushion, 2010). In such environments, engaging individuals to fulfill their potential cultivates satisfaction, accountability, and cognitive activity (Moneta & Csikszentmihalyi, 1996). The physical nature of sport may also explain the importance of challenge, as applications of Confirmation theory, within the context of weight management, note the salience of challenge for determining exercise patterns (Dailey et al., 2016; Dailey, Richards, & Romo, 2010). These observations offer potential avenues for the further refinement of Proposition 2 or the creation of new propositions. However, further investigations across a wider array of athlete populations, especially among youth athletes, are needed to ensure that such observations are not attributable to the characteristics of competitive high school and collegiate athletes, which are addressed in the holistic section below.

A theory that addresses coaching effectiveness is highly *practical* for multiple stakeholders and offers implications for real world settings. Most coaching practitioners agree that effectiveness is their central concern (Horn, 2002; Potrac, Denison, & Gilbert, 2013). By providing specific communicative means through which a diverse array of desired outcomes can be achieved, Confirmation theory offers tools to millions of coaches who oversee organized sporting environments. Coach confirmation promotes stimulating and prosocial athlete-coach interactions that foster healthy identities, connections with others, sporting skills, needed mindsets, and valuable life lessons. The obvious beneficiaries of these interactions would be the millions of youth and adolescent athletes who participate in organized sport, which is currently marred by hyper-competitiveness, professionalization, aggressive forms of interaction, and turnover (Meân, 2013). Finally, such a theory is of relevance to multiple non-profit organizations (e.g., PCA, The Aspen Institute, and NASPE) that seek to promote coach education (see Chapters 1 and 2). An accessible theory that focuses on effective behaviors within coaches' purview would benefit the programs and educational seminars offered by these organizations. The aforementioned extensions provide flexibility to recognize contextual issues and increase the utility and value of this theory (see the holistic section below).

Why Is Coach Confirmation Effective?

At the heart of theory is the *explanation* for why concepts are related or function in a particular manner (Berger et al., 2010; Monge, 1973). Such identification provides mechanisms through which interactions come to determine human experience. There are two mechanisms that explain why coaches' use of confirmation is effective for determining athletes' sporting experiences. The first mechanism is that *there is an intrinsic, human need to be confirmed by others*. Early investigations of the concept of confirmation largely occurred within psychiatry and family counseling (Friedman, 1983, 1985; Laing, 1961; Sieburg, 1985; Watzalwick, Beavin, & Jackson, 1967). These efforts demonstrated that the need to be confirmed is powerful and when unmet, mental health and wellbeing are at risk. Waltzalwick et al. (1967) would come to describe confirmation as "… the greatest single factor ensuring mental development and stability …" that they observed during their studies of communication (p. 84). Sport is an important context in human development and provides opportunities for coaches to confirm athletes (Cranmer & Brann, 2015). Meeting this psychological need is a mechanism that is consistent with the interpersonal perspective of athletic coaching.

The second mechanism, which is specific to the context of sport, is that confirmation *parallels the aims of coaching*. By its very nature confirmation recognizes, acknowledges, and endorses who we are and what we can become. When applied to a task-oriented environment, like sport, confirmation addresses what individuals are doing well and how they may develop or improve within their roles. Coaches already prepare athletes for competition by reinforcing quality performances and refining future skills (Becker, 2009; Cushion, 2010). Athletes are socialized to value such efforts as an integral part of the sporting experience and an indication of their worth to their teams (Cranmer & Brann, 2015; Cushion, 2010). Thus, using confirmation is quite germane to the purpose of coaching, and meets athletes' expectations and preferences for interaction. Facilitating the development of sporting skill and task accomplishment is a mechanism that is consistent with aspects of the instructional, organizational, and group perspectives of coaching.

Before moving on, it is important to recognize that within general Confirmation theory, Dailey (2006, 2010) forwards that confirmation functions through the relational climates that it fosters between two communicators. These sentiments are echoed within the initial applications of Confirmation theory within coaching research. Yet, such a mechanism creates *internal consistency* issues. Specifically, recent confirmation theorizing posits that confirmation (a) is communication that (in part) makes individuals feel connected to others, (b) functions through relational climates, and (c) produces relational outcomes (e.g., conversation satisfaction and relational attachment). Thus, individuals' assessments of quality relationships are part of the definition of confirmation, its mechanism, and an outcome of confirmation. As part of this extension, athlete-coach relationships are treated as an outcome of effective coaching, rather than a mechanism through which confirmation functions. In other words, I argue it is through meeting athletes' psychological needs and facilitating the functions of sport that confirmation cultivates athlete-coach relationships and other outcomes of effective coaching.

Confirmation as a Holistic Coaching Theory

As mentioned within Chapter 7, researchers are building toward holistic perspectives of coaching, which would require the transcendence of the singular communicative perspectives featured in Chapters 3–6 and the recognition of the contexts in which coaching occurs. Sporting scholars have argued that theoretical development is a means through which such holistic frameworks may be accomplished (Haag, 1994). The proposed extension to Confirmation theory that is featured below forwards means through which holistic features become relevant for the communication and reception of confirmation. These efforts are discussed in two parts: (a) the addition of contextual features as determinants of confirmation or coaching effectiveness and (b) the incorporation of multiple communication perspectives within said extension.

The effectiveness of coach communication is influenced by a nearly unlimited variety of situational features (Horn, 2002; Pedersen et al., 2017). The underlying assumption is that the specific combination of individuals and situations produces unique relational contexts that determine the forms and consequences of human interaction (see Chapter 2). One current need that Confirmation theory does not explicate is why confirmation is communicated to athletes. Within familial and romantic relationships, affection for another would be a potential and logical explanation for why individuals confirm each other. However, within task-oriented environments *coaches' arguably confirm athletes as a function of their task and social goals* (A potential Proposition 4). Coaches may possess a variety of goals that span the entirety of effective coaching outcomes (e.g., learning of sport or life skills, winning, enjoyment, or relationships). Jones and Wallace (2006) recognized that the diversity, and sometimes incompatibility, of coaches' goals requires a prioritization of their efforts and behavior. Simply, coaching is a demanding and complex role that requires a high investment of resources (Kassing et al., 2004; Potrac et al., 2013), which must be managed strategically to maximize personalized conceptions of effectiveness (Cranmer & Myers, 2015). This notion is especially true for coach confirmation, which is not only a psychosocial resource but requires intensive expenditures of coaches' interpersonal knowledge, cognitive effort, emotional investment, communication competence, and most importantly time.

As such, coach confirmation is likely strategic and based upon their task and social goals. This proposition may be tested through explaining the use of confirmation as a function of coach priorities or dispositions toward tasks and relationships. For instance, coaches' prioritization of task-related goals (e.g., winning) may guide efforts to confirm athletes based upon their contributions to team performance. One means of assessing this assertion would be to consider the formal roles that athletes' fulfill (e.g., starters/reserves). Evidence indicates that coaches of competitive teams more readily accept those who contribute most to a team's efforts (Cranmer, Arnson, et al., 2019). This use of acceptance is likely a means of offsetting the face threats that accompany playing time (e.g., public defeats or mistakes) and maximizing continued engagement and participation over the short-term (e.g., a season). The continued success and sustainability of teams over years, however, would require the development and challenge of athletes, regardless of starting status (Cranmer, Arnson, et al., 2019). In this manner, coach confirmation may vary based upon the value coaches place on task objectives and team structures.

Coaches also possess relational goals—like all those who engage in communication (Watzalwick et al., 1967)—that guide their interactions (e.g., disclosures, humor, or affinity seeking). For example, coaches may desire to foster positive climates (e.g., like those that indicate successful groups) or be liked by their athletes. These relational goals may direct the distribution of confirmation, especially acceptance, with all athletes or those deemed as nodes in team social networks. Jointly, the comparative importance of task and relational goals would dictate the confirmation messages utilized by coaches (Jones & Wallace, 2006).

Another need present in coaching literature is to determine how the sporting environment in which athlete-coach interaction occurs may alter the effectiveness of coaches' use of confirmation strategies. Sporting environments vary considerably as a function of the type of sport played, team size, level of interdependence between athletes, league cultures, or game situations—among other features (Horn, 2002). Coaching is a dynamic activity that requires adaption toward meeting the needs of given environments to be successful. Thus, *when coach confirmation meets the demands of a sporting environment, coaches are likely more effective* (A potential Proposition 5). In other words, coaches must consider sporting situations when determining the use and balancing of acceptance and challenge. This proposition may be tested by evaluating the comparative effectiveness of coach confirmation across sport settings and situations (e.g., sporting cultures, types of leagues, or periods during/between seasons).

One potential consideration for coaches is the purpose or culture of the leagues in which they participate as a determinant of their confirmation use.

For example, participation-oriented sports leagues (e.g., Little League) have cultures that emphasize enjoyment, basic skill development, and social connection. Moreover, these leagues are for young children, who are emotionally developing and relatively unskilled physically. Coaches in these sport settings should reflect on their surroundings and seek to coach in a manner that is consistent with the purpose and culture of such a league. Specifically, greater use of acceptance should be of more value within developmental leagues because it builds self-efficacy; mitigates face threats, stress, and uncertainty; and fosters relationships with others. This approach would be ideal with young and inexperienced athletes, who are not solely focused on performative outcomes. In contrast, performance-oriented sport leagues (e.g., AAU) emphasize competition and winning. The athletes who participate in these leagues are highly invested and skilled, and often are seeking to gain access to collegiate athletics. Mindful coaches would be able to increase their effectiveness through challenge within these leagues, as it assists in the refinement of skill and task completion.

Finally, there is a need to understand how receivers' characteristics shape their processing of confirmation. Athlete characteristics (e.g., personalities, psychological orientations, or emotions) create a unique set of communicative and relational needs that influence their preferences, expectations, and goals for athlete-coach communication (Horn, 2002). The extent to which communication meets individual needs is a central mechanism of confirmation and human development theories (e.g., Rhetorical/Relational Goals theory) (Mottet, Frymier, & Beebe, 2006). As such, *when coach confirmation fulfills athletes' needs, coaches are likely more effective* (A potential Proposition 6). This proposition may be tested through examining athletes' characteristics as moderators of the effectiveness of coach confirmation. For example, athletes who are predisposed to value praise and recognition—whether out of a sense of narcissism, entitlement, or need for approval—should respond more favorably to acceptance than athletes without these dispositions. Likewise, athletes who are predisposed to value task-mastery or self-improvement should respond more favorably to challenge than athletes without these dispositions. Researchers might consider Mindset theory (Dweck, 2016) in these efforts. This framework suggests that individuals take a fixed (i.e., performances and behaviors are immutable or enduring) or growth mindset (i.e., performances and behaviors are the product of effort and training) regarding the malleability of their performance and respond to feedback accordingly. Individuals with fixed mindsets should respond favorably to acceptance and ignore/respond negatively to challenge, as they do not believe they can alter or improve their performances; whereas, those with growth mindsets should be far more receptive to coaches' use of challenge and appreciate its contribution to their development.

In addition to recognizing contextual elements that influence coaches' use of confirmation, the extensions to Confirmation theory made within this chapter offer a framework that facilitates the spanning of the four communicative perspectives of coaching (i.e., coaches as instructors, managers, group members, and relational partners). The *instructional perspective* is evident in confirmation's focus on human development and growth via creating engaging learning environments. For instance, the praising and recognition that define acceptance address the relational aspects of teaching, whereas challenge parallels the rhetorical efforts to foster and refine performances (Mottet et al., 2006). These realities are evident in the associations between confirmation and athlete learning, motivation, and evaluations of coaching (*Proposition 2*). The *organizational perspective* is apparent in confirmation's contributions to athletes' performance. Specifically, acceptance reinforces desired efforts or performances, whereas challenge cultivates new or improved abilities—both of which contribute to goal obtainment. These contributions should be apparent in outcomes such as athletes' knowledge of their tasks and roles or winning (*Proposition 2*). Further, the extension recognizes the roles of organizational structures (e.g., league cultures or rules) in evaluations of confirmation (*Proposition 5*), as well as coaches' potential use of team roles and hierarchy as guides for resource investment (*Proposition 4*). The *group perspective* manifests in the relational climates that result from confirmation, as being recognized, acknowledged, and endorsed naturally lead to a sense of belonging among collectives (Laing, 1961). These relationships would be most apparent in athlete perceptions of cohesion or team social climates (*Proposition 2*) or in how team cultures alter the reception of confirmation (*Proposition 5*). Finally, the *interpersonal perspective* is notable in confirmation's focus on identity development and prosocial interaction. A mechanism for the effectiveness of confirmation is the meeting of athletes' interpersonal needs (*Proposition 6*), which subsequently benefits athletes' identities, moral development, assessments of athlete-coach relationships, and self-efficacy regarding sport (*Proposition 2*).

Taken together, when Confirmation theory is applied to coaching it offers a dualistic behavior as a means of promoting athlete development and performance. This framework recognizes that it is what coaches say and do that determines athletes' sporting experiences. Moreover, the outlined extension builds toward a holistic approach because it spans multiple perspectives of coaching and recognizes the importance of the sporting contexts in which coaching occurs. Specifically, it acknowledges the interplay between coach communication, sporting situations, and athletes' dispositions for determining the effectiveness of coaches. The promise of Confirmation theory is highlighted by its potential contributions to professional practice (Dainton & Zelley, 2011). Coach confirmation offers a prosocial means of encouraging skill development, which meets the aims of modern coaching movements and detracts from antisocial patterns of coaching that have become increasingly common (Cranmer et al., 2016). Moreover, confirmation is a psychosocial resource that assists in human development, from which the majority of athletes participating in organized sport could benefit.

Conclusion

The continued refinement of theory is crucial for the development and the application of scientific knowledge. It is important to note that a single chapter is hardly enough to bring about the desired scholarly emphasis on theory within coach communication research. The development of social scientific theory is a process that is refined over time and is done so incrementally (Dainton & Zelley, 2011; Littlejohn, 2009). This is especially true considering that much of theory development depends on the occurrence of contradictory findings. Berger et al. (2010) encouraged researchers to embrace this process and suggested:

> … one alternative to a priori specification of alternative explanations is to let other members of the research community identify and propose them. Of course, this process will play out over time, no matter how many alternatives are considered within the context of a given theory. (p. 15)

As such, this chapter and the forwarding of a working extension to Confirmation theory should be viewed as a starting point for future inquiries. It is the goal of this text, however, to promote scholars' continued efforts to create and synthesize knowledge about athletic coaching, especially that from a communicative perspective. Theory is one of the central means for accomplishing this aim. Together, with clearer conceptualizations, a synthesized understanding of previous research, and a commitment to rigorous means of inquiry, communication researchers can make a sizeable mark on coaching scholarship and their local sporting communities.

Note

1. Brainy Quote. (2019) Dan Gable quotes. BrainyQuote.com. Retrieved from https://www.brainyquote.com/quotes/dan_gable_600840

References

Andersen, P. A. (1989). Philosophy of science. In P. Emmert & L. L. Barker (Eds.), *Measurement of communication behavior* (pp. 3–17). New York, NY: Longman.

Becker, A. J. (2009). It's not what they do, it's how they do it: Athlete experiences of great coaching. *International Journal of Sports Science & Coaching, 4*, 93–119.

Berger, C. R. (1991). Chautauqua: Why are there so few communication theories? Communication theories and other curios. *Communication Monographs, 58*, 101–113.

Berger, C. R. (1995). Interpersonal communication: Theoretical perspectives, future prospects. *Journal of Communication, 55*, 415–447.

Berger, C. R., Roloff, M. E., & Roskos-Ewoldsen, D. R. (2010). What is communication science? In C. R. Berger, M. E. Roloff, & D. R. Roskos-Ewoldsen (Eds.), *The handbook of communication science* (pp. 3–20). Thousand Oaks, CA: Sage.

Buber, M. (1957). Distance and relation. *Psychiatry, 20*, 97–104.

Buber, M. (1965). *The knowledge of man.* New York, NY: Harper & Row.

Case, R. (1998). Leader member exchange theory and sport: Possible application. *Journal of Sport Behavior, 21*, 387–395.

Cassidy, T. (2010). Understanding athlete learning and coaching practice: Utilizing "practice theories" and "theories of practice." In J. Lyle & C. Cushion (Eds.), *Sports coaching: Professionalization and practice* (pp. 177–192). Edinburgh: Churchill Livingstone.

Cattell, R. B. (1966). The Scree test for the number of factors. *Multivariate Behavioral Research, 1*, 245–276.

Cranmer, G. A. (2018). An application of socialization resources theory: Collegiate student-athletes' team socialization as a function of their social exchanges with coaches and teammates. *Communication & Sport, 6*, 349–367.

Cranmer, G. A., Arnson, E., Moore, A., Scott, A., & Peed, J. (2019). High school athletes' reports of confirmation as a function of starting status and leader-member exchange. *Communication & Sport, 7*, 510–528. doi:10.1177/2167479518783838

Cranmer, G. A., & Brann, M. (2015). "It makes me feel like I am an important part of this team": An exploratory study of coach confirmation. *International Journal of Sport Communication, 8*, 193–211.

Cranmer, G. A., Brann, M., & Anzur, C. K. (2016). Putting coach confirmation theory into practice: How to confirm youth and high school athletes and coach more effectively. *Strategies: A Journal for Physical and Sport Educators, 29*(6), 25–29.

Cranmer, G. A., Brann, M., & Weber, K. D. (2017). Quantifying coach confirmation: The development and preliminary validation of the coach confirmation instrument. *Communication & Sport*, 5, 751–769.

Cranmer, G. A., Brann, M., & Weber, K. D. (2018). "Challenge me!": Using confirmation theory to understand coach confirmation as an effective coaching behavior. *Communication & Sport*, 6, 239–259.

Cranmer, G. A., Gagnon, R. J., & Mazer, J. P. (2019). A continued application of confirmation theory: Division-I student-athletes' responses to coach confirmation. *Communication & Sport*. Advanced online publication. Retrieved from https://journals.sagepub.com/doi/pdf/10.1177/2167479518824868

Cranmer, G. A., & Myers, S. A. (2015). Sports teams as organizations: A leader-member exchange perspective of player communication with coaches and teammates. *Communication & Sport*, 3, 100–118.

Cranmer, G. A., & Sollitto, M. (2015). Sport support: Received social support as a predictor of athlete satisfaction. *Communication Research Reports*, 32, 253–264.

Cushion, C. (2010). Coach behavior. In J. Lyle & C. Cushion (Eds.), *Sports coaching: Professionalization and practice* (pp. 43–62). Edinburgh: Churchill Livingstone.

Dailey, R. M. (2006). Confirmation in parent-adolescent relationships and adolescent openness: Toward extending confirmation theory. *Communication Monographs*, 73, 434–458.

Dailey, R. M. (2010). Testing components of confirmation: How acceptance and challenge from mothers, fathers, and siblings are related to adolescent self-concept. *Communication Monographs*, 77, 592–617.

Dailey, R. M., Crook, B., Glowacki, E., Prenger, E., & Winslow, A. A. (2016). Meeting weight management goals: The role of partner confirmation. *Health Communication*, 31, 1482–1494.

Dailey, R. M., Richards, A. A., & Romo, L. K. (2010). Communication with significant other about weight management: The role of confirmation in weight management attitudes and behaviors. *Communication Research*, 37, 644–673.

Dainton, M., & Zelley, E. D. (2011). *Applying communication theory for professional life: A practical introduction* (2nd ed.). Los Angeles, CA: Sage.

Duffy, P., Hartley, H., Bales, J., Crespo, M., Dick, F., Vardhan, D., … Curado, J. (2011). Sport coaching as a "profession": Challenges and future directions. *International Journal of Coaching Science*, 5, 93–123.

Dweck, C. S. (2016). *Mindset: The new psychology of success*. New York, NY: Ballantine.

Friedman, M. S. (1983). *Family, community and society*. New York, NY: Pilgrim Press.

Friedman, M. S. (1985). *The healing dialogue in psychotherapy*. New York, NY: Jason Aronson.

Haag, H. R. (1994). State-of-the-art review of sport pedagogy. *Sport Science Review*, 3, 1–10.

Horn, J. L. (1965). A rationale and test for the number of factors in factor analysis. *Psychometrika*, 30, 179–185.

Horn, T. S. (Ed.). (2002). Coaching effectiveness in the sport domain. In T. S. Horn (Ed.), *Advances in sport psychology* (2nd ed., pp. 309-354). Champaign, IL: Human Kinetics.

Jones, R. L., & Wallace, M. (2006). The coach as "orchestrator": More realistically managing the complex coaching context. In R. L. Jones (Ed.), *The sports coach as educator* (pp. 51–64). New York, NY: Routledge.

Kassing, J. W., Billings, A. C., Brown, R. S., Halone, K. K., Harrison, K., Krizek, B., … Turman, P. D. (2004). Communication in the community of sport: The process of enacting, (re) producing, consuming, and organizing sport. In P. J. Kalbfleisch (Ed.), *Communication yearbook* (Vol. 28, pp. 373–409). Mahwah, NJ: Erlbaum.

Laing, R. D. (1961). *Self and others.* London: Tavistock Publications.

Lewin, K. (1951). *Field theory in social science: Selected theoretical papers.* New York, NY: Harper & Row.

Littlejohn, S. W. (2009). Theory. In S. W. Littlejohn & K. A. Foss (Eds.), *Encyclopedia of communication theory* (pp. 957–958). Thousand Oaks, CA: Sage.

Lockwood, P., & Perlman, D. (2008). Enhancing the youth sport experience: A re-examination of methods, coaching style, and motivational climate. *The Journal of Youth Sports, 4,* 30–34.

Meân, L. J. (2013). The communicative complexity of youth sport: Maintaining benefits, managing discourses, and challenging identities. In P. M. Pedersen (Ed.), *Routledge handbook of sport communication* (pp. 338–349). New York, NY: Routledge.

Miller, K. (2005). *Communication theories: Perspectives, processes, and context.* Boston, MA: McGraw-Hill Education.

Moneta, G. B., & Csikszentmihalyi, M. (1996). The effect of perceived challenges and skills on the quality of subjective experience. *Journal of Personality, 64,* 274–310.

Monge, P. R. (1973). Theory construction in the study of communication: The system paradigm. *Journal of Communication, 23,* 5–16.

Mottet, T. P., Frymier, A. B., & Beebe, S. A. (2006). Theorizing about instructional communication. In T. P. Mottet, V. P. Richmond, & J. C. McCroskey (Eds.), *Handbook of instructional communication: Rhetorical and relational perspectives* (pp. 255–282). Boston, MA: Pearson.

Pedersen, P. M., Laucella, P. C., Kian, E. M., & Geurin, A. N. (2017). *Strategic sport communication* (2nd ed.). Champaign, IL: Human Kinetics.

Potrac, P., Denison, J., & Gilbert, W. (2013). Introduction. In P. Potrac, W. Gilbert, & J. Denison (Eds.), *Routledge handbook of sports coaching* (pp. 1–2). New York, NY: Routledge.

Redding, W. C. (1970). Research settings: Field studies. In P. Emmert & W. D. Brooks (Eds.), *Methods of research in communication* (pp. 105–159). New York, NY: Houghton Mifflin.

Sieburg, E. (1975). *Interpersonal confirmation: A paradigm for conceptualization and measurement.* San Diego, CA: United States International University.

Sieburg, E. (1985). *Family communication: An integrated systems approach.* Boston, MA: Allyn & Bacon.

Turman, P. D. (2003). Athletic coaching from an instructional communication perspective: The influence of coach experience of high school wrestlers' preferences and perceptions of coaching behaviors across a season. *Communication Education, 23,* 73–86.

Turman, P. D. (2005). Coaches' use of anticipatory and counterfactual regret messages during competition. *Journal of Applied Communication Research, 33,* 116–138.

Turman, P. D. (2007). The influence of athlete sex, context, and performance on high school basketball coaches' use of regret messages during competition. *Communication Education*, 56, 333–353.

Turman, P. D. (2008). Coaches' immediacy behaviors as predictors of athletes' perceptions of satisfaction and team cohesion. *Western Journal of Communication*, 72, 162–179.

Waldeck, J. H., Kearney, P., & Plax, T. G. (2001). Instructional and developmental communication theory and research in the 1990s: Extending the agenda for the 21st century. In W. B. Gudykunst (Ed.), *Communication yearbook* (Vol. 25, pp. 207–229). Newbury Park, CA: Sage.

Watzalwick, P., Beavin, J., & Jackson, D. D. (1967). *Pragmatics of human communication*. New York, NY: Norton.

West, R. L., & Turner, L. H. (2018). *Introducing communication theory: Analysis and application* (6th ed.). New York, NY: McGraw-Hill Education.

Yoo, S. K., Smith, L. R., & Kim, D. (2013). Communication theories and sport studies. In P. M. Pedersen (Ed.), *Routledge handbook of sport communication* (pp. 8–19). New York, NY: Routledge.

Lawrence A. Wenner, Andrew C. Billings, and Marie C. Hardin
General Editors

Books in the Communication, Sport, and Society series explore evolving themes and emerging issues in the study of communication, media, and sport, broadly defined. The series provides a venue for key concepts and theories across communication and media studies to be explored in relation to sport. The series features works building on burgeoning media studies engagement with sport, as well as works focusing on interpersonal, group, organizational, rhetorical, and other dynamics in the communication of sport. The series welcomes diverse theoretical standpoints and methodological tactics seen across the social sciences and humanities. While some works may examine the dynamics of institutions and producers, representations and content, reception and fandom, or entertain questions such as those about identities and/or commodification in the contexts of mediated sport, works that consider how communication about sport functions in diverse rhetorical and interpersonal settings, how groups, families, and teams use, adapt, and are affected by the communication of sport, and how the style, nature, and power relations in communication are wielded in sport and media organizations are particularly encouraged. Works examining the communication of sport in international and/or comparative contexts or new, digital, and/or social forms of sport communication are also welcome.

For additional information about this series or for the submission of manuscripts, please contact the series editors or Acquisitions Editor Erika Hendrix:

Lawrence A. Wenner | Andrew C. Billings | Marie C. Hardin | Erika Hendrix
lwenner@lmu.edu | acbillings@ua.edu | mch208@psu.edu | erika.hendrix@plang.com

To order other books in this series, please contact our Customer Service Department:
(800) 770-LANG (within the U.S.)
(212) 647-7706 (outside the U.S.)
(212) 647-7707 FAX

Or browse online by series:
www.peterlang.com